# HADHA BALADUNA

# Made in Michigan Writers Series

GENERAL EDITORS

Michael Delp, Interlochen Center for the Arts
M. L. Liebler, Wayne State University

A complete listing of the books in this series can
be found online at wsupress.wayne.edu.

# HADHA BALADUNA

## ARAB AMERICAN NARRATIVES
## OF BOUNDARY AND BELONGING

*EDITED BY*
*GHASSAN ZEINEDDINE,*
*NABEEL ABRAHAM,*
*AND SALLY HOWELL*

WAYNE STATE UNIVERSITY PRESS
DETROIT

ISBN 978-0-8143-4925-0 (paperback)
ISBN 978-0-8143-4926-7 (e-book)

Library of Congress Control Number: 2021951009

Publication of this book was made possible by a generous gift from The Meijer Foundation.

Cover design and illustration by Lindsey Cleworth.

Wayne State University Press rests on Waawiyaataanong, also referred to as Detroit, the ancestral and contemporary homeland of the Three Fires Confederacy. These sovereign lands were granted by the Ojibwe, Odawa, Potawatomi, and Wyandot nations in 1807 through the Treaty of Detroit. Wayne State University Press affirms Indigenous sovereignty and honors all tribes with a connection to Detroit. With our Native neighbors, the press works to advance educational equity and promote a better future for the earth and all people.

Wayne State University Press
Leonard N. Simons Building
4809 Woodward Avenue
Detroit, Michigan 48201-1309

Visit us online at wsupress.wayne.edu.

# Contents

# INTRODUCTION

*Sally Howell, Ghassan Zeineddine, and Nabeel Abraham*

The voices of Arab Detroit are many. They connect us to homelands throughout the Middle East, from Lebanon and Syria to Yemen and Iraq. They are also rooted in the industrial heartland of the United States and in the history of Detroit itself, which has always been a borderland of one type or another—between lake and shore, French and English, fugitive and free. While Arabs don't really enter Detroit's story until the 1890s, they have been a part of all the things that made the city prominent in the twentieth century and those that ripped it apart: the phoenix-like life cycle of the auto industry; the cauldron of overlapping migrations and diasporas; the cultural efflorescence of Motown and the Concert of Colors; the entrepreneurialism of everything from food to vice; political struggles for a living wage, fair housing, racial equity, clean air and water, religious freedom, and a free Palestine; and the restless movement of industry and people from city to suburb to exurb to city again. For well over a century, Detroit has been a refuge for Arab migrants and a jumping off point for their American dreams, and the contributors to this volume are eager to claim this place and history for themselves. We have titled this collection *Hadha Baladuna* (this is our home/homeland) to reflect the sentiment of belonging that gives these narratives cohesion. At once a birthright and a matter of choice, a place of endearment and of restraint, Arab Detroit is the unambiguous home/homeland of the voices gathered here.

As educators working in Dearborn, the symbolic and demographic capital of Arab Detroit, the editors of this book have been privileged to work with the great diversity of young voices that speak as and for local Arab Americans. In the 1980s, when Nabeel Abraham first began teaching at Henry Ford Community College, the Arab students who arrived in his classroom were mostly Lebanese and Palestinian. They were the children of families displaced by occupation and civil war. Today the classrooms of Ghassan Zeineddine and Sally Howell at the University of Michigan–Dearborn are filled with the grandchildren of this earlier migration and with refugees from war and revolution in Syria, Yemen, and Iraq. When Nabeel began teaching, the Arabs of greater Detroit were a little-known minority, and those who lived in Dearborn were struggling for recognition and a political voice. Today, Dearborn's Arab community is at least half the city's population. It plays a prominent role in the city's political establishment and has reshaped its cultural identity. The surrounding communities in southwest Detroit, Warrendale, Melvindale, and Dearborn Heights have also been Arabized, and when people speak today about a distinctly Arab Dearborn, it is usually to this greater Dearborn that they are referring. And Dearborn, of course, is only one part of the story we share in this volume. The Arab enclave in Hamtramck and the Chaldean one in Macomb County are equally visible, equally dynamic. We recognize that the majority of Arab Detroiters live outside these enclaves today, as they always have. This too lends texture and complexity to the ever-evolving relationship between Arabs and non-Arabs in the region.

It is in the spirit of this constant, remarkable change that we bring to you this new set of stories. From them we learn that each generation's experience of growing up in Arab Detroit is different from that of its predecessors. Each family's journey on the route from migrant to local is specific to them alone. Each individual's understanding of what it means to be an Arab American, or a Michiganian, or a Detroiter, is unique. The stories told here are never static. They are a creative response, both personal and political, to the fluid conditions in which their authors live. It is the dynamism and diversity of these experiences that we hope to share with readers.

*Hadha Baladuna* is the third installment in the Arab Detroit series. It follows *Arab Detroit: From Margin to Mainstream* (Abraham and Shryock, 2000) and *Arab Detroit 9/11: Life in the Terror Decade* (Abraham, Howell, and Shryock, 2011). These earlier books sought to capture something of the broad diversity of the Arab experience in Michigan by mixing academic writing with generous amounts of memoir, interviews, poetry, photography, and storytelling. As teachers, we use these books regularly with our students, and we have found that the non-academic essays have a kind of persistent truth to them that keeps them relevant even as the community changes and grows.

So we are pleased to diverge from the format of our preceding volumes and to offer a book composed solely of creative works. The voices in this book differ from those of the previous volumes in ways that will capture the reader's attention. They have certainly captured ours. Several contributors have chosen to take on challenging subject matter, including topics that have long felt taboo in the religiously and socially conservative enclave of Dearborn. Mai Jakubowski, for example, writes of her parent's divorce and of coming out as queer to her immigrant father. Teri Bazzi describes a childhood filled with violence and sexual abuse and lacking the kind of support her family needed—still needs—to heal. Yasmin Mohamed relives the frightening period in her life when her father suffered a mental breakdown and was diagnosed with schizophrenia. Her family, too, needed more help than they received. Nabeel Abraham discusses his experiences of anti-Arab racism and stereotyping that were common in the 1980s, the context in which his colleague, Alex Odeh, was murdered. Abraham recounts his experiences of being Arab American—on national television, as a college student, as a scholar, on the job, on the street—demonstrating the variability of Arab Americanness across time and space. There is anger in these pages, more raw anger than was seen in the earlier volumes.

There is also much that is familiar. There are, for example, plenty of immigrant parents. Some of them suffered the hardships of displacement due to war, brutal dictators, and religious persecution. Some were overjoyed to find Dearborn and Detroit in their search for a place to rebuild their lives and raise their children in peace. Here immigrants can worship, eat, speak Arabic, and dress as they please. And they do, sometimes to the chagrin of their American-born children and just as often to their loving delight. While most of these essays eschew politics, they nonetheless recognize the migrant generation's tremendous relief and appreciation for living in an environment of relative security, where the rule of law is generally adhered to. Rather than criticize the state, the parents who appear in this volume tend to be suspicious of American mores and are eager to protect their children from the consequences of accepting American cultural values in exchange for Arab ones. In other words, our contributors are fully aware of the very real gaps that exist between the generations and of the contrasts between hardship and ease, certainty and confusion, belonging and fear, that shaped their upbringing. Often children and parents stare at one another across these gaps, expressing great love and compassion even when they don't understand and can't quite respect the choices the other generation has made. We see this tension in Yousef Alqamoussi's secret passion for the lyrics of 2Pac, in Hanan Ali Nasser's nostalgia for a homeland she can't remember, and in Yasmin Mohamed's pride in her hard-won educational achievements.

Dearborn itself is an outsized character throughout this book. The city looms large in most of the narratives. For Kamelya Omayma Youssef, it is a site of joyful nostalgia. For Sally Howell and Jeff Karoub, it is an ever-changing wellspring of inspiration. Ghassan Zeineddine, a relative newcomer to Dearborn, introduces us to the city as a "bubble," a zone of familiarity and safety, cultural ease and consumption, that is simultaneously a claustrophobic space of judgment, hierarchy, and conservative values. Many contributors share their first impressions of the city, as Alqamoussi and Nasser do, because for their parents Dearborn was a life-changing refuge that enabled them to create meaning out of chaos and suffering. Those who were born in Dearborn, and those who moved here later in life, are equally likely to be amazed by the place. Youssef and Yasmine Rukia, in particular, share an obvious fondness for the city and its peculiar landmarks and associations. Other second-generation writers are less certain that they belong in Dearborn. They struggle to fit in, to feel Arab enough. This is true for Jakubowski, who grew up in Dearborn, and for Karoub, who chose to raise his young family there after having grown up in a nearby suburb. For Bazzi, Dearborn is a place of harsh judgments, but her desire to claim the city, and the Arab identity it radiates, as her own never wavers.

Detroit, too, is a complex, shape-shifting presence in this volume. For the displaced, it is a zone of refuge. Both Dunya Mikhail and Hanan Ali Nasser see in the city a continuity with their families' pasts in war-torn Iraq, but they also see Detroit as a space where lives and perhaps entire civilizations can be rebuilt. For Hayan Charara, who was born in Detroit but is now raising his own family in Texas, Detroit is a touchstone of his childhood and adolescence, a gateway to the past itself, to memory, nostalgia, and a chance to create the world anew through his writing. For Nabeel Abraham, the city is a set of stages for different types of activism. Often, it is a place where no one is convinced, no minds are changed, and hearts are hardened rather than opened. Photographer Rania Matar sees Detroit as a richly textured canvas where past and present intersect in fortuitous ways. Always, the city is variable, full of contradictions, and a vital part of collective life and memory.

Together these essays reflect a changing Arab community that is a by-product of twentieth-century wars in the Middle East that are assuming ominous new shapes in the twenty-first century. Violent conflicts in Sudan, Iraq, Afghanistan, Lebanon, Palestine, Syria, and Yemen have contributed disproportionately to the global refugee crisis. In Michigan, they have added to the demographic complexity, institutional growth, and remarkable cultural efflorescence of Arab Detroit. These wars compound—they grow out of—the ever-hardening structures of anti-Arab and Islamophobic racialization that complicate life for Arab Americans in countless ways. So we find it remarkable that these wars figure in our narratives principally as catalysts for migration. Their viciousness, and their inconclusive endings, are foreclosures on dreams of return, but otherwise these wars are not really part of the conversation. Evidence of anti-Arab and anti-Muslim prejudice is ample in many of these chapters, as is the long shadow of government surveillance over the community, but these are seldom their focus. We find in these absences not a denial of hatred, or a distaste for politics, or even an expression of fear, but rather a small victory for the community, which is large enough and dynamic enough to generate its own centers of gravity. In everyday life, Arab Detroiters struggle and thrive on their own terms, and they are (mostly) free to construct their lives without constant reference to geopolitics or the stereotypical images that non-Arabs, and non-Muslims, impose on their community. This too is a lesson we have learned from the contributors to this volume.

Hadha baladuna. Come and make it yours as well.

# AN ATLAS OF HOMES

*Ghassan Zeineddine*

## THE FIRST TO LEAVE

At twenty years old, my great-grandfather Assad Ali Al-Awar left Mount Lebanon for São Paulo, Brazil, in 1920. Raised in the Druze village of Qornayel, he hoped to put the trauma of his adolescence behind him. A few years earlier, as soldiers fought and died in Europe during the First World War, a terrible famine struck the Levant. The sky turned black with locusts. Crops wilted and springs dried out. People began eating their mules, donkeys, and horses. They ate rats and wild dogs and chewed on boiled leather. Cholera and typhus spread throughout the land. The dead were piled on the roads and later collected by municipal carts and buried in mass graves.

The Allied forces had imposed a blockade on the eastern Mediterranean to prevent supplies from reaching the Ottoman Empire, which controlled Greater Syria. The blockade decimated the economy; matters grew worse when Jamal Pasha, commander of the Ottoman forces in the region and known as "The Butcher," enforced his own blockade on Mount Lebanon. By the end of the famine in 1918, the death count was over 100,000. For Assad, the horror of those days would prove inescapable.

Villagers had been immigrating to the Americas since the late nineteenth century, and some of Assad's relatives had settled in São Paulo. Before boarding the steamship, the *Lotus*, in Beirut's harbor, he visited a fortune-teller in the souks downtown near Martyrs' Square, who read his future in the coffee grounds of a demitasse cup and predicted that he wouldn't live beyond his seventies. Comforted by the belief that he had over fifty years left on earth to achieve something in his life, he boarded the *Lotus* and three weeks later arrived in São Paulo. But São Paulo didn't sing to him, or he failed to learn the lyrics to its song, and nine months later he tried his luck in North America. He was accompanied by two relatives from Qornayel, Ramzi Sabra and Najeeb Sabra. The three young men arrived at Ellis Island on January 8, 1921, not speaking a word of English. According to the Weather Bureau, the average temperature that day was forty-one degrees. I imagine my great-grandfather standing, all five feet and seven inches of him, on the island carrying a leather valise, the tail end of his overcoat flapping in the bitter wind, his black hair ruffled like the ocean. What I know from family stories is that he held a cardboard sign that read: West Virginia. Before leaving São Paulo, he had been told there was work in the coal mines of West Virginia, and that a few Druze families lived in the southeastern towns of the state. Someone on the boat had written those two words for him on the piece of cardboard.

On Ellis Island, my great-grandfather's name was altered at Customs to Assod Allie, and he'd soon be nicknamed Ollie. He ate his first hot dog and crossed into Manhattan, where he flashed his sign at passersby. He and his relatives were directed to Grand Central Station. Several hours later, they hopped off the train in Welch, West Virginia.

Assad or Assod Allie or Ollie never ended up working in the mines. Like so many immigrants who had come before and during his time, he became a peddler and relied on the language of commerce to communicate with Americans. He stuffed a satchel and a suitcase with wares and walked up and down mountain roads and in the depths of valleys, along rivers and around lakes, and across the way into neighboring mining towns. He was at the mercy of the weather, which often left him sunburned or drenched with rain.

He later moved to the town of Princeton and worked at a diner on Main Street called the Virginia Café, and when he had saved enough money, he purchased the diner and the apartment above it. He developed a taste for beer and bowler hats. He wore three-piece suits and patent leather shoes. When he was feeling homesick, he visited the homes of the Druze families, who were also from Mount Lebanon, and joined them for picnics and gatherings at Lake Shawnee. All that was missing in his life was a wife, so he returned to Qornayel to find one.

"Villagers thought he looka funny in the bowler hat," my grandmother told me on an autumn afternoon in 2007 in her apartment in Washington, DC. She spoke English with an accent thick as honey. "Nobody in town wore a bowler hat."

Assad fell for Hafiza Al-Awar, who was considered one of the prettiest women in the village. He spotted her, black hair flowing down her back, walking down the road holding hands with a young girl. She had high cheekbones and a round face. When he called on her and asked for her hand, she didn't think twice about his bowler hat. He was coming from America, which meant he had money. And she was a single mother. Hafiza's first husband had sailed to Argentina in search of fortune, promising to send for her and their daughter, Wasila, in six months. He never sent word, and Hafiza was left to support herself and Wasila by working at the silk factory in the nearby town of Hammana. In the early morning, she strapped Wasila, who was deaf, to her back and walked three miles to the factory, where for hours she sat at a long wooden table among other village women and sifted through cocoons by the light of kerosene lamps. Toward dusk she walked the three miles home with Wasila on her back. She quickly accepted Assad's proposal, which was made with one condition: she'd have to leave Wasila behind. In a decision that still haunts my family, Hafiza left Wasila with relatives and journeyed with Assad to America.

Assad went to bed every night wearing one of his wife's nylons over his head to keep his hair slicked back. In the morning he rose with a perfect hairdo. After breakfast, he walked down a flight of stairs to the Virginia Café and began to work, and in the afternoon Hafiza joined him to help grill hamburgers. She gave birth to two daughters a year apart: Sally and Geneva, the latter my teta. Assad had insisted on Western names.

By 1938, when my teta was two, Assad had been in America for seventeen years, and he was still terrified to venture down the street after sunset. There were signs hung on storefront windows that read:

No Blacks and No Dogs, No Jews. Assad feared that whoever hung the signs wouldn't hesitate to lynch an Arab. This wasn't an environment he wanted his daughters to grow up in. He also preferred they think and speak in Arabic. And so, he decided that his wife and daughters would live in Lebanon while he remained in Princeton. He'd build them a limestone house in Qornayel and send them money every month. That year he relocated his family to the village, keeping them with relatives while their house was being built. Hafiza was thrilled to return to Lebanon, as she had detested rural life in America, though she'd miss her morning cup of coffee with two glazed donuts and licking custard ice cream from a cone.

In Qornayel, Teta (a.k.a. Geneva) became known as Inaam and her older sister as Souad. On the day Assad was to return to America, Teta clung to his leg. She was too young to understand that she wouldn't see him again until the following summer. "I'm going out to buy apples," he told her. "I'll be right back."

On November 18, 1942, Assad, already in his forties, enrolled in the army to fight the Nazis, only he was never sent to Europe. Instead, he became a member of the Army Civilian Service. For years a portrait of him in a military cap and suit hung in Teta's apartment. In the photograph his angular face is posed for combat. Teta called him a war hero.

Assad eventually sold the Virginia Café and returned to Qornayel to live out the remainder of his life. Since alcohol wasn't served in the village, he walked down to Hammana to drink Almaza beer at the café in the main square. True to the fortune-teller's prediction, he never reached his eightieth birthday. He died at seventy-eight on November 15, 1978, two years before I was born.

A century has passed since Assad first stepped foot in America. Unbeknownst to him, he left his descendants on an interminable search for home.

## FROM THE MOUNTAINS TO WASHINGTON, DC

Teta returned to Princeton as a twenty-two-year-old mother of three girls in 1959. She had been raised in Qornayel, longing for the summers when her father visited from America. At seventeen, her mother, Hafiza, pressured her into marrying her first cousin, Touffic Al-Awar, who was from Qornayel and worked the terraced fields of the village. His hands were big and callused, and he smelled of the earth. When Touffic struggled to support his family, which included my mother and her younger sisters, Teta suggested they live in Princeton, where her father Assad was still running the Virginia Café and could help Touffic find a better paying job. They could live with him in the apartment above the diner. Touffic agreed, and the young family of five set off for West Virginia. It wasn't the pull of America that had tugged at Teta, for she had no memories of her country of birth. She simply wanted to be closer to her father.

Touffic worked alongside Assad at the Virginia Café while Teta raised their daughters. My mother and her sisters began to learn how to speak and read in English. But Teta wasn't happy in her marriage, and three years later, when my mother was eight, she divorced Touffic. Feeling sorry for him (and also respecting their family connection), Assad sent him south to North Carolina, where my great-grandfather had a good friend who owned a restaurant in the small town of Snow Hill and needed help around the place.

Despite his love for Teta, Assad discouraged her from raising her daughters in America, let alone as a single mother. Lebanon was safer, he told her. He'd help pay her bills. She returned to Qornayel with her girls, and when she could afford to travel, she visited her father over the summers. On one such visit, she met an older man at a Lebanese gathering named Ameen David, who was in town for the weekend. An immigrant, he was tall and slim and wore an impeccable suit. White hair frosted the sides of his bald head. He owned a popular restaurant and nightclub called the Blue Mirror Grill on Fourteenth Street in downtown Washington, DC, having made his start as a peddler in Saint Louis, Missouri. He was also divorced with three grown children and was intent on remarrying. Teta was in her early thirties and looked much younger than her age. Ameen David (in our family, we refer to him by his full name) thought Teta was beautiful, and he proposed to her. She declined. She had three girls

to care for, and in any case, she was headed back to Lebanon. That
December, Ameen David flew to Lebanon to propose to Teta again.
He promised to pay her girls' way through school and university if
she agreed to marry him. This time, Teta accepted, and she put her
girls in boarding school at the Beirut Evangelical School for Girls
(BESG). Like her mother Hafiza, she gave up her children to move
to America, a decision that she'd never recover from.

Teta lived with Ameen David in a three-story brick house with a
red-tile roof on Fessenden Avenue in northwest Washington, DC.
Meanwhile, my mother and her sisters lived for the next several years
at boarding school. Their school uniform consisted of a gray gilet over
a white shirt, a gray skirt, and black or dark brown shoes. Bright colors
were strictly prohibited, including colored hairbands and clips. Students sang hymns every morning in the school chapel, followed by
a full day of classes. Although the teachers refrained from whacking
students with rods or rulers, they reveled in an authoritarian style of
teaching that frightened the poor girls. But it was the fierce Ms. Jureidini,
head of the boarding department, who the girls feared the most. A short
and plump woman, she stormed into the dormitory hall after lights
out and marched between the rows of beds, panning her flashlight
across the sleeping girls and those awake and holding their breath,
making sure everyone was accounted for.

My mother completed most of her schooling at BESG before enroll-
ing in the American University of Beirut (AUB). Her sisters couldn't
bear the boarding school for any longer and joined Teta in DC. As a
university student in the early '70s, Mom lived in the female dormitory.
The wooded campus overlooked the sea and a soccer pitch known
as the green field. On the weekends she and her Egyptian roommate
frequented the movie theaters and cafés in Hamra, a bustling neighborhood above the campus.

But when civil war broke out in the spring of 1975, Mom spent the
entire summer in Qornayel to escape the fighting in Beirut. Like most,
she believed that after a few weeks a ceasefire would be called and
the warring militias would clear their barricades from the streets and the
masked snipers would withdraw from rooftops. The fighting intensified,

and Beirut was divided down the middle by an imaginary green line that cut the city in halves: Muslim West and Christian East. The administration at AUB canceled the fall semester and informed students that classes would resume in January.

Mom spent the rest of autumn in Qornyel, anxious to return to her life in Beirut. She lived with her grandparents, Assad and Hafiza, and learned how to crochet.

"It took me a month to make a table cover," she told me. "I had nothing else to do."

Teta was in DC, catering to the needs of Ameen David, who was in his early eighties. She was petrified that Mom would be killed in the civil war and begged her to come to America. Not one to disobey her mother, Mom left Lebanon in December. On the day before her departure, she visited her dormitory at AUB to say goodbye to friends, but the dorm was empty.

She lived the following year in DC, completing her undergraduate studies at George Washington University. She was miserable.

"I never got to say goodbye to my friends in Beirut," she said.

A year later, she married my father, a civil engineer who hailed from a village neighboring Qornayel, and followed him to Jeddah, Saudi Arabia.

## BORN IN THE USA

I was born blue in DC. I gasped for breath as the doctor uncoiled the umbilical cord wrapped around my neck. Once my lungs filled with air, Mom said I let loose a shattering cry that was louder than the howling of the jackals she had grown up listening to on sleepless nights in Qornayel. I spent the first two months of my life in the house on Fessenden Avenue. In November 1980, Mom and my sister Jana and I flew to Jeddah, where my father was waiting for us.

Unlike most Lebanese expats and foreigners who lived in gated compounds and did as they pleased within the confines of their concrete walls—I used to picture pool parties where half-naked men and women swam together and French kissed—we lived in a ground floor flat among the locals. I grew up playing soccer in the evenings with the neighborhood kids in the front courtyard, imagining myself as Diego Maradona as I dribbled between defenders. The monotone colors of Jeddah defined my childhood palette: the soft yellow of streetlights, the thick white of the walls, the beige of the desert sands. It rarely rained—once or twice a year—and when it did, I ran outside and looked up at the sky, raindrops exploding on my face like revelations.

Mom was obligated to wear an abaya over her clothes when we left the flat. As Dad drove, I scoped out the streets for lovers. I was in search of a kiss on the lips, which I had seen in the Betamax films my parents played at home. Mom would instruct me to close my eyes whenever a kiss appeared in a film, but I stared wide-eyed, entranced. I never found kissers on the street, let alone a couple holding hands, because public displays of affection were punishable by law. The mutaween, religious police, drove around in Toyota pickups prowling the streets for offenders. We heard rumors about them—bearded men in red headscarves and billowing white robes—whacking offenders with batons and whisking them away in their truck beds to prison.

Jana and I attended the Continental International School, which was run by Brits as imperious as their colonialist ancestors. Our friends were all internationals like us, coming from Pakistan, Bangladesh, Denmark, and Lebanon. I still remember Mrs. Haverford, who was my homeroom teacher in fourth grade. We were all wary of her because of her terrifying husband, a fellow teacher. A burly man with a thatch of chestnut hair and a mustache that consumed his upper lip, Mr. Haverford once stopped a boy sprinting down the hallway by grabbing him by his shirt collar, turning him around, and, gripping the front of his shirt, lifting the boy in the air and pinning him to the wall. If I ever misbehaved in Mrs. Haverford's class, I feared she'd feed me to her husband.

I was mostly a quiet and shy boy. But one time, after Mrs. Haverford instructed us to write a short story and gave us the class period to complete it, I stood up from my desk and walked to the front of the classroom. Mrs. Haverford's desk was in the corner by the window.

Sunshine filtered between the blinds, casting her face in bars of light. Her bob cut was as stiff as her character. When I reached her desk, she looked up at me. My voice trembling, I asked if I could use American spelling.

"In America," I explained, "we spell the word *color* differently."

Did she even know that I was born in America? Or that my favorite song was Bruce Springsteen's "Born in the USA"? My second favorite song was Stevie Wonder's "I Just Called to Say I Love You." Mom preferred Stevie Wonder and often played his album in the cassette player in the late afternoon. She had purchased the cassettes in DC, where we vacationed in summer. When Springsteen roared from the speakers, I belted out the chorus: *I was . . . born in the USA.* His song was my anthem.

"Go back to your desk," Mrs. Haverford snapped.

I spelled *color* the British way, with a *u.*

As soon as the school year ended, Mom, Jana, and I were on a plane headed west. For the next three months, we resided at Teta's house, sleeping on single beds in the beige room on the second floor. It was called the beige room because of its beige draperies and wallpaper, and the cream-colored Persian rug. Auntie Hinda slept in the pink room, Uncle Mooney (Ameen David's son) in the blue room, and Auntie Laila in the computer room. Teta's master bedroom had walk-in closets filled with evening gowns and fur coats; she also had a balcony that overlooked the street. I walked in and out of these rooms freely, entering conversations between my aunts and uncle or lying next to Teta on her bed as she watched *The Price Is Right*, the remote control clamped in her hand like a fairy wand.

In the backyard enclosed with bamboo, Ameen David had planted fig trees from fig branches he had brought across the Atlantic from Lebanon. In late August the figs turned blackish purple and hung from the branches like softened bulbs. Jana and I picked them, split each one in half, and ate the red flesh standing in the dappled shade of the trees, our fingers sticky with nectar. Mom would sometimes join us, smiling. After eating one, she said the figs reminded her of home. I was too young to understand the ache of her nostalgia.

Teta drove us around in her big, sky-blue Cadillac with white leather seats. She was a reckless driver, calling anyone who cut into her lane a "jackass" as she popped gum between her teeth. As I had done in Jeddah, I looked out the window in search of kissers. One time, as Teta was driving up M Street in Georgetown, I spotted a couple in their early twenties kissing on the sidewalk by the entrance to a clothing store. I turned around in my seat and watched them through the rear window as they exchanged rapid-fire pecks. If only I could be shot at with kisses all over my mouth.

Oh America, land of public kissing and ice cream sundaes at Swenson's on Wisconsin Avenue; land of crushed ice and popsicles; land of Higger's Drugstore on Connecticut Avenue, where we walked to buy Bazooka bubble gum; land of the National Zoo in Cleveland Park; land of fireworks on the Fourth of July, all of us, my aunts and cousins included, sitting among thousands on the grassy lawn down by the Washington Monument, waving glow sticks, our skin hot and sticky; land of movie theaters and arcades; land of musicals at the Kennedy Center and Wolf Trap; land of the majestic Metro, which took us underground to the Smithsonian museums; land of fishing in Rock Creek Park; land of thunderstorms that blew out the electricity; land of the scent of freshly cut grass; land of "lightning bugs" at dusk, the flickering green dots of light more magical than the stars because we could reach them.

In 1990, toward the end of summer, Mom received a long-distance telephone call from Dad, who was calling from Jeddah. Mom sat at the office desk, which was peculiarly situated in a corner of the kitchen. She spoke to Dad in Arabic as Jana and I stood behind her, waiting for our turn to say hello. About three weeks earlier, Iraq had invaded Kuwait, and there was fear that Saddam Hussein would invade Saudi Arabia next. Mom hung up the phone before we had a chance to greet Dad and turned around in her chair. "Kids," she said, "we're not returning to Jeddah. We're staying in America."

Jana and I looked at each other, our eyes widening, and embraced. "We're staying!" we cheered. "We're staying!"

It was because of the threat of Saddam Hussein that my parents decided to relocate to America. I almost wanted to thank him. But once our euphoria subsided, Jana and I realized we'd never see our friends in Jeddah again. There would be no opportunity to tell them goodbye.

## ANOTHER AMERICA

We lived in Teta's house our first year in America. Afterward, we moved to the Maryland suburbs, where every few years over the course of nearly two decades, we packed up our belongings and moved from one rented house to another.

On my first day of school, Mom walked me to Mr. Macy's classroom. The school had been founded by three French sisters in 1911 and stood a few blocks from the National Cathedral in DC. The administration had admitted Jana and me only three days before the start of the school year, taking pity on our circumstances.

Except for one African American boy, the classroom consisted entirely of white Americans. Mom pointed to an empty desk in the front row. I looked up at her, not wanting to leave her side. She combed my black hair from my eyes.

"I'll see you later," she said.

I sat down, noticing how white and freckled all the boys and girls were, their hair light brown and blond. My skin was chestnut brown. When the boy sitting next to me asked where I was from, and I answered that I was American, he gave me a questioning look.

"You have an accent," he said.

At the sound of the bell, Mr. Macy welcomed us to fifth grade and opened his attendance book. His blond hair was swept to the side in a floppy arc. He coughed, cleared his throat, and began to take roll call. My legal family name is Abou-Zeineddine, and so I was at the top of the list.

"Hassan," he said, "Abou, um, Abou-Zeeneddine"? He looked directly at me, the Arab, sitting in the front row. He had pronounced the name *Hassan* with an emphatic stress on the *H*, his gravelly voice filled with phlegm from years of smoking. Whenever he had coughing fits in class, his face reddening, I feared he was about to regurgitate his soul.

My palms were sweating. "My first name starts with a *G*," I said. Mr. Macy must not have heard me, or perhaps he did, because he then said: "Welcome, *H*assan."

Although my British teachers at the Continental International School had routinely mispronounced my name, they had also mispronounced the names of most students in class because all of us were from elsewhere; our otherness was a trait we all shared. From my first day at school in DC throughout my years in college, I dreaded roll call. My name was invariably the first one announced, and although some conscientious teachers would put all their effort into pronouncing my name correctly, their attention exacerbated my sense of otherness.

That winter Jana and I both got sick from the flu—I vomited all over the table during Ms. Knapp's science class. Mom bought us downy winter coats, scarves, and gloves, and still we froze. School was torture. Students made fun of our brightly colored clothes, our accents, our funny sounding names. I was always embarrassed when Mom or Dad came to pick us up from school because they looked so different from my classmates' parents. On the occasion we went out to a shopping mall, I kept my head on a swivel, anxious of bumping into a classmate who would see the foreignness of my family. I hated these outings because there was nowhere to hide if I indeed bumped into a classmate, and it was during these moments that I wished I had the power to metamorphose into a blond boy with white skin and freckles. Although I never named my imaginary Blond Boy, who I visualized with his baseball cap on backward, I pined for the power to become him.

It didn't take Jana and me long to understand that the America we were experiencing wasn't the America of our former summers. The two were irreconcilable, and it was in this dissonance that we yearned to return to Jeddah. The following year our accents turned American and our skin paled. We still, however, had no friends.

At the end of sixth grade, Mom informed us that we were headed to Lebanon for the summer. The civil war had ended a year earlier in 1990, following fifteen years of bloodshed that had killed a hundred thousand Lebanese. It was finally safe to return to our ancestral land.

## WAR STORIES

My first glimpse of Beirut was from thousands of feet up in the air, my face glued to the frosty window of a Middle East Airlines jet descending for landing. The Corniche, formally known as Rue de Paris, wrapped around the triangular shores of Beirut, high-rise buildings flanking one side and a line of palm trees and the Mediterranean on the other. Mom pointed out the campus of AUB, which was easy to spot: a green oasis with red-tile buildings and a clock tower.

Looking through that airplane window, I realized Beirut was a swarming metropolis, a real city like Boston or New York. But unlike these great American cities, the buildings were riddled with bullets, which I noticed on a drive through downtown with one of my aunts. Some had gaping holes where rocket shells had struck. My family's apartment building in Karakol Druze on the western side of Beirut was also sieved with bullets. My cousins inundated me with stories about surviving the traumatic years of the war: the constant electricity cuts and water shortages, nights lit by candles and spent in the stairwell or the shelter downstairs during bombing raids. Their lives were restricted to school and home. It was too risky to wander the streets at night. Snipers hunted from rooftops. Hoodlums broke into cars.

Auntie May told me that as she was cooking in the kitchen one afternoon, a sniper's bullet ricocheted off a pan she was holding. She was lucky to survive.

My cousin Ramzi, who was fourteen and went by Rambo, pulled me aside to show me something in his bedroom closet. A high-ranking cub scout, Rambo was tall and skinny, his forearms laced with veins. He had curly brown hair and a sprawling unibrow. He refused to wear deodorant. His pocket bulged with a Zippo lighter and cigarettes he had pilfered from his father's pack. That day Rambo had returned home from school with blood spots on his T-shirt. He showed me a fresh cut on his knuckle.

"I punched a kid at school and got my knuckle stuck in his braces," he said. I looked at his fist with wonderment, imagining what it felt like to hit someone.

Rambo swung back the hanging clothes in his closet and reached for a Kalashnikov. He slipped the gun strap over his shoulder, aimed the automatic rifle at the window, and squinted. Body odor wafted from his armpits.

"Please don't shoot," I said.

He lowered the rifle. "It's unloaded. Let me teach you how to use it."

Rambo showed me how to pull and release the charging handle and pointed out the safety. I removed the clip, blew on it, and stuck it back in. The feel of the cold barrel and the wood of the butt, the spring of the trigger and the metallic smell of the instrument, empowered me, for I had the resource now to fight any man of any size.

Almost all Beirutis were armed during the war. Without a viable army or police force to protect them, people were left to fend for themselves. Rambo was allowed to keep the family Kalashnikov in his room as long as it remained unloaded. I asked him if he had ever used it on someone during the war.

He shook his head. "No one fucks with me."

Every member of my family had a war story. I began to yearn for one myself, because it seemed to me, even at that age, that these stories were a currency for belonging. You couldn't be Lebanese if you didn't have a war story to share.

For fifteen years, my family never ventured to East Beirut, the Christian side, for fear of being killed. At that time, people's throats were slit at roadblocks because of their religion, which was printed on their identity cards.

At least my family had the Corniche in west Beirut. The sea was their fleeting escape from a city, and a life, ravaged by war. During that summer of my eleventh year, I went on many drives with my aunts and cousins down the Corniche, mostly in the evenings when the heat dissipated and traffic eased. Vendors planted their handcarts filled with grilled and boiled corn at the edge of the sidewalk or even on the street itself. Auntie Waddad would order several corn on the cob from her open window and the vendor would pass them through. I'd receive a piping hot cob on a paper plate, and without a moment's hesitation, bite into the crispy blackened kernels dusted with salt. I held the cob at either end and twirled it about, chewing down on it until not a kernel remained, my teeth flaked with yellow and black skin.

On the weekends, Mom took Jana and me to the family house in Qornayel that Assad had built, and it was on these occasions that she became a girl again, pointing out the fruit trees in the garden she used to climb. We'd watch the sunset from the balcony overlooking the valley covered in pines. Once, a sliver of the sea appeared beyond the mountain ranges, shimmering like a shard of glass.

I began to think Lebanon was a place in which I could settle. We would return for a couple of more summers, and with each visit, I was drawn to the mountains and Beirut, places where my name was never mispronounced and my dark looks didn't stand out. As a teenager, I decided that as soon as I turned eighteen, I'd join the Lebanese Army. I bought customized dog tags from an army surplus store in Beirut and wore them throughout my freshman year of high school. The sound of the tags clinking against each other as I moved about reminded me of my military aspiration. Like Assad, I, too, would serve a nation's army, only Lebanon's, and I'd actually fight in combat if war broke out. I was prepared to die for my ancestral land!

Our summer visits to Lebanon came to an end when my family began to struggle financially, and it wouldn't be until my early twenties that I could afford to pay my own way to the Levant.

## THE CITY BY THE SEA

After obtaining my master's degree in creative writing, I left America and moved to Lebanon in 2005. As I had matured into adulthood, my sense of alienation only swelled. Perhaps in Lebanon I'd find some semblance of home.

At the time, Lebanon was in the midst of major political change. On February 14, 2005, former Prime Minister Rafic Hariri was assassinated by a car bomb as his motorcade was passing the St. George's Yacht Club, at a bend in the road leading to the main thoroughfare of the Corniche. An SUV packed with explosives was detonated by a suicide bomber. Twenty-one others were also killed. Hariri's assassination sparked the Cedar Revolution, a people's revolution that led to the withdrawal of Syrian troops from Lebanon after a presence of nearly thirty years.

I rented a studio in Beirut with a partial view of the Mediterranean. In no time, walking on the Corniche in the late afternoons or evenings became my Saturday ritual. It was the only place in the city where I could escape from my life as a middle school teacher and quell my feelings of lonesomeness and dislocation.

I had landed a position at Rawdah Middle School days before classes were scheduled to begin. I lacked teaching experience, but I was a native English speaker, and the school was desperate to fill the position of an eighth grade English and Social Studies teacher. I thought teaching would be a prime way to better understand Lebanon, as I would have the chance to see it through the eyes of its youth.

Before the first day of class, Mr. Hassan Choeir, chair of the English Department, gave me this advice: "The students come from the streets. They're animals. If they give you trouble, yell at them! Understand? Yell at them!"

Mr. Choeir was one year from retiring—he had been teaching middle school for thirty years and was about ready to throw his students into the sea. He longed to move up to Aley, a mountain town overlooking Beirut, where he could spend his remaining days reading his favorite poet, Alfred, Lord Tennyson, in the quiet serenity of his summer home. A short, bald man with purple lips, he had a smoker's cough as bad as Mr. Macy's. He wore big glasses that consumed half his face. Between classes and during lunch break, he chain-smoked in the teacher's lounge. Whenever I had supervising duties on the playground during recess, I overheard students mimicking Mr. Choeir's voice. They all sounded like Marlon Brando from *The Godfather*. I tried my best to stifle my laughter. But to my dismay, I discovered I wasn't spared the students' impersonations. I overheard them snapping at one another: "You think that's funny?" a phrase I used with troublemakers when they misbehaved.

On my first day, I entered a classroom hot and stuffy with thirty eighth graders who all looked up at me from their wooden desks. In my anxiousness, I gave them a big smile.

"Hey, guys. My name is Mr. Zeineddine."

That smile would haunt me for the entire year. In that moment, my students, who were terrified of the older, authoritarian teachers, became the hunters for a change.

I struggled from September until June to control my classroom. I once got sprayed in the face with cologne by a pudgy troublemaker as I was standing in the hallway; I was called a motherfucker in Arabic by a seventh grader, who got suspended; and one winter morning I had to calm down a classroom full of pro-Hezbollah seventh graders who were cheering the assassination of a rival politician, Gibran Tueni. One class clown, Firas Saffiedine, a smart but mischievous teen, followed me home from school—it was a twenty-minute walk home. When I answered his knock at the door, I found him grinning like a genie.

One day, I was guiding my eighth graders through an excerpt from Mark Twain's *Life on the Mississippi* when a student named Nour, a bright and mature teenager, raised her hand and asked me where I was on September 11.

"I was in my apartment in Washington, DC," I told my class, "in my final year of university. My classes were canceled for the day. My friends and I gathered around the TV and watched with horror the images of those planes crashing into the twin towers."

"America deserved it," Nour said. "Look what's going on in Palestine."

I looked at Nour with concern, not wanting politics to enter the classroom.

"But I'm American. Do you think I deserved it?" I asked her.

"You're *Lebanese*," Nour said.

At that moment, I felt immense pride: I *was* Lebanese. But still, I had to address Nour's problematic statement, which I then did.

The school day left me exhausted and stressed. I had nightmares in which my students were screaming in class and I was powerless to stop them.

On the weekends, I went out for long walks on the Corniche. I relied on these walks not only to forget about my failings as a teacher, but also to forget Beirut. As much as I enjoyed the frenetic vibe of the city—its countless cafés, five-star cuisine, pubs, bars, nightclubs, and movie theaters—I also found it claustrophobic. All those concrete buildings began to look the same. And the traffic was insufferable. But it was more than this. The superficiality of many Lebanese taxed me. You could stand on Hamra Street and watch the most expensive cars pass you by one after the other: Lamborghinis, Ferraris, Porches, Alfa Romeos, Mercedes, BMWs, and the occasional Rolls-Royce. Lebanese spend all their money buying fancy cars but have none left over to fill their tanks, a saying goes. I was a teacher with a lousy salary who relied on public transportation.

I didn't quite fit in, either. My cleaning lady, a short, hijabi woman with a massive belly, asked me if I was Armenian.

"I'm Lebanese," I said.

"Then why do you speak funny?"

My Arabic was broken. The cleaning lady assumed I was Armenian because older generations of Armenians who had migrated to Lebanon following the Armenian genocide spoke broken Arabic and often confused the male and female pronouns.

I didn't even have to speak for others to recognize I was coming from abroad. I once sat down at a table at Starbucks on Hamra Street when a middle-aged man sitting across from me put down his newspaper on his lap and asked me where I came from.

"I'm Lebanese," I told him in my accented Arabic.

"But where were you living before?"

"America . . . How did you know?"

"By your clothes, by the way you walked to your chair. A Lebanese man will enter a room as if he owns it, and he'll be wearing a tight fancy shirt and slim pants. Look at you."

My shirt was loose over faded jeans. I was wearing sandals. Unlike Lebanese men who slicked back their hair with gel, mine hung down to my shoulders.

Among the many people I encountered—taxi drivers, bakers, delivery boys, florists, barbers—all wanted to know why I had come to Lebanon. Although I'd explain my reasons for coming, they were rarely convinced. They couldn't understand how someone could leave America for a country with so few opportunities and low-paying jobs.

The only thing keeping them in Lebanon was the fact that they had nowhere else to go.

I was unable to make Lebanese friends. The men and women my age had grown up together, gone to the same schools and universities, and had survived the civil war. They spoke in a language I lacked the personal history to acquire.

My walks on the Corniche came to an abrupt end in the summer of 2006 when Israel and Hezbollah went to war. The Israeli Defense Forces (IDF) began bombing the country in retaliation for Hezbollah's kidnapping of two of its soldiers.

I stayed with my aunts and cousins in an apartment building in Hamra. The first few days and nights of the bombing were terrifying. IDF jets were pounding Dahieh, a Shiite suburb of Beirut and home to Hezbollah leader Hassan Nasrallah. Reverberations from the bombs were felt throughout the city, rattling windows and saucers on tables. Black, swirling fumes hung in the sky.

We were eight living in a one-bedroom apartment. I realized you didn't survive a war alone. You endured it with those closest to you. We spent our time in front of the TV, watching the news obsessively. We never lacked for food or water, as grocery stores remained open and were well stocked, and electricity, thankfully, wasn't an issue, as the apartment building had two generators. Across from our apartment building, the Weiner Haus Hotel, a three-star German hotel under renovation, had opened its rooms to refugees from southern Lebanon and Dahieh. Thousands of refugees were flooding into Beirut to escape the bombings, and they soon occupied hotels, public schools, and even Sanayeh, the public garden.

After several days of my family and I waking up to the sound of bombs, watching the news, squeezing ourselves next to one another on the couch or at the dinner table, our hair greasy and our skin oily, we got on one another's nerves. During the day we'd leave the apartment for an hour or so to walk the empty streets, buy a few supplies, and at night, if we weren't watching the news or discussing the war, we were playing card games, smoking hookahs on the veranda, or simply gritting our teeth.

My aunts urged me to evacuate with the thousands of foreigners leaving the country by ship or by car across the border into Syria. I refused. How could I leave my family behind? There was another reason, however, why I didn't want to leave, a rather self-serving one. I had the opportunity to suffer as a Lebanese. If we were going to die, we'd die together. For so many years I had been hearing tales about the civil war, seen documentaries, and read novels and books about it, that it had produced in me a nostalgic longing for it and envy of the people who had suffered through it. Now I could suffer, fear for my life, and hopefully live to talk and write about it. I'd finally have my own war story.

After the summer war I left the middle school to teach at AUB. I walked down the same paths Mom had traversed in the seventies, taught in the same buildings in which she had once been a student.

"Make sure to eat at Universal," Mom told me over the phone from Maryland.

Universal was a hamburger joint on the corner of Jean D'Arc and Bliss Streets, across from the main entrance to the university. In operation since the early seventies, it was famous for its hamburgers made the Lebanese way: packed with french fries and coleslaw lathered with ketchup.

By that point I had found my own community of misfits in Beirut: foreign-born Lebanese or those who had studied and worked abroad and internationals who taught at the university. I came to the realization that I'd be a misfit wherever I went. Despite my personal troubles in Beirut, as well as Lebanon's political instability, life in the city was always vibrant—not simply because of the nightlife and the urban rush but because you never knew when war might break out; everyone lived each day as if it were their last, believing sooner or later the bombs would fall from the sky.

During my time off and when the weather was warmer, I took the bus up to the family house in Qornayel. I spent hours reading on the balcony, the scent of pine in the air, the trees filled with birdsong. A villager was invariably chopping wood or hammering nails into beams or cutting metal with a miter saw. The tolling of the church bells on the other side of the village swept down from the mountaintop. On a few occasions I heard the announcement of a death over the loudspeakers. In summer, especially on Sundays, I watched wedding motorcades drive up and down the roads, the cars honking, hazard lights flashing. I pictured Assad strolling down the road in a bowler hat, thirsty for beer. I, too, liked beer and hats, though I favored fedoras.

As the years passed, I was unable to get promoted at work without a doctoral degree, and so in August 2011, I moved to Milwaukee, Wisconsin, to pursue a PhD in English. My plan was to eventually come back to Beirut to secure a better position at AUB. Life plans, however, are about as elusive as childhood dreams.

## ARAB AMERICA

Seven years later, in 2018, I landed in Dearborn, Michigan, the so-called capital of Arab America. I was hired to teach Arab American literature and creative writing at the University of Michigan–Dearborn (UM-D). Beirut would have to wait.

I had heard of Dearborn back in high school. My parents occasionally ordered boxes of baklava from the Shatila Bakery, which was in Dearborn. All I knew was that a lot of Arabs lived up north. I began to learn more about Dearborn during graduate school, where I researched the Arab American experience and came across the city in various Arab American novels, such as Diana Abu-Jaber's *Crescent* and Alia Yunis's *The Night Counter*. When I began teaching Arab American literature as a visiting professor at a liberal arts college in central Ohio before moving to Dearborn, I started to mythologize the place. I shared articles about Dearborn and showed pictures and video clips of the city to my students. Although Arab migrants had made their way to Detroit earlier in the twentieth century, I explained, many more were lured to Michigan when the Ford Motor Company started paying their employees five dollars a day in 1914.

"Dearborn has the largest concentration of Arabs in America," I said. "There are even store signs in Arabic. Isn't that interesting?"

I fantasized about living in an Arab American community, without knowing what that entailed.

In Beirut, it wasn't uncommon for taxi drivers, once they heard me speak Arabic and asked where I was coming from, and I answered "America," to then ask, "From Michigan?" A few even followed with: "From Dearborn?"

In the summer before moving to Dearborn, I had spent a month in Beirut. At a funeral reception held for a relative at Beit el Tayfeh, a Druze community building, I sat in the men's section. Most of the men were Al-Awars from Qornayel. As I sweated through my suit, they asked me where I lived, and when I answered that I was moving to Dearborn, one said: "Dearborn is Dahieh and the Jnoub." Jnoub is a word for southern Lebanon, which has a high concentration of Shiites. This man had never even been to Dearborn, but he had heard stories.

Lara Rizk,* a librarian at AUB, where I spent my mornings writing in a small cubicle in the library, told me that Dearborn was shaabiyeh (a broad negative connotation for the poor and underdeveloped) and to stay clear of it. We were sitting in her office on the first floor of the library. She had earned a Master of Library Sciences from Wayne State University and had lived for two years in Detroit. "I never went into Dearborn," she told me. "The people," she said, shaking her head. She was about to continue but stopped, worried that I'd judge her. Lara had been raised in a Christian household in Beirut, and although she had studied with Muslims and had Muslim friends, that didn't mean she was comfortable living in a Muslim community.

"I plan to live in Dearborn," I told her.

"Good luck," she said.

---

* Personal names Lara, Noha, and Ali are pseudonyms.

If living in Beirut wasn't viable, then the next best option was living in a place that reminded me of the city by the sea. A place filled with Arabs that had the conveniences of America.

My wife Rana's parents were delighted that we were moving to Dearborn, as it would facilitate Rana's transition from Lebanon to America. Rana and I had met in Beirut in the summer of 2016, before I started my teaching position in Ohio. She is originally from Baalbek (amazingly not Qornayel), a city in the Bekaa Valley famous for its Roman ruins, and grew up in Dahieh. Fortunately, her family's apartment building escaped destruction during the 2006 summer war.

Rana's parents had seen TV reports about the Arab community in Dearborn and had heard stories about the city from those who traveled back and forth between Dahieh and Dearborn.

"There's halal meat in Dearborn," Rana's mother told her.

"Nothing will change for you," Rana's father said.

Rana's older brother, Youssef, who lives in Warsaw, was perplexed. "You're crossing the ocean to live among Arabs?" he asked her.

In May 2018, four months before the start of my new job at UM-D, Rana and I looked to buy a house in Dearborn (we were still unmarried). Neither of us had ever owned property. I was especially keen on purchasing a house instead of renting, remembering the disorienting feeling my family experienced packing and unpacking boxes. I wanted Rana and I to feel that we belonged to a place, even though we hardly knew Dearborn.

We drove north up I-75 from Ohio and arrived in Dearborn in the early evening. After checking in at a motel, we drove to the east side of town, which was predominantly Arab. We were eager to see the Dearborn I had mythologized for the past several years. Our first stop was the Shatila Bakery, which I typed into Google Maps. On our way to the bakery, we found an Arabic station on the radio—the DJ only spoke in Arabic and played Arabic songs—and as the voice of Melhem Zein, a singer from Baalbek, soared through our speakers, we drove down Michigan Avenue, past the Arab American National Museum, and took a left on Schaefer Road. Grocery stores and restaurants on either side of the road bore signs in Arabic and English. We took a left on Warren Avenue and arrived at Shatila's on the corner of Schaefer and Williamson. The bakery was packed with Middle Easterners, the majority of the women wearing headscarves. Artificial palm trees decorated with string lights arched over the patrons sitting at the tables. Behind a glass counter were tempting cakes and pastries that we usually found in the patisseries in Beirut. Around the counter was a display of Arabic cookies, baklava, and trays of kanafi. Rana and I bought kanafi and a pot of Turkish coffee flavored with cardamom and sat under a palm tree. A mix of Arabic and English buzzed in the air.

"It feels like we're in Beirut," Rana said.

With sugar and caffeine coursing through our blood, we drove through the neighborhoods. The modest brick houses were built close together, with narrow driveways barely separating them. A gaudy mansion would suddenly appear like a spoiled child demanding attention, fashioned with stone pillars and big entrance doors with brass knockers. At one such mansion, statues of lion sentinels stood on either side of the front staircase. I was reminded of the Lebanese expats who erected huge houses in their native villages in Mount Lebanon and in southern Lebanon, houses that dwarfed all others and remained empty, gathering dust, for the majority of the year.

Arab families sat on their front porches, drinking coffee. A man in a sleeveless white undershirt, the cotton stretched over his belly, sat back in a beach chair smoking a hookah. Some families sat in plastic chairs in their garages with the door open. Hijabi women walked down the sidewalks, trailed by children.

"Amazing!" I kept repeating. This was the first time either of us had entered an Arab community outside of the Middle East. "We made the right decision to come here," I said.

Following our night out, Rana and I met our real-estate agent, a Lebanese American named Noha. She was born and raised in Dearborn and couldn't see herself living elsewhere. A mother of two young daughters, she spoke English with a Midwestern accent and Arabic as a native speaker, which I found surprising. Growing up, Jana and I would always respond in English when spoken to in Arabic, and as such, we were better at understanding Arabic than speaking it. But Noha spoke as if she had lived her entire life in Lebanon.

Noha referred us to a local lender named Ali. Like Noha, he was a Lebanese American born and raised in Dearborn. In scheduling an appointment with him, I told him that my partner and I were in the area and would arrive shortly at his office. In his late thirties, Ali had a neatly trimmed beard and short, black hair combed to the side and frozen in mousse. He was dressed in a black suit with a blue tie. He shook our hands and sat in a swivel chair at his computer. On his desk was a donation box for Al-Mabarrat, a Lebanese Shiite humanitarian organization dedicated to aiding orphans in Lebanon.

Before discussing the prospect of a loan, Ali leaned toward me, grinning.

"When you said that you and your partner were on your way," he said, "I thought you were two men coming to see me." Rana and I exchanged glances. Ali expected us to laugh as if he were telling a joke, but we remained silent. He turned to his computer.

"Are you married?" he asked me, looking at his screen.

"No," I said.

He turned to me. "Engaged?"

"No."

He looked at Rana. "Just friends?"

"No," she said.

He went back to typing on his keyboard to alleviate the awkward silence.

We declined Ali's services, and later I began seeing his face in advertisements on highway billboards and on signs fixed to the back grille of the shopping carts at the Kroger grocery store. "You are not a loan," all the signs said, with Ali smiling, his hair glowing like a waxed bowling ball. Rana and I hoped that the younger generation of Arab Americans in Dearborn didn't share Ali's apparent conservatism.

An Iraqi American student who I met that summer in the office of the English department at the university advised me not to live in east Dearborn.

"Do you like children?" she asked me.

I nodded.

"Well, do you like children running across your yard from morning to night? Or random strangers parking in your driveway? Because that's east Dearborn for you. Stay away from the Arabs."

Rana and I preferred to live among Arabs, but we started to think a little space from the community might be healthy. We bought a house in west Dearborn.

## PORTALS TO LEBANON

When Rana and I grocery shopped at the Middle Eastern stores, whether it was Greenland (a.k.a. Mustapha's) or Dearborn Fresh (a.k.a. Al-Medina), as soon as we entered the front door, we were transported to a grocery store in Beirut from that first whiff of roasted nuts and coffee beans. There was also the smell of raw meat at the butcher's in the back; the bags of thyme, sumac, bulgur, moograbieh, and fava beans stacked on metal shelves; the jars of pickled eggplant, radishes, and hot peppers; the strained yogurt and kashkaval cheese; the loaves of pita bread and boxes of ka'ak; the Ghandour biscuits and Unica chocolate; and the Rani and Shani juices that Rana used to drink as a child. As in Beirut, we'd catch the patrons sampling the fruits on display—they'd pick grapes or loquats and eat them in the aisle. It wasn't uncommon to find olive pits left on the edge of the olive counter. As soon as we left the grocery store and a blast of icy wind hit our faces, we were reminded that we were in the Midwest.

Many of the small businesses in the city that weren't outwardly Middle Eastern were owned by Middle Easterners, such that most of their patrons were Arab. Rana and I were always confused whether to speak in English or Arabic to the cashiers. Even American establishments like Starbucks were somehow Arabized, or should I say, Dearbornized. When I entered the Starbucks on Michigan Avenue in west Dearborn, I often found a group of Lebanese men sitting in the leather armchairs in the main seating area carrying on a conversation in Arabic over espressos as they must have done in the coffeehouses in the Middle East.

"Dearborn isn't America," Rana once told me. "It's Dahieh."

High-rise buildings dominate the Beirut suburb, its narrow streets crisscrossed above with electric lines. Martyr posters of Hezbollah soldiers are pasted on walls and streetlamps. Yellow Hezbollah flags flutter from balconies and telephone poles. Although Rana grew up in Dahieh, she attended the Lycée National and Saint Joseph University, the latter a Catholic school founded by Jesuits in 1875, and previously worked in companies with no religious affiliations, so she never quite embraced the Islamic atmosphere of Dahieh or the fact that most of the women, including her mother, wore headscarves. But she still dressed conservatively. There were eyes watching her every move, especially the neighbors. As frustrated as she was by Dahieh, Rana accepted her reality because this was a side of Lebanon that wasn't going to change.

When we began living in Dearborn, Rana had expected her life to change. "I thought America was this place where I'd care less about what others thought of me. You do what you want," she said. "But in Dearborn, I still worry that others are judging me." Rana particularly felt this way when buying groceries. The salespeople and patrons could tell that she was coming from abroad by the terms she used when she spoke, sometimes saying kilos instead of pounds. "When did you arrive here?" they asked her, followed by, "Why'd you come here?" They wanted to know her religion, to see if she was a practicing Muslim. Fortunately, Rana didn't feel the same way in west Dearborn, where we frequented bars without anyone judging us.

My work at the university reminded me of my experience at AUB in that I was teaching Arabs again. The majority of my students in my Arab American Women Writers seminar were Arab, and as the university was a commuter campus, almost all were from the area and had attended the local high schools. I had Lebanese, Syrian, Iraqi, Palestinian, and Yemeni students. I had never taught Yemeni or Iraqi students before. I made it a point to stress to my students through the various works we read that semester that the Arab American experience was not monolithic, that there was a diverse range of experiences when it came to being Arab and Muslim in America, and that we should avoid all generalizations.

"The Arab American experience in Dearborn is unique," I told them. "My sister and I were the only Arabs in our school." I wanted my students to appreciate their good fortune to have grown up in Dearborn and, except for the times they left the city, to have rarely felt like outsiders because of their ethnicity. Later that day in my office, I wondered if my students had heard the envy in my voice.

## COEXISTENCE

One day, Rana came back home distressed from an outing with a Lebanese friend she knew from Beirut. This friend, a well-educated and successful woman, told Rana that the other Arabs—specifically the Iraqis and Yemenis—weren't as "classy" as the Lebanese. "They don't even respect the law," the friend said. Rana's friend only associated with Lebanese.

I was curious about what the other Arabs in town thought of the Lebanese community. My student Fatima Al-Rasool shared her impressions with me. Fatima is an Iraqi American who was born in Amman, Jordan, and immigrated to America with her family in 1998. After brief stops in Arizona and Detroit, they settled in Dearborn, and later, Dearborn Heights. In my campus office, Fatima explained that in school, most of her friends were Americanized Lebanese who didn't distinguish Arabs from one another. But the differences between the Arab ethnicities in Dearborn were marked. There was a hierarchy in Dearborn, Fatima explained, with Lebanese at the top followed by Iraqis and then Yemenis. "Growing up," she said, "I always felt like Lebanese people were better." She attributed this feeling of inferiority to whiteness in America. "Lebanese know that they're more white than other Arabs, and there are privileges to being white in America. But Lebanese Americans have been here a lot longer, so that might also factor into it."

Several of Fatima's Iraqi and Yemeni friends abhorred Dearborn and were desperate to leave, and not simply because of the Lebanese majority. "Dearborn is a bubble," Fatima said. "People are always watching you." This was especially true for the Arab women in regard to what they were "allowed" to do.

Many of my other Arab American students explained that they felt safe only in Dearborn. By safe they meant being protected from racist bigotry, particularly in the wake of Trump's presidency. When I was discussing the impact of the attacks of 9/11 on Arab America in my seminar in the fall, my student Nour said that whenever she had to leave Dearborn, she removed her hijab in fear of being stared at or even antagonized by white people. Jawad, who had a big, bushy black beard, said that he avoided driving into rural Michigan, where he clearly stood out. At the end of the spring semester, my student Heba came to my office and described a harrowing incident she had experienced as a hijabi woman in November 2015, a week after the suicide bombings in Paris. At the time, Heba was eighteen and had recently been issued her driver's license. "When I got my license," she said, "I got my freedom." With the exception of a few summer trips to her family's native village, Tibnin, in southern Lebanon, she had primarily remained in Dearborn. "I have a really limited experience in life," she admitted. When she was offered an internship at the law offices of Joumana Kayrouz in Southfield, about twelve miles northwest of Dearborn, she left Dearborn on her own for the first time. "It was a culture shock," she said, in that she wasn't in an Arab American enclave. One day, she stepped into the elevator with a male colleague from the law firm. An elderly white man followed them inside. As soon as the doors closed, the elderly man looked at Heba, and then stepped up to her and spat in her face.

"It's because of you people that innocents are dying," he said. "Go back to ISIS."

"Stop man, this isn't right," Heba's colleague said.

Heba and her colleague got off on the eighth floor. "I went to the bathroom and started crying," she said. "It struck me that someone could have so much hate in their heart for me without even knowing who I am all because of the hijab I wear around my head."

Heba had never experienced any discrimination or hostility for being Muslim in Dearborn. But elsewhere, she had been singled out. "When I was younger," she said, "I'd visit Cedar Point in Ohio with my family, and people would stare and snicker at me if I walked by.

I asked my mother why people did that; she said because they're ignorant."

I asked Heba if she had ever considered removing her hijab for safety precautions. It had crossed her mind, but she'd been wearing the hijab since she was seven. "I wear it for myself; it's part of my identity. If I have to lose a part of my identity to feel safe, that's wrong."

She went on to describe her upbringing in Dearborn, which like Fatima, she called a "bubble," and that she felt more of a sense of community here than in Tibnin. "My generation [in Dearborn] understands me. We're all struggling with our identity, so we get it." The villagers in Tibnin didn't understand her Arab American upbringing. "This is my motto: Born in Dearborn, live in Dearborn, die in Dearborn. I even went to Dearborn High."

Heba's notion of belonging to Dearborn on the basis of a shared struggle over identity resonated with what I had been contemplating about my own experience in Dearborn. Could one feel at home in a place where many of its inhabitants were conflicted about the idea of home? Heba explained that there was a look that she and her Arab friends shared that spoke of this conflict. It was a look of familiarity that said, I don't quite know where I'm from or where I belong, but neither do you.

I questioned how truly "safe" Dearborn was for my Arab American students and for Rana and me. Those who despised Arabs and Muslims knew exactly where to find us.

One day in late April, with the sun out and the buds of trees starting to bloom, Rana and I went to Ford Field Park to play badminton. Our version of badminton consisted of swatting the shuttlecock back and forth to each other without a net, which we did on the paved area of the park. Our objective was simply to keep the shuttlecock high up in the air. We must have been a ridiculous sight to onlookers, the way we nearly threw our bodies to the ground to keep the shuttlecock afloat. On that spring day, a few hijabi women sat on the benches by the river.

Three young Arab men were kicking a soccer ball around on the grass. Arab children swung back and forth on the swings. As I was about to serve, I noticed a middle-aged white man cycling slowly on the asphalt, making wide circles as he turned his head from side to side. He wore a baseball cap and a backpack over a T-shirt. He was the only non-Arab in the park. What was inside his backpack? I served the shuttlecock to Rana but kept my eye on him. If he pulled out a gun, I was prepared to run to Rana and cover her body with my own to protect her from the oncoming bullets. This image made me swing at air when the shuttlecock came back to me.

"Let's take a break," I said.

We stood next to each other. I pointed out the cyclist, who was now talking on his cell phone. I expressed my concerns to Rana, who stood in silence. The cyclist returned his phone inside his pocket and cycled over the grass, approaching the hijabi women on the benches. I held my breath. The cyclist stopped at the river, peered at the rapids, and then sped over the footbridge and into the parking lot and was gone.

My anxiety was borne from the continuing mass shootings and the growing rise of white supremacists, from the anti-immigration rhetoric spewed by the White House and right-wing media outlets. The cyclist may have been a decent man, but I had been unwilling to give him the benefit of the doubt.

Rana and I spent most of our time in Dearborn. To celebrate the end of the academic year, we met up with American friends from the university at a pizza joint in Ferndale, a hip, liberal suburb of Detroit thirteen miles northeast of Dearborn. As we washed down our pizza with craft beer, we noticed that we were the only Arabs in the restaurant. I took a quick glance out the window to see if I could spot any Arabs on the sidewalk. There were none. We were minorities, I reminded myself. Outsiders. This was how it had always been for me in DC, Milwaukee, and Ohio. I felt an intense yearning to be among Arabs, and when I shared this sentiment with Rana on our drive back to Dearborn, she said she had felt the same way at the restaurant. It was as if we had traveled far from our country and had begun to long for it and its people. In less than a half hour, we were in Dearborn. Like my student Heba, we had experienced our own culture shock.

A couple of weeks later, the holy month of Ramadan commenced in early May. Restaurants, bakeries, cafés, and hookah lounges remained open into the early hours, festooned with Ramadan decorations—crescent moons, stars, and paper lanterns. "Our best business is between one and three a.m.," Ibrahim, owner of Qahwa House, a popular Yemeni coffeehouse in east Dearborn, told me. At night, following iftar, which was when the sunrise-to-sunset fast was broken, small tents appeared outside restaurants and in parking lots, where late-night (or early morning) food, the suhoor meal, was sold. Every Friday and Saturday night, a suhoor festival was held in Dearborn Heights on the grounds next to an athletic facility. Festivities began at 11:45 p.m. and lasted until 4:00 a.m. This was the second year the festival was being held, and an estimated eight thousand participants attended opening night, requiring Dearborn Police to direct traffic. Rana and I made it a point to visit the festival every weekend, walking among hundreds of Arab Americans, mostly teenagers. String lights bathed food and merchandise tables in a soft, golden hue. We squeezed between the long lines stretching from the food stalls, where a variety of meals were sold, from pancakes, barbeque, hamburgers, corn on the cob, and potatoes, to crepes and cotton candy. The smell of hookah smoke drifted in the cool air—one stall sold portable hookahs made out of disposable cups and mouth stems. Several underage teens walked around puffing on these hookahs, taking turns inhaling mouthfuls of flavored tobacco. Only in Dearborn was a festival like this possible.

I bumped into a student named Sara Bazzi, who was helping her brother sell knickknacks at a table. She had recently graduated and was now contemplating her next step.

"I went to Ann Arbor to check out their MBA program," she said, "but I couldn't stand the place. I felt so different. I want to stay in Dearborn."

"I understand," I told her. I truly did.

## THE METAMORPHOSES OF DEARBORN

Dearborn's identity as a bustling Arab American city is a recent phenomenon. Nader Seif, a software developer based in Auburn Hills, lived in Dearborn in the '80s and early '90s. Of Palestinian descent, Nader was born and raised in Amman, Jordan, and came to America in 1983 for college. Following a brief stint in North Carolina, he moved up to Michigan to attend Henry Ford Community College in Dearborn, and later transferred to Wayne State University. After his apartment in Detroit was broken into, he moved to Dearborn, which was considered safer, sharing an apartment with a friend on the east side. In 1984 the area was desolate, pocked with big, empty lots. There were only three Arab establishments in town, all located between Wyoming and Schaefer Streets: the Lebanese Restaurant; Yasmine Bakery; and an Arabic bookstore. Nader lived seven houses south of the Lebanese Restaurant. Most of his neighbors were American. When he married in 1988, he and his wife Wejdan Azzou, an Iraqi Chaldean, moved into a nearby apartment. In the late '80s, Dearborn still had few Arab establishments, but Lebanese families had begun to trickle into the neighborhoods. Nader and Wejdan hosted many parties for their Arab and American friends that lasted into the early hours, playing loud music and serving plenty of food and alcohol. It wasn't unusual for their friends to spend the night. In the morning, Nader and Wejdan's landlord, Abu Ali, appeared at their door with the moral righteousness of the religious police. Abu Ali monitored who came in and out of their apartment, and he criticized Nader and Wejdan for their late-night parties. "I saw the tall woman again," Abu Ali said, in reference to Nader and Wejdan's tall American friend. In 1992, the liquor store across from the Lebanese Restaurant where Nader and Wejdan bought their alcohol closed down. The Chaldean owner doubted his store could survive in a neighborhood that was quickly turning Muslim. Nader didn't feel that he was living in America anymore. He was confused about what was considered appropriate and inappropriate in the way he interacted with his new Arab neighbors, who watched his comings and goings with inquisitive eyes. He had grown tired of Abu Ali's visits. In 1993, Nader and Wejdan left Dearborn. They were expecting a baby girl and wanted to move into a better school district. They also preferred to live in a place where they weren't required to conform to the conservatism of a Muslim community.

The Dearborn that I've come to know began to take shape in 2003, following the US invasion of Iraq and the subsequent influx of Iraqi refugees and immigrants. "As much as I complain about Dearborn," Nader told me, "it makes up for not visiting the Arab world. It's like going back to the Old Country."

Nader and Wejdan now live in west Bloomfield, close to twenty miles northwest of Dearborn. They visit Dearborn for the restaurants, the grocery stores and bakeries, and events at the Arab American National Museum. "We're so proud of how much our community has accomplished," Nader said. "We really did something positive. Dearborn was once a sleepy town, and now it's thriving."

I asked him if he'd ever consider moving back to Dearborn.

"Yeah, but not really."

## DEARBORNITES

Today, Rana and I recognize faces at community events and banquets (Dearborn loves its banquets), and at the grocery stores, restaurants, and cafés. We've made a few friends.

I still don't call Dearborn home. A job brought us here. We could have ended up elsewhere. When we visited my parents in Maryland over Christmas break, we packed a carry-on with wheat, cheese, and thyme manakeesh; loaves of pita bread; frozen kanafi; ka'ak; sesame cookies; and nougat candies. We had followed the custom of bringing back food from the homeland for loved ones.

Dearborn isn't Lebanon, nor is it entirely America. Although I'm taken back to Beirut whenever I step into the grocery stores or the hookah cafés, or when I hear the Lebanese dialect in the streets or happen to watch Lebanese cable TV at someone's house, I'm not in Lebanon. One has to walk the streets of Lebanon to be in Lebanon, to gaze at the Mediterranean and the snowcapped mountains looming in the distance, to hop in a taxi in Beirut and feel the stickiness of the seat against your legs, to suffer the daily anxieties of its people.

My great-grandfather's decision to come to America has, after all these years, led me to Dearborn. From everything I've learned about Assad Ali Al-Awar, I think he would have felt secure raising a family in the Dearborn of today. He wouldn't have needed to send his wife and daughters back to Lebanon to live among Arabs. They would have settled right here.

# WAṬAN

*Hanan Ali Nasser*

Dear Nour,

I remember little of myself at your age. I recall being a child—sensitive, not unlike yourself, but silly and unfledged and too shy.

I believe that my consciousness began the day you were born. I remember thinking as I watched your wrapped, newborn body: *Now I am finally awake. From now on I will remember.* It was then I felt I had finally grown into consciousness, finally able to fully remember what I had seen and felt. With your birth, I began knowing and remembering. And with your growth, I met a glimpse of my once lost childhood self.

As you may now know, our parents have not always lived here. I, too, was not born here. In 1997, when I was three years old, our family fled Baghdad following the Iraqi Civil War, which was a series of uprisings during the Persian Gulf War. It was a turbulent and violent time that made life very dangerous for Iraqis. We traveled to Jordan, where we waited for eighteen months before being granted permission to enter the United States. I do not remember much of these transition years, nor much of those following our settling into America. I did not find it difficult to imagine, however, how our parents must have felt during these early years. I later witnessed these emotions when finding photographs taken of them as they walked through the aisles of the Detroit Metropolitan Airport for the first time. In the photographs, Mama and Baba stood tall and smiling, our brother, sister, and I below them, seemingly unaware of our surroundings.

Our parents' lives as children, though not free from the economic troubles that afflicted many Iraqis, were not much unlike ours. Before coming to America, Mama and Baba lived in Baghdad with their parents, siblings, and relatives. Baba, like his father and older brothers, worked as a carpenter and built and repaired houses, a trade job which he continued after settling in America. He was also a student and athlete, becoming the top-rated boxer in Iraq at the age of twenty. Mama also went to school and was the eldest of her siblings. She always describes her life as a very happy one, where her mornings began with the voice of Fairuz and the evenings came with anticipation of seeing her father return home from work.

Our parents were forced to leave Baghdad due to a strict and violent regime led by Saddam Hussein. Any hint of discontent or rebellion led to interrogation, something that was not uncommon for many of the men in our family's community to experience. During this time, Baba's oldest brother, a former soldier, was to be drafted into the army. Due to Saddam's harsh regulations, he had not abided. One night, our home was raided and searched by a group of government soldiers in hopes of locating our uncle and forcing his draft. Mama tells me that this terrified our family, which included Baba's parents and siblings, who themselves had children. Baba found himself confronting the soldiers, objecting to their mistreatment of the family and their endangering of the women and children's safety and privacy. For this, he was immediately arrested and imprisoned. Since Saddam's soldiers had failed to find our uncle in our home, they threatened to use Baba as a replacement for his brother if he was not found. A close friend and relative of our family sought to help Baba. He protested the injustice of his arrest to state police members and officials, finally convincing them that he had done no wrong. After four long days, Baba returned home, weary and starving, in the same clothes he had been arrested in. Mama says that Baba's condition was so poor that his unclean clothing caused a serious case of pox in some of our family members, including my infant sister. Baba recalls the many other innocent men who were imprisoned with him, expressing his contempt of the government's severe and unjust treatment of them. Many of these men never returned to their families, and many more like them—fathers, brothers, uncles, sons, even soldiers—continued to be brutally arrested and tortured.

And so our parents sought to leave Iraq. They did not know what to do or what would happen. It was, as Baba describes, "like walking into a dark cave." They did not know where their travels would lead, though their only hope was to escape their situation. Several years before this time and shortly after I was born, when economic turmoil still distressed many Iraqi citizens, Baba was compelled to travel to Jordan in search of work. Many Iraqis had visited there in hopes of finding a safer place to bring their families. This Baba also hoped to do, and after eight long, strenuous months, he returned home. After a year and a half, we were finally able to prepare passports for travel. Baba was forced to take out a loan to pay for this, one he was unable to repay until he had worked in Jordan for some time. But we were unable to leave together. Mama, our siblings, and I traveled to Jordan as refugees, while Baba, due to the effects of being once imprisoned by the Iraqi government, was forced to walk across the border and seek entrance without a passport. Our time in Jordan, however, was at least as difficult as it had been in Iraq, due to the country's economic conditions.

We lived in a small room attached to a landholder's house, which opened onto the side of a mountainous area. In it was one window and one door, a corner where we stored our blankets and few belongings, and a sink we used for washing. Mama tells me that we slept and ate on the floor and that it was very challenging for them to support our family, even though Baba worked daily in manual labor. This was especially difficult when our siblings and I were ill. Finding work was extremely important, so much so that a day without work meant no food. Gathering the remains of bones from a butcher's shop for a meal of soup was not uncommon for our parents.

After eight months in Jordan, our parents received news that we were accepted as refugees and could travel to America, news not all families like ours had the opportunity to hear. Afterward, our family began to receive funds from the government, making our last months in Jordan far easier and more comfortable than they had been.

Our first home in America was a small house in Detroit. In settling into America, though finally having reached a new state of peace and safety, our parents' new life caused fear and loneliness. Their few social relationships included those they had with families who also sought refuge from Iraq. Their biggest hope now was to care for us, to begin to build a future that would prove safer than the one they left behind. Though the ideas, customs, and values of the American people were unfamiliar to our parents and very different from those they had lived with, they found many of these things to be better than they had been back home. They found comfort in the organized manner of laws and in discovering that they, like those in their new community, could live independently and in privacy, something once strange to them. With this, they learned to alter their own lives in respect of these laws and the people they lived among.

We lived in our Detroit house for several months before moving between many different apartments and tenements in Dearborn and Detroit. During this time, after we had lived for a year in America, Baba was injured at work and was unable to return to full-time work. Afterward, he worked only when his physical state allowed him.

We eventually settled into a small three-bedroom home in Detroit. It was surrounded by many little houses in a diverse community, and just a couple of streets away began the city of Dearborn, to which we would return in another eight years. As our parents sometimes reminisce, not all our neighbors in Detroit were comfortable or accustomed to living near Muslim Americans, especially during the early aughts. This, amid the moderate safety of the area, occasionally caused fear and unease. Nevertheless, we grew to love our home and eventually made friends with some of our neighbors. We had a large backyard, which, over the years, slowly became encircled by the gathering of small houses, garages, and sheds Baba loved to build.

Growing up, my siblings and I quickly learned to read and write English. And though this was something constantly embraced, our parents encouraged us to speak Arabic at home. They felt it was important that we not forget our native language or lose the benefits that came with it. Although they soon became accustomed to their new home, our parents held firm to the manners and values of their own religion and culture. They believed in the quality of these and viewed them as indispensable elements of their identity and character, for these were the tools they applied in living and in their regard for and understanding of others. Baba often reminds me that he and Mama learned many things since coming to America, knowledge he believes would not have been gained had they remained in Iraq. They found in the struggles of settling in a new country an opportunity for self-growth, for meeting people they would not have had the chance to meet, for ideas and values they could not have had the experience to understand.

It took many years before our parents received their American citizenship. I recall Mama studying for her citizenship test and sensing a feeling of gratefulness and pride in her. Yet I did not know then why becoming citizens was so important to our parents. I recall many times over the years our parents, even after receiving their citizenship, telling us that we would return to our watan, our homeland, as soon as we were able. They explained that we left only to flee the war so that we could be safe, so that we could go to school, and that we would one day return.

During grade school, I attended a small charter school in Dearborn. Many students there, if not most, were from the Middle East, and many from Iraq. Their parents, like ours, spoke little to no English, and their families had not been living in America long. Many of these families were large, with school-aged children. Some had relatives who also came to America, and a few had grandparents who lived with them. All our parents seemed content to bring their children to school each day, especially to one with many teachers and families who could speak their language. Our siblings and I spent many years in this school, which I remember seemed to form a community of families we would always see outside of school. I would come to encounter them in the mosques our family visited and during religious holidays and gatherings.

I recall often speaking Arabic with my friends and exchanging stories about coming to America (stories mainly heard from our parents). I did not think, having so few memories of coming to America, that I would have discussed this topic, but it seems now that I must have been somewhat conscious of it. I think my friends and I felt proud to be of both worlds, of Iraq and America, perhaps because that is what defined our similarities. That is why I never felt out of place then. Now, having grown up in cities filled with people like us in many ways, who have experienced many of the same things our family did, I still do not feel out of place. And that is comforting.

Iraq, to my child self, was an emotion more than it was a place. It meant our grandparents and relatives I had not met. It meant the dread in Mama's voice when we received phone calls from family in Baghdad, calls which often brought news of loss or death. It meant old VHS tapes of our grandparents, recorded in Baba's few visits to Baghdad, rarely touched because they could not be watched without tears. America meant home, but it felt like an extended one. For Iraq was a daily memory, whether on the television news each morning or whispered in Mama's prayers.

During the US occupation of Iraq, these vague emotions became tied to clearer images, many of them on TV: the twin towers falling, a little boy inside a mound of gray dust hurling a rock at a US tank, American soldiers capturing an Iraqi father in his home. I also began slowly to see that it wasn't only my homeland that was in danger but many countries like it. I did not fully understand what it all meant, but I could see that our parents were troubled.

I think that I sensed, though subconsciously, a strange uprooting. For it was during our early years in America that I began to understand what home was, but this understanding was quickly lost. I felt detached emotionally, both drawn to a country I was no longer physically a part of and pulled away from a country that had welcomed us. I imagine that I felt the need for a kind of uninterrupted cord between Iraq and America so that I could find comfort in remembering Baghdad while feeling at home in America. Many years later, during the 2017 travel ban, many new immigrant families in our community lived in unease, in constant fear of being questioned or banished. To see people like us cast away from the country in which they sought refuge, with no choice but to return to lands they escaped, I was again forced to question my understanding of home. With the growing political tension, this was perhaps true for our parents as well. Though they often declared, sadly but firmly, that we would return to our waṭan, they began to remind us about America: "Hadha Baladuna" (this is our country).

I remember when our paternal grandmother visited us in our little home in Detroit. I had heard stories of her, that she was kindhearted and pious, and that she had raised me as an infant. Our parents had tried for years to complete the necessary paperwork that would allow her to come to America. As refugees, some of our family details had to be changed or altered for a time, even our names, in order to transition into Jordan and eventually reach the United States. This made it more difficult for us to obtain an authentic travel application for her.

I remember coming home from school the day she arrived. She was sitting on the floor of our parents' bedroom, family and friends surrounding her. As I imagine her now, she was angelic, saint-like, her head and body covered in her black abaya, her face like the full moon, her voice deep and tired but gentle and wise. I remember greeting her without words as I placed my small face and body in her arms, tight against her chest.

When she came, she brought a little bit of Baghdad with her. In her face I saw the Iraqi women, like Mama, with their black abayas and faces filled with memories of both joy and sorrow. I learned from her that, though it was a wounded place, a land darkened and scarred by war, Iraq was a treasured home to very good people. She was an emotional image of Baghdad for me, of our family back home, of our paternal grandfather (who had passed away a few years before), and our other grandparents, most of whom I did not get the chance to meet. When I recall her presence, I find in it all that I had missed or forgotten and all that I have since come to cherish about Iraq.

I now envision her short stay to have been somewhat surreal. For not long after her arrival, she was diagnosed with cancer. Being a child, I did not realize the pain our parents were going through during this time. They had not seen her since they left for America, and here she was, less than a month into her stay, falling ill. She was not in pain, Mama said, something unusual for a person with her illness.

Baba traveled back to Iraq with her. She did not want to die here. I recall seeing her for the last time. She sat in a wheelchair at the airport, near the doors leading to the airplane that would carry her home, her round face still bright and ethereal. Not long after, I heard that she had passed away, and I remember that it was not easy comprehending the fact. But I must have since I clearly remember burying my face in Mama's lap and sobbing. I know our grandmother would have loved to meet you.

I questioned myself and our parents. Why could she not have visited us earlier or stayed longer? Why did we leave her in the first place? Why did she not come with us? Why was our homeland in such a condition? Would it always be this way? When could we return?

Baba once told me he wished he could go back in time to when he was a young boy in Baghdad, to be with his family and to play with his friends and forget his responsibilities.

A few summers ago, here in our current home in Dearborn Heights, Baba planted a young fig tree. He planted it in a round ceramic pot and placed it in the sun. In the heat it grew tall, its straight branches thin and its sandpaper-like leaves round and strong, the shape of Baba's hands. He would visit the tree every day to see if its fruits had blossomed. And when they did, though few and delicate the ripe, light-green figs were, he would pluck them, admire them, and save them for us to eat.

When it rained or became too hot, he would wheel the tree into the shade under the patio, and when the late autumn came, he would carry the heavy pot into the warm kitchen. And there it stood during the winter beside another young fig tree. I watched him as he cared for each, and though the slender branches still grew tall and their leaves wide, the figs only budded into tiny solid bulbs. Yet he quietly watched them and looked for their fruits each day.

Last summer, Baba transferred one of the trees to the garden and planted another in its place. He would then care for his two cherry trees at the end of the garden and the soft grape leaves that surrounded it. But he would always come back to the fig tree. Under the sun sprung its leaves and one or two figs, though seldom ripe enough to pick. The fruits came and went, some quick and plump and others shrunken and withered. When the winter came again, he covered the newly planted tree, gently tucking its sides with a blanket against the cold wind.

Now the fig trees in the kitchen have grown taller, and Baba has tied their highest branch to the ceiling by a string. Their old copper-colored leaves have curled and floated to the ground, leaving them bare. But every now and then, at the hint of warmth, their leaves appear again, this time soft like mint.

I wondered at Baba's persistence. I think these trees reminded him of Iraq, of its warmth and its tall date trees. Perhaps he wished he could grow something like them. He knew they weren't meant to blossom in this weather, but that did not concern him.

After thirteen years in America, Mama lost her father. She had not seen him since she left Baghdad for Jordan. "I could never go and leave you and your siblings behind," she would explain. Of all my memories of this time, I remember her sadness the most.

Mama visited Iraq a year after our grandfather's passing but found a similar emptiness to what she had felt when entering America years earlier. Though she at last saw the family she had separated from as a young woman, she also sensed the void left by her father. In returning home, she hoped to find all the people she was forced to leave behind. This untimely emptiness led her to see Iraq differently, to realize how much time and the war had changed her life and that of her family. The once-promising hope of returning to Iraq permanently seemed now only an old dream.

It was then that I felt I had witnessed the most difficult part of our parents' refugee experience. Seeking refuge in America, a journey that would never have been made but for consideration of their children's freedom and well-being, was for our parents a sacrifice as much as it was a vital decision. For in leaving, they left behind all that they had known and cherished: their homeland and their families. Though their physical distance from it grew each day and year since they left its borders, Iraq could never be forgotten. No matter the burden of grief which belonged to it, and despite their gratefulness for their new country, their love and longing for Iraq only grew.

You will be turning eight later this year. I watch you now as you head into the morning to the swing Baba built for you. You are tall for your age and very kind. You ask many questions and prefer to sit and mix baking soda with vinegar all day rather than read a book. You often tell us about the newly arrived immigrant children in your classroom, and I sense your pride in being able to speak their language, to understand their concerns when others cannot.

A few years ago, you traveled with our parents and some of our siblings to Iraq. You have already grown attached to it, especially to our cousins and our maternal grandmother. I have yet to visit Iraq, to see it again for the first time. To have accompanied you and our family would have been a long-yearned opportunity, but one which was not possible at the time due to educational responsibilities. But I hope that when I do return, no matter how temporary, it will bring with it some lasting service. As an adult, I feel a duty to our homeland, a kind of obligation to it and those who stayed behind.

If you ever sense such a responsibility, let it be first to understand the road our family and those like ours took to arrive where we are today, to come to know the individuals, places, and events that shaped this road, and to welcome the questions and uncertainties of belonging. You may find this to be important in recognizing your identity and all it represents, in connecting to the struggle our parents and grandparents and those children your age still face today.

I often think of the young girl in the photo who walked through the airport the first day she arrived and question my relationship to her. I feel that though she entered this country as a refugee and is the child of refugees, she was too young to have experienced it consciously, and so she cannot take credit for being one. I feel that the real experience, with all its struggles, belongs to our parents. I feel I do not have the right to claim that I was oppressed or once in danger and forced to flee my country and leave loved ones behind and seek refuge across the sea—only that my parents did. But I ask myself: Do the thousands of migrant children now separated from their parents on the American border not have the right to claim that they are oppressed and in danger, that even though they may one day not remember every detail of their experience, do they not have the right to be recognized for their struggles? Do their parents' struggles in some way invalidate theirs or make them any less significant? And what of fear that knows no age or time?

I also ask: must we have consciously experienced our identity to claim it? And perhaps there is more than one way we might experience our identity. Perhaps not remembering or comprehending an experience which the cultivation of our identity depends on allows us to see it in newer eyes, allows us to view it from a perspective made especially for us. Perhaps I experienced my identity as a refugee through meeting our grandmother and then losing her, or through watching our parents struggle for a living in a strange country far from home.

When you one day question your lack of memory, know that it was only a natural unawareness, nothing more. It does not mean that you do not have an identity or that you are not part of the struggle. Perhaps, like Baba's fig trees, it is the presence of these few memories, the patient tending of them, that matters most. Though they may be broken or incomplete, they signify only a finite image of the faces and events they represent. And their roots, though plucked suddenly and harshly, can always be resown in a soil not so unlike that in which they once flourished.

Now I know it was not simply the trees, their few fruits and modest leaves, that Baba tended but rather the idea of them—the hope they harvested and the memories they revived. And I imagine he will take the trees into the summer again, mend them, and watch their heavy leaves dance in the sun.

# BAGHDAD IN DETROIT

*Dunya Mikhail*


On the Fourth of July
here in Detroit
I hear the echo of Baghdad explosions.
They say it is the sound of fireworks.

Song by song
I scatter my birds
away from the fog of smoke.
They say it is ordinary clouds in the sky.

A butterfly from the Tigris shore
alights on my hand.
No bombs today to scare her away.
They say this is the Detroit River.

I enter a shelter
with the others in the crowd.
We will leave at the end of the raid.
They say this is the tunnel to Canada.

# IN RETROSPECT

*Yasmin Mohamed*

I was raised in Dearborn the way a good Arab girl from a Yemeni village is supposed to be raised. At thirteen, I could prepare dinner for twenty guests and keep the house spotless. I knew how to sew clothing and garden. I was clever but quiet. I respected my elders and guarded my family's honor by guarding my own. This was the way my mother had prepared me to one day be a good wife.

I was raised to believe that my future would consist of marriage with children. I would have a house of my own to take care of and children to raise, and my husband would manage the finances. At twenty-one, I was married and had a boy. My son was less than a year old when I asked my husband for a divorce.

I grew up with parents who were very close and loving toward each other. I had not heard of any of my relatives divorcing. I would be the first. I didn't have anyone to confide in, except Allah, so I prayed every chance I could. I remember looking in the Qur'an for a reason to give up on my so-called marriage. I needed a strong justification to convince myself, and I found it. I came to the realization that Allah didn't create me to accept feeling oppressed as a daily expectation. I had the ability to get myself out of such a state of being, and I owed it to myself and my son to do so. After this epiphany, I called my older brother. He came over to my house to help me pack my belongings and move everything to my parents' house.

Mom had done her part by teaching me the skills she thought I needed to succeed as a wife. She taught me what she had been taught by her mother. As the eldest daughter, she carried the burden of not only assuming chores for her mother but also looking after her younger siblings in a village in Yemen. I could only imagine how hard her mother must have worked her, because I know how demanding she was with me. She had impossibly high standards that I still cannot meet today. She would often recall with great pride what an efficient daughter, and then housewife, she had been. She would wake up before dawn to milk the cow, fetch water, and grind wheat kernels into flour. She would then prepare breakfast from this flour by the time the household got up. The family would wake up to a hot breakfast made from scratch. This was expected of me as well, although I didn't have to grind my own flour in America. I wasn't about to wake up before dawn to prepare a huge breakfast from scratch on a daily basis.

As good as my mother was with her duties, my father was also good at his. He worked very hard to support our immediate family as well as his family back in Yemen. He even made sure to find a wife for his brother and brought his brother to America so that he could make a better life for his new family. He always walked with his head held high, a smile on his face. He walked quickly—like he had somewhere to go and things to do. He had broad shoulders and strong hands. When Dad came to America, he eventually joined the US Merchant Marine. I know this because I found his ID card. It stated his height at 5'10" and his ethnicity as "Arabian." He then got a job with Ford Motor Company. That was when he brought us in, because he then had steady work and a good income. He was a wonderful, playful father. He made each one of us siblings feel like we were his favorite. As much as we loved him, he could be very scary when he needed to be. When we were mischievous, he would roar at us. My mother wasn't able to tame us with her mihwash, a Yemeni wooden spoon, but my father had no problem doing so just with his voice.

I had a particularly close relationship with Dad. Although he never called me "princess," I always felt like one with him. He protected me from my mother's anger, which usually revolved around chores not being completed. For example, I would be locked in my bedroom listening to music and doing homework. My mother would yell at me to wash the dishes and lecture me on how shameful it was to have dirty dishes in the sink. Dad would intervene and say, "Don't yell at

my daughter. I will do the dishes. Leave her alone," as he rolled up his
sleeves and washed the dishes for me. This was his "I love you" to me.
We didn't grow up saying those words to each other like the families on
TV did. It would be demonstrated in actions and said in other ways. I
was in awe of him. I knew that each gender had strict roles to play, but
he would set that aside to protect me from my mother's anger.

When I was a year old, my "girliness" had almost kept me from
coming to America. Dad had thought that I should remain with
my eight-year-old sister, but my mother refused to leave me behind
because I was a baby. My grandparents wanted to keep my sister with
them so that my parents would return to them. They knew they were
going to a distant land that had a different language and way of living.
They were afraid to lose all of us, so they held on to my sister. Dad's
cousin, who lived in America, tried to convince him that America
wasn't a good place for a girl to grow up in, and that his girls should
remain in Yemen. In the end, they agreed that my sister would stay
with my grandparents and that I would go to America with my parents
and older brother. I often wonder how my life would have turned out
if I had stayed in Yemen with my sister.

Our journey to America started when Dad needed to decide about
how best to support our family. Following the death of Al-Imam
Ahmad, the king of North Yemen, in 1962, Yemen fell into civil war.
At that time, Dad's options were to either join in the fighting or try to
look for opportunities to make a living elsewhere. To build a better
future for our family, he knew he had to look outside of Yemen for
work. Mom agreed with him. So, he walked barefoot (everyone in
our village was too poor to afford shoes) from our village in the Ibb
province to the southern port city of Aden. The distance is roughly one
hundred miles, and it took him a week to get there. He had made this
trek several times before for different reasons, including, according to
my mother, to skip school with her brother.

After many months of walking back and forth to Aden, he gained
entry into Bahrain by becoming, according to my mother, an eskary,
which means he joined the military. We have a picture of him and
another man from our village posing in their uniforms. He would send

letters and money to the family regularly. Later, through the help of his cousin in America, he immigrated to California, where he worked picking grapes and asparagus on farms. He returned to Yemen in early 1971 to be at my birth. When he first laid his eyes on me, he commented on the size of my nose and that it authenticated me as a member of his side of the family. We have larger noses than my mom's side.

We arrived in America in 1972. I was a year old, the youngest of three siblings, and my mother was pregnant with my brother, who was born later that year.

Although growing up in America gave me more opportunities, as a girl I was still restricted in the man's world of my community. I was a good student, and I loved to read for fun. I would often look for inspirational quotes that I would write all over my notebooks and folders. Some were quotes from holy books of various religions, and others just words of wisdom from philosophers and intellectuals. I also liked to write poetry, and I read anything about or written by Edgar Allan Poe, my favorite author.

After I graduated from junior high, I was thrilled for the start of high school. There would be so many more students and teachers and a variety of electives that I could enroll in. I was to attend Fordson High School, the first high school in the United States that cost more than a million dollars to build. It was designed in the collegiate Gothic style, which resembles the style of universities that were built in the late nineteenth and early twentieth centuries. This made it look like a castle, which was very exciting to me. However, when it was time to report to school, my parents told me that I wouldn't be going. High school was full of boys who were looking for girlfriends, so for my own protection, I was prohibited from attending.

There wasn't a worse thing that my parents could have done to me. My life was school and learning. I felt like I had nothing else. Since the age of ten, my play time had been interrupted because I had to start learning how to cook and clean. When I was thirteen, I wasn't allowed to play outside because I was considered too old for that. Mom would call me in from playing outside and teach me how to cook. I was a marah, a woman, so I had to learn the cooking skills that a woman needed to know to succeed as a wife and mother. I would promptly return outside after the cooking was done. The best time in my life was when I was a child playing outside with my brothers, without a care in the world.

I wasn't allowed to ride a bike like my brothers were. I was told that it wasn't good for girls to ride bikes, that it was 'ayb, shameful or not honorable, so I never learned how to ride one. I watched as my brothers got new bikes and zipped right passed me, laughing and having fun as I stood there watching them. Dad bought me roller skates instead. Not actual roller skates, but the ones that are just wheels and that can be attached to the bottoms of shoes. When I went down the sidewalk on my skates, the Yemeni neighbor who always sat on the porch of her upstairs flat would push her face between the wrought iron fence posts and say in Arabic, "You are so ghawiah." She was accusing me of acting childishly. I ignored her. Now, little Yemeni girls wearing hijabs ride bikes all over the Southend. It isn't 'ayb anymore.

When it was time to enroll in Fordson High, my parents decided that it would be better for me to stay at home.

"You can't keep me from school, it's against the law!" I raised my voice at Mom in the kitchen.

"We've decided," she said.

"Other Yemeni girls are going. I won't be alone. Why can't I go? What am I supposed to do?"

I ran to my room crying.

The next day I tried again but to no avail. Then Dad told me I had to stay at home, and what my father said was the law. I was able to raise my voice with Mom but not with Dad. I accepted my fate because I had no other recourse. My brothers had seen what had happened to me but said and did nothing. Despite my restrictions, I knew that I was loved, and I loved my family back.

I got used to staying at home very quickly. I turned to the TV as a way to escape my reality. I loved to watch the *The Price Is Right*, *Family Feud*, reruns of *I Dream of Jeannie*, *Bewitched*, *The Munsters*, *Good Times*, *The Jeffersons*, *Three's Company*, *Laverne & Shirley*, *Happy Days*, *Diff'rent Strokes*, *The Facts of Life*, and *The Golden Girls*, just to name a few. I became lazy, and I loved it! I enjoyed going to the grocery store with my parents and plopping back down on the sofa to watch the next show. Staying home and watching TV while my brothers went to school and then came back to do homework was somehow very satisfying. They would then go outside and play on their bikes while I remained inside. I put on weight from not doing anything besides eating and some chores. My parents didn't like what they saw.

It was a chilly day in November 1985, about eleven weeks into the school year. I got up at 9 a.m. I went through my morning routine of washing up and making the morning prayer. My brothers had already left for school, so the only sounds were coming from the oven door being closed and opened and a metal tray being placed in it. The house had the buttery sweet aroma of ka'ak that Mom always baked. She told me to eat a fresh hot ka'ak, but I wasn't hungry yet. I started to head toward my spot on the sofa. Dad came out of his room and said, "Put your coat on and go to the car." I assumed this would be another fun run to the grocery store, but I noticed that Mom was still in the kitchen, cooking. She didn't stop to put her coat on. I got my coat from my room.

"Ya'bah, where are we going?" I asked while slipping into my winter coat.

"You're going to school," he said in Arabic.

"I don't want to go to school anymore. I like staying here at home. You don't have to take me!"

I was annoyed. First, I was made to stay home against my will, and then I was made to go back against my will. How would we explain why I hadn't attended school, especially when it was against the law? My parents insisted that I go for my own good.

Later, I found out that someone my parents knew from our village and had grown up with had talked them into not sending me to school. He had seven daughters of his own. He had filled my parents' ears with all kinds of stories. In the end, they knew me and knew I would make the right choices and could be trusted. They relented and pushed me to attend high school after seeing the effect that staying home had had on me. After all, we were in America. There was opportunity for more.

I remember Dad always expecting me to do more. He used to hold my hands when I was little, kiss them, and say, "These hands are going to write." He would point to the anchorwoman on TV and tell me that I would do that one day. That I would be educated. He brought us to America for that very reason: to make a way for ourselves and to have better lives.

Dad drove me to Fordson High. We parked and I was immediately taken aback by how beautiful the architecture was. I felt a bit hesitant, not sure that I wanted to be there. I reluctantly opened the car door and walked up to the school. We entered, looked down a long hallway with shiny floors, and headed toward the counseling office. Dad said that I shouldn't say a word, that he would handle it. I listened. I was concerned about what we would tell the school. Dad was my heart. If he asked me to hang upside down from a tree branch like a bat, I would without hesitation.

We entered the counseling office, which had many smaller offices located inside. Dad told the receptionist that he wanted to enroll me in school. She asked Mr. Derda, one of the counselors, to speak with us. Mr. Derda, who had a thick mustache, asked where I had been because the school year had already begun. Dad said that I had gone on a trip to Yemen. Mr. Derda asked for evidence. Dad said it wasn't with him. Mr. Derda gave him a look and then asked us to follow him to his office, where he pulled out a worksheet that looked like something you would find in a kindergarten class. It had a grid on it, with an image in each box. He pointed to an image, looked at me, and said in a loud, slow voice, "Can you tell me what this picture is?"

I looked at Dad, who nodded.

"Ball," I said.

He pointed to the next image.

"Top."

After the third image of a rake, the counselor asked me if I spoke English.

"Yes."

"What school did you attend?"

"Salina Junior High," I said, smiling.

He searched for my file in his drawer. He gave Dad that look again and commenced signing me up for classes.

I found myself excited to start school once I was in the actual building. All of that love and excitement for learning came back to me. I did well enough in my classes but had some problems because of my traditional clothes.

I grew up in an enclave of Dearborn that was flanked by the Ford Rouge Factory on one side and Detroit on the other. By the time I went to high school, the Southend of Dearborn had a lot of Arab families, including many from Yemen. Most of the white people had moved out. The older Palestinian women would cover their hair and wear thobes, the traditional Palestinian dress with hand-embroidered designs. But the younger generations, particularly the Lebanese, dressed in American clothes. As for the Yemeni women, they wore traditional dresses, while the Yemeni men mostly wore American clothing. At the time, I wore traditional dresses made from fabric that had floral or other prints on it. The dresses were fitted from my neck to my waist, with the skirt cut in an A-line style reaching below my knees. I always wore pants under the dresses. My scarves had floral prints or were solid in color.

Fordson was in another part of the city and had students from all over Dearborn. Many students hadn't seen someone like me before, and I knew this because they were vocal about it. One girl in particular stands out in my memory. I don't remember her name, but she was a bit shorter than me and had long and wavy blond hair down to her waist. She wore a lot of makeup and tight-fitting clothes. She stood in front of me one day, looked me up and down, and said, "What's the world coming to?" I couldn't bring myself to say anything back to her. I felt like I understood why she said it. I knew I didn't fit in. She was the quintessential American girl. I was an immigrant kid who wore traditional dresses. We had them sewn in styles that were popular in my village at the time. I wore a scarf that looked like old Russian babushkas. They were square with roses printed on them. She looked like the people I saw on TV, and I didn't.

One day, boys from the school drove to the Southend. They saw me walking down the sidewalk on my block, shouted at me as they drove by, and then laughed. I wondered if they had made their way to the Southend just to torment me, or if they had other business and just saw me and decided they should bully me along the way.

One thing did happen to make those kids who made me feel like an outsider have some respect for me. We were in Mr. Moss's biology class. This was soon after I started high school. The teacher had given me a textbook and showed me all the chapters that they had already covered so I could study them at home. Mr. Moss wanted us to review for the chapter test, so he led us in a game where a student would sit on a stool in front of the class and other students, one by one, would ask them a question about what we were learning. The objective was to ask a question that the student on the stool couldn't answer in order to replace them. Essentially, whoever stayed on the stool the longest was declared the winner. My turn came to ask the student on the stool a question. They didn't know the answer, so I had to go and sit on the stool in front of the class. In this class was the blond and the boy who was involved in the drive-by bullying. He sat in the front row. Needless to say, I was petrified. I listened carefully to the question. I knew the answer. I listened to the next question. I knew that answer. I listened to the third, and I knew that answer as well. I'm not sure how many questions I was asked, but I got all of the answers right. At this point, students were starting to cheer for me, and so did Mr. Moss. Most notably, so was the drive-by bully. I glanced over at him, and he was cheering me on. I couldn't believe it. I got another answer correct. The class cheered me on. The bell rang, ending the period. I was the winner.

It was not easy navigating my bicultural life. I am American and Yemeni. In one instance, a female student in my language arts class, who dreamed of becoming a doctor, worked at a gas station and told us about it in class. I went home and told Mom that I wanted to get a job so that I could save money, too. Her scolding made it clear to me that I should never think of working in my life. Women didn't get jobs, and if they did, they weren't honorable women, and our Yemeni society looked down on them. Only marriage awaited me after high school. She told me to get those ideas out of my head, and I did. Afterward, I didn't care too much about my grades. I knew that it wouldn't matter if

I did well academically because I was to marry, and university wasn't in my future. Even though intellectually I accepted that attending college wasn't an option for me, deep down in my soul I didn't lose hope.

As a sophomore, the most tragic thing in my early life occurred. This changed all of our lives. Dad began saying strange things. He asked my brother to write a letter to the White House. My brother refused. I found out and told Dad that I would write it for him. I don't remember what I wrote or if it was ever mailed, but that was the first strange thing that happened that I remember. He then began saying that the neighbor's son had listening devices in his shoes and that he was working with the government and trying to listen in on us. This was confusing to me. I didn't understand. Why would he have listening devices in his shoes?

One day we came home from school and Mom was very agitated. We asked what happened, and she said that there was an incident with Dad that required his hospitalization. She gave us the details. When I heard them, I felt like the room was spinning all around me as I stood still. My world was shattered and flipped upside down. My father had schizophrenia. My family would never be the same again. Months later, Dad finally came back home from the hospital. He was not the same strong Yemeni man I had known my entire life. He was medicated and looked much older and weaker. He even looked shorter. I ran to my room, devastated.

It was very difficult for our family when our beloved father became ill, not only because of how he was affected but also because of how the community responded. Some illnesses, when mentioned, elicit responses of sympathy and compassion, and others not so much, even though they cause just as much pain and agony to the one suffering and their family. Schizophrenia is one of those illnesses that is not talked about. People don't raise money to help those afflicted or offer other forms of comfort.

Instead, men from our village came to our house after my father had his breakdown and was hospitalized. They told us that they had gathered funds so that we could go back to Yemen. They wanted my whole family to return. Mom refused to take the money and insisted that we stay in America. I didn't understand why they would send us back because of my father's condition. It seemed that they were trying to shame us rather than offer us sympathy and support. We managed to continue with our lives in Dearborn because life goes on despite tragedies. My older brother took on my father's role. He worked hard to support us the way Dad had so we didn't have to go back to Yemen. To this day, I have an enormous amount of love and respect for him because of how he stepped up to his new role when he was just as hurt as we were.

Thankfully, today people have started to change their attitudes toward mental illness as more and more understand that it is a medical problem, just like cancer is. The brain is an organ, and it can get sick just like other organs of the body can. People have to take care of their emotional and mental well-being just like they have to care for their bodies to stay healthy. For this reason, it is important for me to say that it's OK that my father suffered from schizophrenia. I refuse to be ashamed. There was not a more honorable, generous, kind, and respected man than my dad.

When I went back to high school, students who were from the Southend came up to me and asked me if what happened to Dad was true. I told them that it was. They offered words of support. I, however, had changed. My teachers noticed it and spoke to my counselor, Mr. Derda. He pulled me into his office and let me know that everyone was concerned. I didn't tell him what happened with my father. I just told him that I had too much work to do at home, and that's why my grades had gone down and I seemed different in class. I was so hurt by my father's illness that it consumed me and I didn't care about anything else anymore. I didn't want to talk about it with anyone because I knew they wouldn't understand. How could I explain the devastation that I felt? I couldn't.

After I graduated from Fordson, I stayed home until I got married. My would-be husband had told my family that he wanted to continue his studies after we married. That this was a goal of his. This alone made me agree to marry him. I was hopeful that I could go to college under the right circumstances. Perhaps I could go with him. Once we were married, however, when I asked him if I could attend college, he told me that I wouldn't go and neither would he. He had just said that to impress me so that I would marry him. It had worked. It had also ended my hopes of obtaining a college degree. Instead, I had a baby. This was the one solid accomplishment, if it can be called that, of my marriage. By twenty-one I had my son, who was born in 1992. He was the most amazing thing that had happened—or will ever happen—to me.

Meanwhile, I became aware of a Yemeni woman who worked as a nurse in a doctor's office that we went to. She had decided to work for a living. The fact that she worked "like a man," caused some people in the community to laugh at her, to try to put her down by making fun of her. What she was doing was different and new and very threatening. Not only did people look down on her, they also looked down on her village because one of their women was working like a man. When I saw how she was treated, this reinforced the idea that I was just going to be a housewife and mother. Not that that was a bad thing; it wasn't. But I wanted to leave my mark on the world in some way. I didn't want to have lived without making some kind of difference beyond my family.

My son was the only light in the darkness of my marriage. One of the most challenging aspects of my life at that point was that I was not allowed to leave the house without my husband's permission. I lived next door to my family's house; we were neighbors. I had to get approval anytime I wanted to visit them. To some extent I acquiesced to this condition. I didn't fight him about it. I thought that I was being an obedient wife, and that was a good thing to be. I believed that we each should know where the other was. I knew he was at work, and he knew if I was at home or at my family's house. I was very naive, to say the least. This wasn't a "normal" practice in my community. Needless to say, I gave up too much of my power to him. In my Yemeni Muslim culture, we don't traditionally get to know the men that we are marrying before we get married. We get to know them after the wedding.

There's an assumption that they are good Muslims, which means that they are automatically going to be good, kind, trusting, and loving. He had his issues like everyone else.

I didn't leave the house very much. I would leave when we'd go grocery shopping, which only happened at night. I became very pale. I remember my brother's reaction after seeing me; he said that I should sit in the sun a while to get some color back in my skin. I have always loved being outside in the sun. So, I usually have a tan during the warmer months. When I was married, all of that went away. This wasn't because he was a religious fanatic. In fact, I was much more religious than he was. My religion was what helped me get through all of the bad times, from my father's breakdown to my marriage, and then everything else that came after. As bad as that time in my life was, it was a learning experience for me. I learned that I am not meant to live in such a way. I learned that it's OK to think for myself and not just obey someone without question because of their gender, especially if their rules don't make sense.

After leaving my husband and moving back into my parents' house, I explained to my family why I had asked for a divorce. They were upset with me for having put up with so much. I hadn't shared what I was going through because I thought it would be wrong to do so. I believed that what happened between a married couple should stay between them, and that I shouldn't talk about it with anyone else. I had kept everything to myself and prayed about it. I really wanted the marriage to work because we had a child. Although they were displeased, I was grateful that I didn't have to interact with that man again, except for issues concerning our son.

After the divorce, my son and I became a financial burden on the family. I was only receiving seventy-two dollars per month in child support from my ex-husband. Mom sat me down one day and suggested that I get a job and work to support myself and my son. That was a strong blow coming from her. I began to cry. I was always taught that men supported women, so why weren't they supporting me? I tried to wipe the tears as quickly as they came down so that I could see her face. I told her that I would have to go to college in order to find a decent job. She agreed. My youngest brother was about to start school at Henry Ford Community College. She suggested that I register and go to school with him.

I attended Henry Ford Community College and then transferred to the University of Michigan–Dearborn, where I earned scholarships to help me pay my way through school. Since I was finally in school, I didn't want to leave. I earned two bachelor's degrees—one in social sciences and the other in education. One last hurdle remained before I could become a teacher. I needed to complete my student teacher training, which commenced in January 2002, just months following the attacks of 9/11. This was not good timing for me because of my visibility as an Arab Muslim.

I was assigned to Palmer Elementary School in Melvindale. My cooperating teacher was Mrs. K. She taught a third-grade class of thirty-four students. I met the students as they were leaving their art class in two lines of seventeen. As they walked past me, some handed me their works of art. I told them that their parents would love to receive them, but they insisted, so I left that day with several art projects. I didn't know that I could fall in love with a class of students. I was very anxious to start teaching them.

I've always taken pride in my religion, even though it's misunderstood by so many in the West. I am a proud Muslim woman. I wear a scarf and I dress in an ankle-length coat called a jilbab. This is how I choose to project myself to the world. I dress modestly because I want to be judged by my merits, not by my looks or physical attributes. I don't put on makeup to look prettier. But does this mean that I don't ever put on makeup or try to look a certain way? No. There is a difference between public and private spaces. A public space can also constitute my home if men who are not my immediate family are present. I would dress in front of them like I would if I were in a public. When I'm in my private space, like my home, with only immediate family around,

I do not wear a scarf or jilbab. If I plan to go to a party or wedding that is only attended by women, I would prepare for it. I may want to get khudhab done. Khudhab is like henna, but black, and consists of a beautiful design that is painted on the hands, arms, feet, and legs. It can last a week or so and eventually fades away. I would visit a salon to get my hair and makeup done and then dress up in a beautiful gown. On the way to the party, I'll wear modest clothing on top of my dress and make sure that my hair and made-up face is covered, but when I arrive at the party, I'll remove the outer clothing to reveal my glamorous-looking self. At these parties, the DJ (a woman, of course) plays the latest Arabic and American dance music and we all gather and dance the night away. So, Muslim women do wear makeup and dress up but at times that we deem to be appropriate and in spaces where men are not allowed. Men are not allowed to enter a woman's space, such as a party or wedding. To do so is dishonorable and may bring him some repercussions. I'd always been strong enough to stick to this dress code, but student teaching at this school after 9/11 was a challenge that shook me. It changed the way I dressed in public.

At the elementary school where I did my student teaching, most of the students were from middle-class and lower-income families. Some of the students lived in a nearby trailer park. The principal and other staff members were welcoming and supportive. The students were easy to love and work hard for. My cooperating teacher, unfortunately, was not so easy to like at first.

When my student teaching started, I couldn't wait to work with Mrs. K and her students, but it all started on the wrong foot. Mrs. K got the class's attention and told them that she was only working with me because she was a professional and that she was asked to work with me. I looked at the class to see if I could get a sense of whether or not they understood what she was talking about. After all, they were third graders. I couldn't tell. They were just listening closely. I looked at her and then at the class. I couldn't believe what she was saying. How dare she? She was telling them that she would not work with me if it were her own choice. Was this because I was a Muslim? She didn't give a reason why. We looked at each other. I didn't say anything and kept a straight face. I didn't want to argue with her in front of the class.

I started to think that others shared Mrs. K's thoughts of me and felt scared. So, I decided to stop dressing the way I always had. I went shopping and purchased some blouses and trousers and dresses. I didn't take my scarf off, but I didn't wear my jilbab again while at that school. I was genuinely worried that someone would attack me if I dressed too differently. I mean, if my cooperating teacher could say that about me to the class like she did, what else could happen there?

I worked hard and cared deeply about the students. The teacher started to notice that. She saw that the students liked me and didn't treat me any differently than they treated her. One day, the teacher asked the students to look carefully at her and then carefully at me and to tell her what was different about us. One student raised his hand and proclaimed that I had brown shoes on and she had black shoes on. She seemed to be disappointed by that response. I felt relieved. So, she asked the students to look closely and tell her what was very different between us. Another student raised their hand and shared that I had brown eyes and she had blue eyes. Again, she reacted like that wasn't what she wanted them to say. The students didn't mention my scarf. Kids see past that stuff. They know if someone cares for them or if they don't. They are sensitive that way.

There was a particular student in class that I felt connected to. James didn't fit in because he had a different religion. He belonged to a Christian group that didn't celebrate holidays. I'm not sure which group he belonged to, though. One day his parents were standing at the classroom door with him. They nudged him toward me. They looked so proud. He hesitated but then approached me and gave me pamphlets about Jesus. I looked at them and then back down at him. I forced a smile and said, "Thank you," just to make him feel successful and for his parents to go away.

It was approaching Easter, and the teacher told me that we would have an Easter party. She had purchased little gifts for the students that were Easter themed. I brought up James because his religion forbade him from celebrating any holidays. She said that he would just have to sit there and not participate, and that it was his parents' fault that he couldn't participate, not ours. She didn't feel as bad for him as I did. I knew what it felt like to be left out, to be the "other." I wasn't going to let him just sit there and watch the rest of the class have fun. The evening before the party, I purchased erasers and some fancy pencils that were not Easter themed. I thought that he could at least get a gift like the rest of the students.

During the party, he looked depressed. He was sitting at his desk with his head hanging down while all the other students were talking excitedly, waiting for their gifts. When the teacher began passing out the gifts, I called him over to me. I pulled out the pencils and erasers and told him that I also did not celebrate Easter, so I understood how he felt, and that I just wanted to give him something, and that it had nothing to do with the holiday celebration. His eyes grew two sizes and he threw his arms around my waist and squeezed as hard as he could. He was overjoyed, and so was I. He ran back to his desk and stared at the glittery pencils with a huge smile on his face.

The teacher got to know me as a person by the end of my student-teaching experience. She liked some of my ideas and wanted to use them after I left her. She appreciated my connection with the students. On my last day, as we walked to the parking lot, she told me that she would be proud to have me as her children's teacher and that she had put me on her Christmas card list. I was taken aback by what she said. We embraced each other and wished each other good luck. She sent me Christmas cards for a few years after that.

Throughout my education, Mom helped me take care of my son. I lived at home with my family. My son grew up in the same house that I grew up in. When I graduated from college, I was finally able to support him and tried to give him everything he needed. He was sixteen and got into arguments with my brothers, who also lived at the house. I could tell that we needed a space of our own.

I was able to purchase a house in 2009 at an affordable price during the economic recession. I sold my gold jewelry to pay for necessary repairs to the house. My older brother, an electrician, helped me with the electrical wiring and with the plumbing. Other family members helped me paint the house and hang my prized chandelier. My nephews gutted the basement. I replaced the roof and repaved the driveway. My son and I finally moved in on Halloween that year. I carried my final items into the house as ghouls and goblins walked by.

Initially, all was well. We were happily living in our new house. I moved my mother in with us so that I could take care of her. She had spent so many years taking care of us, and then my dad, that I wanted to give her a room to herself and a bit of peace and quiet. I didn't want her to have to worry about anything. A few of my brothers lived with Dad at our original home, where they took care of him there, so this arrangement was fine. Family visited me. My son had his friends over. I was working at a charter school in Dearborn called Riverside Academy. In 2009, I was able to finally travel to Yemen and meet the family that we left behind. I also completed my master's degree in education that year.

Unfortunately, my mother did not stay with us long. She moved back to the family house because she found my house a bit lonely. One reason was that we didn't have a local mosque like the Dix Mosque that she could walk to for Friday prayers and halaqahs. She couldn't visit with her friends as easily as she had always done in the Southend.

My son was going to school at that time. I was very proud of him. I even bragged to my colleagues about how his college instructor told him that he should be a doctor. He was taking biology and chemistry classes at Henry Ford Community College and getting good grades. At the same time, he was working for Art Van, loading furniture in people's cars. He kept busy with his work and studies, and I was busy with my job. In 2011, I left the charter school and began working for Dearborn Public Schools at Salina Intermediate, the same school that I attended as a child, formerly called Salina Junior High. I was hired to teach social studies and language arts.

It wasn't an easy journey to get to where I am today. Looking back at my life, I am in awe at how brave my parents were to leave everything they knew to settle in such a very different culture, to achieve an American dream of their own. They sacrificed everything they had and everyone they knew to make a better life for our family. Their sacrifices didn't end when we grew up. When I went to college, Mom took care of my son for me. I wouldn't have been able to earn my degrees without her support. Their choices led to my eventually becoming a successful professional working woman who supports herself and her family. To say I am grateful for what they've done for me is an understatement. Without them, I wouldn't be where I am today.

Dad passed away in October 2013. I was at school when I received a phone call in my class. My eighth-grade students had just completed the MEAP state assessment test. It was transition time, and they just left my class. I answered the phone and the secretary said that I had to come to the office because my brother was there and he looked like he'd been crying. My brothers never cried. I hung up the phone and started mentally going through family members who might have passed away. I walked to the office, hoping that my knees would get me there because they felt like they were melting. I saw my youngest brother. His eyes were red and teary. He said, "I tried to call you, but you didn't answer your phone." I told him that my phone was on silent. He said, "Dad died, Allah yirhemih."

I rushed to my family's house, which wasn't far from the school. There was a police car with an officer in it parked outside the house. I entered the house to find my family sitting in the living room, silently staring ahead. I asked them where my dad was. They said his bed-room. I ran to his bedside. He was lying on his bed with a bedsheet covering his face. *Is he really dead?* I wondered. I took off the sheet and touched his cheek. It was cold. I started screaming "Ya'bah! Ya'bah!" hoping he would hear me and come back. My screams woke my family from their trance, and they ran into the room and surrounded me. I sobbed. He didn't come back.

I just want him to know that these hands that he kissed are writing, that he will forever be my hero.

# WORD MAN

## A Quest for Self-Discovery Through Shakespeare, 2Pac, and the Holy Qur'an

### *Yousef Alqamoussi*

Anything can be a microphone. An empty soda bottle serves just as well as a banana. I preferred the stack of mini Legos because I loved the colors, and beyond a certain height, I could even bend it like a real mic stand. Once it was assembled, I took my place on the couch in the living room, sitting crossed-legged with a bedsheet over my shoulders and a towel-turban upon my head. I tapped the Lego mic with my finger, closed my eyes, placed my open palm over my ear, and began: "Bismillah i' Rahman i' Raheem . . ."

The plan was simple: Grow up and become Sheikh Yousef, just like the Sheikh Yousef from the majma' down the road from our second-story flat on Appoline Street, or like the reciter from the audio cassette who incanted my favorite Qur'anic sura of all: Chapter 12, Yusuf.

By the age of four, I was ready to launch my career. I knew enough suras by heart to get started. Mama and Baba had been teaching me ever since I was a toddler in Kuwait. I had memorized most of the qisar, or short suras, as well as the Throne Verse—al-Baqarah, Chapter Two, Verse 255—and the majority of surat al-Wāqiah, Chapter 56. Best of all, I was already landing gigs. I was often selected to recite the Qur'an during Islamic school functions, where I could perform all that I was practicing at home. I usually opted for the shorter suras I knew so well, but one day, I hoped to recite surat Yusuf, just like the sheikh on the cassette. Not only was Yousef my name, but I shared it with the great prophet of the Qur'an whose miracles were his wisdom, patience, and beauty; who rose up from the pit of a well, abandoned and betrayed, to become a great king of Egypt; who dreamed of the planets and the sun and the moon prostrating to him. It was, as the Qur'an calls it, the best of stories.

This wasn't a terribly original aspiration. I wasn't the first sheikh or the first Yousef in my family. My mother's father was also named Yousef. Though not a king of Egypt, he did survive the family curse. His mother, Sukayna, had endured a terrible streak of dead babies, and after losing several in a row, her neighbors in Chehour, Lebanon, offered this antidotal advice: name your child after an animal and it will live. Sukayna obliged and named her next two children Deeb—wolf—and Nimri—tigress. Both survived. The spell had been broken. She named the next three boys Yousef, Suleiman, and Ali.

Yousef grew up and married a girl from the village. They moved to Kuwait to work but ended up settling there and raising six children. My mother was the second child and oldest girl of the bunch. Although Yousef had established his life in Kuwait working for the Ministry of Communications, he had always intended to return to Lebanon, where he often vacationed. "I want to wash my mother's feet and drink its water," he used to say.

In the spring of 1980, Yousef arranged such a vacation for his wife and children. "Go ahead," he said. "I'll follow you." He arrived in Lebanon soon after as promised. In a casket. The story goes that he had gone to the bathroom to make ablution for prayer and had dropped dead from a heart attack right where he stood. "I couldn't have saved him had I been standing next to him," the family doctor reported. Yousef was laid to rest among his other siblings in Chehour, the hometown he so longed to return to. He was forty-two.

As for the sheikh, that honor belonged to my paternal grandfather, Sadik. He was the ultimate man of letters. "Word Man" is perhaps the most simplified translation of my last name, Alqamoussi. That laqab, or title, traces its roots to Najaf, Iraq. It was first attributed to one of my great-grandfathers, a scholar whose verbal expertise was so renowned that it earned him the reputation of al-Qamoosi: "He [who is] the dictionary." Sadik carried on this legacy, studying at the eminent Shia seminary of Hawzat al-Najaf and establishing a bookstore in Baghdad, where he eventually settled and authored works of prose and poetry.

Yousef Assaf and Sadik al-Qamoosi likely did not imagine that their grandson would be a Qur'an-reciting Kuwaiti-born Iraqi-Lebanese immigrant to the United States, of all places, but that's how it played out. My father's emigration from Iraq at the start of the Iran-Iraq War eventually led him to Kuwait, where he met and married my mother, a daughter of Lebanese expatriates. When I was three, my family was selected to come to America through the Diversity Immigrant Visa program. After a short stay in the Emirates, and an even shorter one with my uncle in Wales, we finally made our way to America.

My parents had no idea where to live in America. They spoke little English and feared that the move to a Western country would dissolve their children's bond to the language, religion, and heritage of their homeland. Friends of my father recommended a town in metro Detroit called Dearborn, which was known for its large Muslim Arab population. Lebanese and Iraqis lived there, including one of my grandfather's friends from Iraq. He generously offered to receive us and help us get settled.

Our first stop in America was New York's JFK International Airport on Friday, July 20, 1990, just days before Saddam Hussein's invasion of Kuwait sparked the Gulf War. My mother recalls the hot, stormy evening, and often recounts our first exchange with an American. Noticing us lugging our possessions across the terminal, a man kindly offered to help. My father obliged. But once we reached our next gate bound for Detroit, the man gestured for a tip. Newly arrived from Wales, my father had nothing in his pocket but British coins. He placed a fistful into the attendant's hand and braved a flurry of violent curses in return. We rushed off, fleeing the man's "F and F's," as my mother puts it. That wasn't our only British faux pas in America. Weeks later, at a Pizza Hut down the street from our Michigan Avenue motel in Dearborn, we realized we were the only ones eating our pie with forks and knives. You might imagine our bewilderment at the KFC across the street when we ordered "chips" and were told they didn't serve "chips," even though we were staring at a heap of them in the fryer behind the counter.

We arrived at Detroit Metropolitan Airport sometime before midnight. My grandfather's friend and his son received us at the gate. We stayed with them for a couple of nights, and then moved into the motel on Michigan Ave where we spent our first two months in America. Other Arab families were also staying there. Two Lebanese families were immigrating from Sierra Leone to Canada and were finalizing the process in Detroit. Another family had arrived from Kuwait, to my mother's elation, and we quickly became friends during their brief stay.

In our first month, we had no kitchen in our room, so we had to frequent nearby restaurants to get our meals. This was a challenge since our diet was restricted to halal food, so we got by eating at Big Boy, Pizza Hut, and La Shish, the only nearby Middle Eastern restaurant. We also had to walk. Without a car for weeks, I absorbed the streets of my future hometown from my stroller, pushed along through the midsummer heat by my mother, who was carrying my soon-to-be American brother in the womb.

We also witnessed our first tornado. We were startled one evening by a wailing that overcame the city, followed by a knock at the door. My parents were instructed in obscure English that they had to leave immediately. After much confusion, they eventually figured out that they were being temporarily relocated to a basement to seek shelter from some kind of storm. As for the wailing, these were warning sirens from the city.

During the second month, my parents managed to upgrade to a room with a kitchen and stove. Mama was cooking mujaddara one evening when the aroma captivated the neighbors, drawing a crowd to the door. With instinctual hospitality, she diced up some tomatoes and cucumbers, laid out some pita bread, and on that warm summer night, we all sat around outside the motel room laughing and sharing mujaddara sandwiches.

As her pregnancy matured, my mother needed medical care. She was directed to a center called ACCESS, a social services provider for immigrants and community support. They connected her with a doctor and a hospital in nearby Lincoln Park. For transportation, they recommended a taxi service. The first cab we called to take us to the hospital had a white, or "American," driver. He got lost along the way, to the ire and panic of my parents. The second cab was driven by an Arab man. He was kind and welcoming.

"Where are you from?" he asked. My parents knew from his accent that he was Lebanese.

"We are new to America from Kuwait," my mother said. "I'm Lebanese."

"*I'm* Lebanese!" exclaimed the driver.

"And my husband is Iraqi."

"My *sister's* husband is Iraqi! And *she's* Lebanese!"

The driver dropped us off at the hospital and insisted on waiting for us. On the way back, he made this offer: "I'd like to introduce you to my sister today. I'll drive you to her house. I can pick you up after my shift is over."

As promised, he met us in front of the motel that afternoon and drove us over. His sister and her family lived in a lower-level flat across town, near Wyoming and Tireman. She was called Umm Mustafa since her son's name was Mustafa. Her husband, predictably, was Abu Mustafa, thereby honoring the familiar Arab tradition of referring to parents by the name of their eldest son. By this tradition, my parents were known as Umm Yousef and Abu Yousef, respectively.

Our families hit it off that day. Umm Mustafa introduced us to other Arab families in Dearborn. We were also told about an Islamic center called the majma' which held prayers, sermons, and community functions. Near the majma', there were Arab grocery stores and restaurants that served halal meat.

Throughout that sweltering August, my pregnant mother would pack me into a stroller and walk the two miles across town from Michigan Ave to Warren to get her groceries and attend the majma' services. Those days coincided with the Islamic month of Muharram, in which the Ashura commemoration was held. The majma' offered two daily sessions: The first was held after noon prayer and was for women only.

The second was held before evening prayer and was open to all, but seating was segregated. Women were seated on one side of the hall, and men were seated on the other. As a child, I could attend both sessions and sit on either side, so my mother would take me with her in the afternoon, and then we would go back with my father in the evening. The typical program was delivered entirely in Arabic. It began with a recitation of the Qur'an, followed by a sermon and elegy commemorating the events of Ashura, and concluded with a prayer. I found the lectures boring, and I'd grow restless, so my parents used to bring a notebook and some markers with them so that I could draw and color during the lecture. But whenever the sheikh assumed the podium to recite the Ashura majlis or the incantations of the Qur'an, I would perk up and listen intently, mesmerized. The magic of their voices and the passion behind their words inspired me to do the same one day before a congregation of my own.

As the name suggests, the majma' was truly a community center of congregation. This is where we met many of the families that would become our friends in America. My father recalls one of the first friends he made there. He overheard a man nearby speaking to his daughter in an Iraqi dialect.

"You're Iraqi?" my father asked.

"I am Iraqi," the man replied.

They chatted through the requisites. Where are you from? How long have you been here? Are you married?

"Yes," my father replied. "My wife is Lebanese."

The man beamed. "*My* wife is Lebanese." His name was Abu Israa.

We met many families that year. We would converge at the majma' or invite each other to our homes. Some families were Iraqi, such as Abu Reda and Abu Baqir's. Others were Lebanese, such as Umm Hassan and Umm Ali's. Many were Iraqi men who were married to non-Iraqi women. Like my father, Abu Yaseen, Abu Israa, and Abu Mustafa's wives were Lebanese. Abu Ali and Abu Ahmed's wives were white "Americans." Abu Jawad's wife was Filipino. Abu Hadi's wife was Costa Rican.

In the fall of 1990, we moved to the flat on Appoline Street, near Warren Ave. We spent those warm fall days walking around the neighborhood and splashing in a plastic wading pool and those stuffy nights sleeping on the floor of the living room, since the bedrooms were too hot. My father bought his first car and got his first job as a gas station attendant at a 76 in Detroit. We bought a couch, some beds, and a television. The flat on Appoline was our first home in America.

I've always had an odd relationship with words. For example, I can taste them. The taste of particular foods triggers certain words and phonemes in my mind's eye. It happens in both English and Arabic.

The taste of watermelon produces *grow*. Doritos Nacho Cheese chips produce the word *one*, and ك ف ر words like كافِر and كُفّار. *Two* and *twenty* are inspired by the taste of my mother's homemade orange zest sponge cake, as are the words *king*, *pick*, and *kick*. The government cheese of my childhood tasted precisely like *chase*, *charge*, and *chance*, but other store-bought American cheeses like Kraft did not. Frosted Flakes elicits *taxi*, *fox*, *call*, and *because*. With milk, it's *tiger*, نمر, and مُنكَر. Nestle Kit Kat bars—*not* Hershey's—elicit ش ك ر, words like شُكر and شاكِر, but not the English equivalent *thank*. Oil-cured black olives inspire نور and بَلَد. Za'atar in olive oil elicits ز د, words like زاد and يَزيد, the English *magic*, and other -*ic* words like *tragic* and *romantic*. Red meat produces بَعد, *meeting*, and *met*, but not *meat*. Well-salted plain omelets produce *back*, *come*, *return*, and *at once*.

Pizza is complicated. Generally, the taste of pizza elicits *v* words such as *move*, *vote*, and *invite*. But my mother's homemade thick-crust pizzas bring about an additional -*tion* at the end, as in *elevation* and *motivation*. That's just plain cheese pizza. With toppings, pizza can produce such a dizzying array of combinations that I won't go into it.

To date, I have no explanation for this sensory mystery. There's a technical term for it: lexical-gustatory synesthesia. However, there might be a clue to its origins in the fact that I am also an anosmiac. I can't smell and never could.

In addition to tasting words, I used to combine them into stories long before I could read or write them. When I wasn't draped in bedsheets reciting Qur'an, I would sit beside my mother dictating full-length narratives which I had invented using characters from my favorite films and cartoons, such as *Snow White*, *The Jungle Book*, *Tom and Jerry*, and *Bugs Bunny*. I drew my stories on colorful sheets of construction paper, then brought them over to my mother and dictated the words that she should write.

"Mama, write 'The cat chase the mouse!'"

With little knowledge of English herself, she botched the spelling as she set my words to print. But eventually, we worked together to compose a substantial body of storybooks. It would be years before I learned to read them.

When my mother wasn't helping me write stories, she was telling them. My mother is a fantastic storyteller, and some of my fondest memories involve me and my siblings seated at the dining table eating stew and rice while she told and retold a number of fables and folktales. Among my favorites were *The Wolf and the Seven Young Kids*, *The Boy Who Cried Wolf*, and *Laila wal Thi'b* (Little Red Riding Hood). On weekdays after school, she would sit us down and read to us, and every night at bedtime, she would tuck us in and recite the Qur'an for us until we fell asleep.

Words were magic. They healed me when I was sick, comforted me when I was scared, and guided me when I was lost and alone. The best words of all were the words of the Qur'an, the literal Word of God. Those words could alter the universe. I summoned hope and patience by reciting Chapter 94, ash-Sharh. If frightened, I recited Chapters 113 and 114—al-Falaq and an-Nas. In the face of oppression, I found strength in the struggle of Musa against the pharaoh in Chapters 20, Taha, and 28, al-Qasas. I beheld God's justice against evildoers in Chapter 105, al-Fil. I began and ended each day with Chapter One, al-Fatiha, and 112, al-Ikhlas. In grief, I found solace in Chapters 36, Yaseen, and Two, al-Baqarah, Verses 153 to 157.

When confused, I consulted the Qur'an through kheerah. When sick, I recited the Lord's name through tasbeeh. When thirsty, I drank from the brass cup inscribed with the Throne Verse. If I lost something, I incanted the besmalah and I would find it. We hung calligraphy on the walls and wore jewelry with Islamic inscriptions. When we entered the house, we announced our arrival with "Salam" so that evil spirits would flee.

I wanted to know these words, to harness them, to command the world with chants that summon courage, comfort grief, and inspire change, to declare them among throngs of listeners and to hear their echoes in the distance. I wanted to be a sheikh, a reciter of great words.

But I didn't become a sheikh. I became a gangsta rapper instead.

Years later, as an eighth grader at Woodworth Middle School, I found a word which came to define my emerging adolescence. I was browsing the bookshelves in language arts class one day when I came upon a thesaurus and looked under the word *angry*. I skimmed down the list: *hostile*.

I was hostile, and I had every right to be. Middle school didn't make any sense. If you were mean, people liked you. If you were nice, people were mean. If you teased girls, they smiled and laughed. If you complimented them, they frowned and walked away. If you were bad in class, you were hailed in the hallway. If you were good in class, you were bullied in the locker room. The pretty girls dated the ugly boys, and the only friends you had were the ones you didn't want.

If school wasn't bad enough, things were even more confusing at home. Suddenly, there were all sorts of rules, and everything I did fell into one of two categories: 'ayb or mafrooth. 'Ayb was shameful, discouraged behavior that hurt and offended others or demonstrated disrespect. I was forewarned that such behavior not only reflected upon me as an individual, but also my family and community. With the whole of the Collective at stake, compliance was nonnegotiable. But many of the things that were considered 'ayb did not seem 'ayb to me. What shame was there in wearing a hat, or chewing gum in the company of guests, or sitting in a manner that exposed the soles of one's feet? What was so disgraceful about bright-colored clothing or a high-fade hairdo? Then, there were things that were mafrooth, or required by expectation, but they seemed just as arbitrary. It was mafrooth to greet elders with "Salam" in Arabic, but the English "Hello"—or, God forbid, "What's up?"—was 'ayb. You could wear shorts outside, but inside, especially among elders, wearing long pants was mafrooth. When it was time to eat, it was mafrooth that the eldest or most distinguished guests be served first, followed by the remaining elders, followed by the children.

The social rules were buttressed by religious rules that classified behaviors as wajib (mandatory) or haram (forbidden). The religious rules were easier for me to obey, partly because they were consistent. What was wajib and haram in adolescence had been so in childhood. The rules weren't arbitrary, either. They were derived from an arduous evaluation process called fiqh, or Islamic jurisprudence, which establishes laws of conduct through the study of the Qur'an and the Hadith. But the social and religious didn't always correlate. Wearing shorts was 'ayb but not haram. Rising when elders entered the room was mafrooth but not wajib. If hats were 'ayb, then why were sheikhs supposed to wear turbans, which are functionally hats?

Worst of all, what was cool in school was 'ayb at home, and what was mafrooth at home was humiliating at school. Speaking Arabic in the house was mafrooth, but doing so in school, other than in jest, was grounds for being labeled a "boater," the common slur for a newly arrived immigrant. Brandishing brand names was a social must at school, but begging my parents for material vanity was 'ayb, since my value as a person was supposed to be reflected in my character, not my clothing.

Many of these expectations seemed to contrive and enforce a collective respect. But as an adolescent, it didn't make any sense to me. The lists of dos and don'ts were so contradictory and inconsistent that the only conclusion I could gather was that it was 'ayb to be an individual. I was nothing more than a cog in a greater wheel of blind conformity in which my only role was to pay homage to others and suppress my personal identity. Any attempt to stand out or establish my individuality, whether by dressing or talking uniquely, was somehow disrespecting the Collective. At least, that was how it seemed.

No wonder I was hostile.

Music was the most baffling paradox of all. At home, music was out of the question; it was both 'ayb and haram. It was not permissible to perform it, listen to it, or attend events in its presence. The laws of fiqh prohibited music as a gateway sin, since it was often accompanied by gender mixing, alcohol and drug use, and suggestive dancing, which all invariably lead to cardinal sins. Although some scholars permitted instrumental or classical music, most of them strictly forbade it. In addition, the content of most music was unmistakably 'ayb. At home, we substituted music for recitations of the Qur'an, the nasheed—or Islamic hymns—and the occasional latmiyyah, the cadenced elegy poems of Ashura.

But at school, musical knowledge was a social code of conduct. You were expected to keep up with the latest trends in music and to recognize and sing along with any and all teen references. If anyone so much as *suspected* that you couldn't rattle off the week's latest hits on 93.1 WDRQ, then you were instantly labeled a pariah. I made sure to avoid that irrevocable law of teen nature by secretly tuning in to my clock radio when I was alone in my room, which at least kept me armed with the latest lingo for evading social humiliation: "britney spears backstreet boys nsync vida loca noscrubs kissmegenieina blah blah blah . . ."

The music paradox infuriated me. What was so bad about music? What *is* music, anyway? Any inflection of sound, from the chirps of birds to the jingle of wind chimes, was musical, wasn't it? What was the basis for the sweeping assumption that music inevitably leads to sin? I could just as easily sin without music, couldn't I? And was I the only one who noticed that what we were listening to instead of music was actually music? Call it what you want, but the Qur'an reciter was singing, the nasheed was a song, and the latmiyyah was a ritual dance. Besides a language shift and the religious overtones, there wasn't a lick of difference. Nevertheless, calling them "music"—especially the Qur'an—was haram. But incanting the Qur'an was wajib and mafrooth! I had been wearing towel-hats and singing Qur'an all my life, to the admiration of adults and peers alike, yet suddenly, if the words were in English or the song didn't praise God, I was violating some cosmic ancestral order!

In time, music became more than social currency. I listened to Britney Spears and the Backstreet Boys to survive the peer pressure of middle school, but Jay-Z, Eminem, and DMX made me feel alive. This was the most haram music of all: gangsta rap. It was profane, sexual, and violent, but it revved my soul and gave voice to my rage against the duplicitous world around me. It was real, raw, 'ayb, and proud. It shunned the rules and defied social norms. It was hostile. But most of all, rap was individualistic. It asserted the rapper's right to be who he is. It defied establishments in the name of individual expression, and did so with unapologetic courage. It was the most precise expression of my personal hostility against the cultural conformity of my environment.

I had to devise all sorts of schemes to gain access to gangsta rap. Since it was rarely played on the radio due to its explicit content, I could only listen to it on CD. Up until that time, I had always honored my parents' directive that music CDs, cassettes, and instruments were not allowed in the house. But technically, if I happened to be over a friend's house and he happened to own a large rap CD collection, then I wasn't exactly breaking their rule. So, I'd visit friends and we would listen to DMX, Eminem, Jay-Z, Snoop Dogg, and Dr. Dre. I committed many of the songs to memory and would rap them to myself when I was alone. Eventually, I started to compose my own rap lyrics in my head to match the beats of my favorite songs. And in the course of that process, without realizing what was happening, I underwent some serious changes.

One evening in the summer of 2001, right before the start of my high school freshman year, I was at a friend's house browsing Napster for the names of songs I'd heard on the radio: "Country Grammar," "Bye Bye Bye," "The Real Slim Shady." I typed in a name I'd heard in passing but had never listened to before. It was called "Changes," performed by somebody named 2Pac.

A flutter of piano introduced the track, and then this couplet: "Wake up in the morning and I ask myself / Is life worth living should I blast myself?" It went on to admonish selling "crack to the kids," lament the "hungry mouth[s] on the welfare," caution against "misplaced hate," and defy police who "jack you up, back you up, crack you up, and pimp-smack you up." The song ended and I played it again. Then again.

I entered "2Pac" into the search bar and found another song: "Hail Mary." Its opening declaration brought me to my feet: "I ain't a killer but don't push me / Revenge is like the sweetest joy next to gettin' pussy." I listened to that more than fifteen times in a row. I needed more: "Pain," "Hit 'Em Up," "Troublesome '96," "Me Against the World," "2 of Amerikaz Most Wanted." I might never have left if my parents hadn't arrived and practically dragged me away from the screen.

Holy shit. 2Pac.

My sole mission that summer was to get my hands on a 2Pac album. To my relief, I had recently managed to upgrade my clock radio to a boom box with cassette and CD players, so half of the battle was already won. But how was I going to convince my parents to purchase a rap CD for me?

I wasn't. I was going to have to do it myself.

I had been plotting the operation for weeks. I'd managed to sneak away from my mother while shopping at Target to scope out the shelves of the music department, and I'd found just what I was looking for: a two-disc album called *2Pac: Greatest Hits*. From there, the plan was simple: take the forty bucks I'd been saving from my allowance, ride my bike the one mile from my house to the store, purchase the album, and ride back home before anyone could suspect anything. Since my little brother and I often went bike riding, nothing would seem out of place. The only obstacle I could foresee was my age. Since I was clearly under eighteen and trying to purchase a CD which brandished that infamous black-and-white PARENTAL ADVISORY EXPLICIT CONTENT label, what was I going to do if the cashier refused me? I was going to have to risk it and find out, because there was no other way to get that album.

I casually approached my father one afternoon and said, "Jay and I are going to ride bikes. We'll be back in an hour." My unsuspecting brother came along only to find himself pulling up to Target after an unusually hasty ride.

"Watch the bikes," I instructed. I wasted no time and permitted no distractions. I darted to the back of the store, grabbed the album, raced to the cashier, and, appearing as casual as possible, handed the attendant the album and a pack of gum. She rang it up, cashed me out, and offered a receipt. "No thanks," I stammered as I ran out of the store, stuffing the album into my pants. We were there and back in less than forty-five minutes.

Disc one of *2Pac: Greatest Hits* begins with a "holla to [the] sistas on welfare" and asks, "since we all came from a woman . . . I wonder why we take from our women / . . . do we hate our women?" It continues with a toast to gangsta recklessness, a plea to God from temptation, an ode to the dead, a phantasmagorical resurrection, and concludes with the most ruthless diss track of all time. Disc two opens with a boast to all the troublemakers, a caveat on teen pregnancy, an apology to old friends, a call for change, and a tribute to a mother. The scope and range of human expression astounded me. How was gangsta rap capable of such magnificence? I saw myself reflected in every aspect of 2Pac's music. His biblical references and Christian iconography validated my passion for my own faith and the Qur'an. His iconoclastic vigor and lust for vengeance fueled my rage against social and religious conformity. His odes to friends and family epitomized my aspirations for love and friendship. 2Pac was proud to be a man, an individual, a force for truth and change, and I loved him and idolized him for it.

I tried to tell my father about "Changes" in the car one day, tying in his career as an accountant with the themes in the song. After working at the gas station for several months, my father found a job as an accountant at a juice distribution company, a task which was consistent with his professional training. He had studied and worked as an accountant in Iraq. Later, he managed accounting departments in Kuwait and the Emirates before immigrating to the United States. Since then, he has owned and operated his own accounting and book-keeping business in Dearborn.

"He talks about the government and taxes and everything," I told him, "and about how to make society better."

"Haatha very good, bes shino hal kalam," my father countered with a wince. "Why this *language*?"

"That's his reality," I explained. "That's how they talk in his world. It's not his fault."

"Yes bes you can say it without the bad word," my father insisted.

"It's not bad words!" I said. "He's just telling it like it is. He's being *real*."

"There is no need," he scoffed. He couldn't get past the "kalam," the "words," and his fixation on them was preventing him from seeing the bigger picture: that 2Pac's music transcends all kalam and speaks directly to the heart. It is a burst of raw truth. "*'Ayb* hal kalam," he added.

I rolled my eyes and stared out the window. He didn't understand. Nobody did.

But 2Pac understood. He'd been dead for five years, but his words still addressed the crises of the present age. I would watch the pan-Arab operetta *al-Hilm il-Arabi* (the Arab Dream) on our satellite Arabic TV, and 2Pac's words "Can't a brother get a little peace? / There's war on the streets and the war in the Middle East" would resonate within me. His vitriol toward the injustice of American police paralleled my revulsion of the Israeli military's oppression of the Palestinians. And his heartfelt advice "the old way wasn't working so it's on us to do what we gotta do to survive" pushed me away from the traditional backdrop of my upbringing onto a new path of self-actualization as I entered high school: to speak the truth of life through rap.

By the fall of 2001, I had officially become a gangsta. Just like 'Pac, it was me against the world, and the only course of action for a troublesome outlaw was the Thug Life. So, with all eyez on me, I threw my hat on backward and pictured me rollin' down to Hemlock Park to shoot some ball with my lil' homies. My father practically keeled over when he caught me one afternoon.

"'Ayb!" he cried. But life goes on.

I was producing rap songs under my new alias, Anonymous, and my latest eighteen-track album *Aspects of da Corpse* featured such self-declared hits as "Manifestation Theory," "Repentance," "Don't Mourn Me," and "Long Live Da King." I was also running a makeshift mafia on the side under the name Snakeyes, and with the help of my associates—Bugsy, Wite-Out, and Chainsaw—we roamed the halls of Fordson High demanding kids give us their money and pushing them out of their seats, which only resulted in a slew of tardies and the resentment of our peers. Our recruitment flyer read "Give it to us, or we'll give it to YOU!!!" We even had a contract for new members.

Hostile, gangsta, and mafioso as I thought I was, my peers would've likely disagreed. They might've described me as nice or smart. I certainly wasn't hot, popular, athletic, or funny—attributes I would've strongly preferred—but quite an agreeable and cooperative young man. I didn't want to be.

Smart or not, I wasn't shining as a student. I completed eighth grade at Woodworth with a 2.7 GPA, and by the time I arrived at Fordson that fall, I was all but completely checked out. I didn't care about school, because being "smart" wasn't exactly a badge of pride for a fourteen-year-old. What I really wanted was the validation of my peers. I was more interested in girls, friends, and basketball than I was in being smart. And so, due to my apathy in middle school, I didn't advance to the honors courses with the rest of my classmates that freshman year. Instead, I was relegated to a special "team" where I was required to repeat my previous math class.

But I didn't care because I was a gangsta. I had bigger things to worry about. I was updating my rapper name to ELKAMUZI, the gangsta-rappin' OG from the D. I had traded in those Qur'anic verses for rap lyrics, dropped the bayati scale for the hip-hop tetrameter, and dreamed of a jannah in which Heaven got a ghetto.

It was all going great until I discovered allusions.

That year in English class, my teacher, Mr. Peters, was introducing our next unit about a play called *Romeo and Juliet*, written by a guy in tights named William Shakespeare. As Mr. Peters was distributing the worksheet, I felt it was appropriate to voice my opinion on the matter.

"Poetry sucks!" I declared.

Mr. Peters looked up. "It does?"

"It's stupid!" I continued. "Just a bunch of old people moping about love or whatever. Why are we even reading this? It doesn't even make any sense. We should be learning about life!" And then, rising from my seat, I proclaimed, "We should be listening to 2Pac!"

"2Pac," echoed Mr. Peters.

"Yeah! 2Pac. He talks about life."

Mr. Peters allowed me to finish, then carried on with the lesson. The next day, we found him standing at the front of the room with a boom box. A classmate distributed the day's worksheet. When I got mine, I read the title at the top: "'Dear Mama' by 2Pac."

I screamed and jumped up and down from one side of the room to the other. We took our seats and Mr. Peters played the song. I bobbed my head and rapped along to the amusement of the class. When it was over, Mr. Peters began the lesson.

"Now, everyone look down near the bottom of that first stanza. By the way, a *stanza* is what we call a paragraph in a poem. Notice how the sentences have numbers next to them. That's because the lines in poetry are usually numbered. Would somebody read lines seventeen through twenty out loud for us?"

My hand shot up. Mr. Peters picked me.

"And even as a crack fiend, Mama, you always was a black queen, Mama, I finally understand, for a woman it ain't easy trying to raise a man."

"Thank you," he said. He wrote "black queen" on the board. "Now, does anyone know why 2Pac refers to his mother as a *black queen*?"

Someone responded that it was because she's black and a queen is respected and appreciated.

"Good," said Mr. Peters. "Any other ideas?"

No one answered.

"Well, back in the 1970s and '80s, there were a lot of poor African American women on welfare. These women were sometimes called black queens." Then, next to those words on the board, Mr. Peters wrote *allusion*. "If 2Pac is referring to this phrase, then we would call it an *allusion*, which is when a poet makes a reference to something else."

On my worksheet, I wrote *allusion*.

"But that raises a question. If *black queen* means both *respected woman* and *woman on welfare*, then which meaning does 2Pac intend in this line?" The class broke out into discussion. Mr. Peters settled us down and suggested, "We can't know for sure. But could it mean both of those things at the same time?" And then, under the word *allusion*, he wrote *pun*.

On my worksheet, I wrote *pun*. By the end of the lesson, I had added *meter*, *rhyme*, *AABB*, and *refrain*.

I went home and listened to "Dear Mama" again. It felt like seeing in color for the first time. This simple tribute was brimming with multidimensional meaning and complexity. "Mama catch me put a whoopin' to my backside" is imagery. "Make it through the night there's a brighter day" is a metaphor. The whole song was composed in AABB rhyming couplets of four beats per line, the traditional meter of rap. 2Pac's music was more intricate than I ever could've imagined.

The next day, I asked Mr. Peters if we could listen to another song.

"Sure," he said. "What do you have in mind?"

I knew that most of 2Pac's music was not school appropriate, but I had one suggestion. "There's a song called 'Keep Ya Head Up,'" I offered. "There's no swearing and it's full of positive ideas."

"I'll listen to it and get back to you," he said. But the next day, Mr. Peters declined.

"Really?" I was surprised. "Why?"

"Well," he explained, "that first line, 'Some say the blacker the berry, the sweeter the juice' . . . I'm concerned that it might . . ." he hesitated. "I believe that it's referring to the *fruit* of a woman."

"Huh?"

"Which, if it is, would be a metaphor," he grinned.

"Makaveli in this killuminati" is layered with puns and allusions. "Had a church of kids" is hyperbole. "Steal from the ones without possessions / the message I stress" is loaded with inner rhyme. One day, the truth of Mr. Peters's lesson finally hit me:

Rap is poetry.

2Pac is a poet.

And I the rapper was in fact writing poems.

Alone in my room, the next words I wrote seemed to magically appear before my eyes:

*Oh my Mariah, my candle, my moon*
*My chills in December, my warmth in June*
*A look in your eyes, and creation lies dormant*
*And you leave me bawling, incensed with torment*
*The angels look up, yet you still rise higher*
*But I swear I will reach you, my sweet Mariah*

"My Mariah" was the first poem I ever wrote. Mr. Peters let me read it aloud in front of the class.

By the time we got to *Romeo and Juliet*, I had studied and learned all that I could about figurative language. One of the first things I noticed about the play was that the parallels between Shakespeare and 2Pac were unmistakable. *Romeo and Juliet* was composed almost entirely in pentameter, with lines slightly longer than 2Pac's tetrameter. Shakespeare employed various rhyme schemes, including 2Pac's AABB sequence and a more rigid form in the prologue called a sonnet. I borrowed *Hamlet* from the library, almost immediately pairing "To be or not to be, that is the question" with "Changes'" "Wake up in the morning and I ask myself / Is life worth living should I blast myself?" When I came upon Polonius's advice to his son Laertes, I was reminded of something I had heard long ago, but it wasn't 2Pac. It was the advice of Luqman to his son in Chapter 31 of the Qur'an. Come to think of it, the Qur'an had a rhyme scheme as well. In many cases, it followed AAA . . . , as in Chapters 19, Maryam; 20, Taha; and 55, ar-Rahman. And as for Chapter 48, Verse 10—"God's hand is placed on theirs"—that's a metaphor. So are the final verses of Chapter 59, al-Hashr. Chapter 24, Verse 35—"Allah is the light of the heavens and the earth . . ."—weaves a breathtaking allegory. And Yusuf's dream of eleven planets and the sun and the moon prostrating to him is symbolism. And foreshadowing.

All I wanted to do was write poetry. I wrote about love, unity, racism, and even paper clips. By the fall of my junior year, I had filled several notebooks and folders with hundreds of poems. I was sorting them by preference and quality when it dawned on me that I had written enough poems to create a book. I approached my father about the idea. Although he had been supportive of my newfound passion for poetry, he thought that it was too soon to publish a book.

"Not yet," he advised. "Keep reading and writing. And *memorize*."

But I disagreed with him. What good would memorizing other people's poems do for me? I had my own poems, and they were ready to be published. We went back and forth about it, but he insisted that although I was writing a lot, and he was very proud and impressed, I was not ready to publish. I conceded. I wasn't going to break his word. At least, not while he was around.

But in September of 2003, I got my chance. Earlier in March, the United States had invaded Iraq and overthrown the regime of Saddam Hussein. For many Iraqis, this was a fantastic, unfathomable impossibility. For the first time since he had left his homeland in 1980, presumably forever, my father could consider the possibility of going back. Like many Iraqi refugees, he had been forced to leave his friends and family behind. Since then, his parents had died, his friends had fled to countries like Syria, Canada, and the United Kingdom, and his brother had gotten married and had children whom my father had never met nor expected to meet. Iraqis were convinced that the tyrannical Saddam would be succeeded by his even more tyrannical sons. Now, the nightmare was over. My father booked a flight as soon as he could and left that fall. He wouldn't be back for weeks.

It was the perfect opportunity to create my book.

I gathered my poems, sorted them by topic, solicited a friend to create some illustrations, and designed the cover. I called a digital printing company to discuss my options. I had saved some money while working weekends at a banquet hall, and by the time my father returned, I was ready to show him the whole plan.

"Here are the poems," I said. "I designed the cover. These are the photos I'll have on the front and back. I took them myself. These are the drawings, and here is where they'll go. I called a printing company, the same one that the mosque uses to print its magazine. They said that I could print five hundred copies for two thousand dollars. Look, I saved the money from the banquet hall. It's all ready. I just need you to drive me there."

He was silent. He reviewed the pictures and poems. He sat back, took a moment to think, and then said, "OK."

I published my first collection of poems in the spring of 2004. It was called *Renegade Rebel*. I asked the school administration if they would allow me to sell it. I was permitted to set up a table in lower B Hall between the main staircase and the Fordson tractor. Students were very supportive. Some would stop by during passing times and buy my book. I signed their copies and they patted me on the shoulder, shook my hand, and hugged me. Others offered to sell copies to their friends and family. Parents came by to congratulate me and offer encouragement. Teachers advised me. Mrs. Ameer met with me after school to proofread and revise my poetry. Mr. Salam would chat with me in the hallway about listings in *The Writer's Market* so that I could submit my poems to publishers. Mr. Mortensen suggested that I contact agents who accept unsolicited manuscripts.

"Use punctuation in your poems," said one teacher. "Don't leave it out unless you're making a point."

"Get away from rhyming," said another. "If it's not purposeful, it can be limiting."

"*Memorize*," my father insisted. That's what his father, Sadik the Word Man, had told him in his youth. "Read the masters and memorize." It was advice I generally neglected in the beginning. But today, it stands as perhaps the greatest piece of writing wisdom I've ever received. I would rephrase it to say, "Memorize poetry now so that you have it when you need it later."

I'm glad I did. I needed it later.

When I graduated from Fordson High in 2005, my plan was to carry on the legacy of my high school teachers by becoming an English teacher myself. At the time, I envisioned the classroom as a Platonic academy of radiant learners engaged in passionate discussion and innovation. But to put it mildly, I discovered that eighth-grade language arts is not that.

After working as a parapro at Universal Academy in Detroit, my first full-time classroom position was at Woodworth, my middle school alma mater. In addition to the challenges of large class sizes, complicated schedules, and the all-encompassing enigma that is the "middle schooler," there was the largely impossible task of keeping one hundred fifty children seated, engaged, and academically functional for an entire hour, every day. This was a doomed objective from the start; despite my best efforts, I couldn't get my students to listen. No matter how straight they sat up, how dead-eyed they stared forward, or how tightly they pressed their lips, I couldn't penetrate their firewalls of distraction. Despite their sincere intentions, they could only manage to sustain that yogic position of classroom etiquette for so long before dissembling into chaos and disarray.

The only time they actually gave me their full attention was when I played videos on the Promethean Board. As soon as the lights and sounds appeared on the screen, their conversations ceased, their bodies oriented toward the front of the room, and almost in unison, they leaned forward in transfixed hypnosis. But the moment the motion on the screen stopped and I approached the podium to discuss, they fell back into mayhem and distraction.

Ahmed, in particular, *never* listened to me. In fact, he never listened to anyone. He was so notorious for his horseplay and disruption that he'd been dubbed a frequent flier at the principal's office. The students, however, really liked Ahmed and often joined him in his antics. And despite our frustration as teachers, we were generally fond of him. For me especially, Ahmed bore a unique significance. He might not have known it, but his presence in my class inspired one of the most important developments of my teaching career.

In the fall of 2014, my students were reading Edgar Allan Poe's "The Tell-Tale Heart," and by reading, I mean they were throwing erasers, passing notes, and falling asleep in their seats. However, I did manage to capture their attention at the end of the hour when I mentioned in passing that the *SpongeBob SquarePants* episode "Squeaky Boots" so uncannily paralleled Poe's short story that it would be reasonable to assume that the episode was based on it.

"We should watch it," Ahmed said.

*That's a good idea*, I thought. I went home and found the full episode online, and when the students arrived the next day, I was excited to announce their lesson.

"Today, we're going to watch *SpongeBob*!"

They were ecstatic and fell into complete silence once the video began. I noted their unwavering focus. Ahmed, in particular, was so absorbed in the episode that I actually felt a bit jealous.

"Is a screen that much more interesting than *me*?" I thought. "Why won't they listen to *me* like that? I bet if I was on the screen, even *Ahmed* would listen to me."

And then, it hit me. If I were on the screen, he *would*.

That afternoon, I searched for a program for making simple videos. An app called 30hands allowed me to upload photos, record and attach audio, and sequence them into one complete video. I skimmed the next day's PowerPoint lesson about figurative language. I was planning to deliver that same lecture to each of my five classes. And so, I simply uploaded my PowerPoint slides to create an eight-minute video lecture. I called it *The Mr. A Show*.

When students arrived the next day, I said, "Today, we're going to watch a video." A huge yellow smiley face appeared on the screen, and then, much to the students' amusement, my voice announced, "Hi everybody! This is Mr. Alqamoussi. And today, we're going to be talking about the differences between figurative and literal language."

I sat in the back of the room and watched the students absorb my lesson. Afterward, I gave them a quiz. Almost every student passed, and most answered every question correctly. Ahmed earned 100 percent. I repeated this process in each class with similar results. It turned out to be my easiest and most effective day of instruction.

"That's so weird," a student said after the show. "*SpongeBob* was just like the story. Even how Mr. Krabs put the boots under the floorboards."

"You could even hear a heartbeat in the background," another student added.

"That's right," I said. "They're very similar. In English, we call that an *allusion*."

On the whiteboard, I wrote *allusion*.

Over the years, I created dozens of *Mr. A Show* episodes that covered a range of topics from figurative language and etymology to poetry and symbolism to Shakespeare and writing strategies. In addition to improving student engagement, the show also resolved other problems in the classroom. I could now walk around the room during the lesson and work with struggling students, which hadn't been possible when I was lecturing. I could assign absent students the lessons they'd missed. I could even assign videos for homework, and students were not only more likely to complete it but were also more likely to be engaged in class the next day. Eventually, they were excited to come to class and watch videos. I continued to use *The Mr. A Show* throughout my five years at Woodworth, as well as two years at Fordson, and eventually at Henry Ford Early College, where I transferred for the 2019–2020 school year.

In March 2020, when Governor Whitmer declared a state of emergency and closed schools, teachers throughout Michigan scrambled to create content, schedule lessons, and learn how to teach online. Fortunately, *The Mr. A Show* facilitated this process for me, allowing me to schedule content and teach remotely. I created playlists and shared them with my colleagues so that they could use them as well. But there was a sadness about it all. It felt like this revolution of virtual learning had been far overdue. From as early as 2008, virtual schools like Khan Academy had demonstrated the limitless potential of online learning. So, why had it taken us so long to get on board? Why did we need a pandemic to force us into such an obvious shift? The internet had always been there, kids were always tech-savvy, and teachers were always looking for innovative ways to make learning easier and more effective. I began to wonder if our frantic adjustment to virtual learning was due to necessity or an overdue matter of course.

Overall, it felt like we were all "late to the party," as my friend Adam would put it. He and I discussed these and other issues on our annual travels, since he was also an educator of sorts who lived and worked as a guide at Zion National Park in Utah. Things like education and a pandemic were topics we would've likely discussed in real time, but that March, as the world was reeling, Adam was still coming out of the woods. He was part of an annual program organized by the Cranbrook Schools of Bloomfield Hills, Michigan, which took students on a ten-day camping trip to the Tennessee–North Carolina border. With no cell phone service or connection to the outside world, the group emerged from the forest on March 20 only to be gravely informed that the United States was on universal lockdown, flights were canceled indefinitely, and their only way back to Michigan was to drive. At first, they generally dismissed these hysterics but quickly discovered the gravity of the situation once signal was restored on their phones and they read the news. Adam also found a voice mail from his employer at Zion, who urged him to call back immediately. He was informed that the park was closed until further notice and that he had been laid off for the summer. Adam returned to Dearborn to assist his parents and family members with grocery shopping and other pandemic-related needs. By the time we managed to regain a sense of normalcy, it was almost midsummer.

And so, in late June, Adam and I started to meet again. We spent much of the summertime in my backyard, socially distant, discussing our own experiences as students and learners. Since high school, Adam and I had taken different educational paths. I attended Henry Ford Community College and Wayne State University and completed a bachelor's in English and a master's in English as a second language. Adam took the roads less traveled by, moving from a speech/physical education major in college to studying at a fire academy, completing EMT/paramedic training, traveling the world, and moving to Utah to work as a guide. In the end, we both became teachers.

I had my gripes with the education system as a whole, and Adam would listen patiently to my rants about it. Those discussions eventually led us into a series of conversations about American education when it comes to language and words. Adam and I explored our own challenges as students, as well as all the misconceptions surrounding language and literature. Most of all, our talks made me realize that my aspirations for teaching transcended classroom instruction. My whole point in becoming a teacher was not so much to train children in "comprehension skills" as to help them discover the magic of words that had so enthralled me since childhood. I wanted to do more. I felt responsible to do more.

After all, words saved me in 2020. That fateful spring, as our nation and the world dissembled into fear and despair, I managed to keep afloat by embracing the magic of words. I read every day. T.S. Eliot's "The Waste Land" reminded me that collapse is a natural course of civilizational growth. Wallace Stevens and Hart Crane represented the fellow Americans who had despaired before but prevailed. Walt Whitman's "Song of Myself" incanted the resilience of the American spirit, and Emily Dickinson's downright creepy fascination with sorrow is almost comical. I also wrote to cope with the chaos and uncertainty that consumed me. As one day of the pandemic blended with the next, I chronicled my thoughts, feelings, and observations in a series of journal-poems which I called *The Apocalypse Diaries*. Between reading and writing, words kept me sane. Words were made for times like these.

From Shakespeare to 2Pac to the Holy Qur'an, the words I knew were there when I needed them. I wanted to share this knowledge with the world; to declare the timeless advice of my grandfather, Sadik the Word Man; and to provide the words that arm and buoy and comfort us through the trials of life.

"I want to teach more than one hundred fifty kids a day," I told Adam. "I want to teach 150,000 kids a day."

"Then do it," Adam said. That's how Adam lives his life. He just *does* it. "Let's start teaching online. What have we got to lose?"

And so, that summer, Adam helped me prepare a series of programs to share my passion and joy for words. I composed poetry, took photographs, recorded and edited videos, and blended words with other multimedia. We tested these creations by posting them on social media and engaging with fellow artists and fans. We used the feedback to formulate long-term plans, and once we had prepared a skeletal framework and developed a promotional strategy, we needed to give the whole thing a name.

"What should we call it?" Adam asked.

I knew right away. "Let's call it WORD MAN."

"It sounds like a corny superhero."

"It's right," I insisted.

# ALIFABET SOUP AT THE LEBANESE–SYRIAN BORDER // I BOUGHT MY BOWL FROM THE KITCHEN WAREHOUSE PLUS ON WARREN ACROSS FROM SHATILA

*Yasmine Rukia*

the angle of incident // smells like a soft-core parade // on the banks of River Rouge // and the east side of Dearborn too // once I thought twice about the power of words // the possibility of protest // but in all kinds of weather // the earth bubbles with more than // the apocalypse called for // that's what you get // sings a shy boy in a trendy saloon // in every pomegranate seed lies the mother of dissent // every country has a stalk of browned barley // already fermented into imagination // at the border // I cry // cackle // crack // what else can we do // where the sea is covered // in barbed wire // where your own brother // turns you away // into fire // only the alphabet // remembers // the echo of a name //

the alphabet soup is strained through my fingers

articulating Arabness / bandit Bedouin brides /cursing Canonized Culture / drone disquieting / eponymous elephants enchant / fine fiery figs / gallows garrote greenery / hopeful homes haqq / immigrants imagining / jahiliyah justice / keif khoder knows / love leads life / mouth mimics mountains / naked narrations negate / ossifying oceans / pillowing prayers / queer queens / relinquishing Riyadh rhetoric / serving semi smiles /      / ubiquitous unions / voluptuous vigilance / why would we / xeric xenophobia / you yourself young / zealot

# ON THE MARGINS

## Queer, Arab, American

### *Mai Jakubowski*

I bound down the stairs, backpack falling slightly off my shoulders. It is close to the end of the school year—this I know from the early morning sun already beating down through our windows and that feeling in your heart that you only get when you know summer is coming. That type of light where you feel as though you're already somewhere else—the smell of fresh-cut grass making its way in through an open door and the sound of sprinklers starting up.

My face glowing, I wear a robin's-egg blue skort and what I think may have been a Lisa Frank top—just a precious early 2000s look. I'm downstairs, ready to walk to school. Today would be the day people wouldn't bully me, because look at how cool I looked! This may have been fourth or fifth grade. It's 8:15 a.m., just enough time to take my time, imagining all that I could on the block-and-a-half walk before the school day set in. What happens between this moment and the second time I look at the clock—8:45 a.m.—is blurry after all these years. So, I'll do my best to reimagine:

The all-familiar groan associated with me fucking up. "Baba?" I ask, tightening up all my muscles, fight or flight kicking in.

"WHAT are you wearing?"

"What am I wearing?"

"Yes, hamara *(donkey, asshole, idiot, take your pick)*. Haram, baba, haram."

"What?"

"Your legs like that—it's 'ayb *(bad, wrong, ensuring eternal damnation, take your pick)*, habibi. You don't do that."

"But I just wore shorts yesterday." Could I have been any more confused? Probably not. The spite and the fire in my dad's voice wasn't necessarily new, but this was the first time I didn't know why it was there.

"Astuffruallah!" And he starts yelling at my mom for raising us so irresponsibly. I start to cry—confused about what I did wrong, embarrassed for not having picked out a cooler outfit (I really thought he was mad that I looked bad or something), preparing for another day of being mercilessly teased. The confidence I had at 8:15 a.m. has long left, sunk into the floor, not to be seen again for at least a decade.

The simple solution would have been to change, right? But I didn't want to—I didn't understand why I had to. I was so excited to wear a skort, the height of early 2000s fashion, so ready to enjoy the sunshine. Why was I being yelled at like I should have known better?

I'm on the couch, sobbing. I'm being yelled at for crying—couldn't I do anything right? It wasn't about whether the skort was haram, or my legs, or whatever else. It was that *I was haram* for choosing to wear a skort, and double that for not wanting to change. *I was the problem.* I look at the clock—it's 8:48 a.m. I'll be late for school because I was crying over skorts and somehow everyone will know that's why—truly embarrassing.

This is the first distinct memory I have of being told by my dad that my choices were both not Arab or Muslim enough, and that they signaled to him that I was an inherently bad person. At age ten or eleven, I should have already known that existing in my body was something to not burden others with. That I didn't know that, or seemingly didn't care, showed my dad that I was already beyond repair and could only change if I followed his every rule and met his every expectation—even if they were moving goalposts of respectability and isolation.

Sexualized and punished before I could understand what that would even mean—arguments where I wasn't sure what was going on—became our primary method of communication. The push and pull of Muslim and Arab standards, decided by my dad on a whim, and the criminality of my assumedly persistent refusal to measure up. Over and over again, the problem wasn't religion or culture—the problem was how my dad saw me. The problem was me.

I tentatively cling to my identities, as an Arab American, white, queer-identified, raised-Muslim who grew up in Dearborn, Michigan. Now that I live in Minneapolis, I am nostalgic for every cultural nuance in Dearborn, the same nuances that as a teenager I absolutely abhorred. I understood Dearborn as a series of exclusionary boundaries—if you could not perform correctly, you were ostracized, belittled, left to figure out what you did or liked wrong on your own.

The passing of time and the growing progress of Dearborn in some senses forces me to rethink my own experiences growing up. I dove headfirst into my queer identity after an entire childhood of ignoring it. I stopped defining myself as the person who is too white to be Arab, because what does that statement even imply? What does it privilege? At the time, for me, whiteness was privileged because whiteness meant freedom. Being Arab did not—and though I've since come to understand that this is incredibly far from true, that does not mean it didn't factor in to how I experienced community as someone from a culturally mixed background. I have always felt like I was forced to choose, or rather, that a choice was thrust upon me before I was even old enough to understand fully what that meant.

I started to understand that the boundaries placed on calling myself queer or not, Arab or not, were in part set by the expectations my father set for me and the ones I set for myself. Since accepting my queer identity and the loss of family that came with it, I have been able to imagine and engage my multiple identities in tangible ways, although these engagements sometimes feel voyeuristic. I go to hookah bars, I stumble through explanations of Islam to well-intentioned but poorly informed white folks. I rarely feel competent or authentic when I am in Arab or Muslim spaces. I am the outsider, the amateur, continuously existing at the margins of Arab and Muslim communities. As much as I know it isn't fair or right, I sometimes feel as though coming out as queer was the ultimate act of choosing whiteness—even though queer Arabs and queer Muslims exist and are thriving in Dearborn and beyond.

Growing up, Arab American was an enforced identity for me—an obligation rather than something I felt comfortable embracing. It was community dinners and not understanding the language despite endless hours of tutoring. It was constantly not being in on inside jokes. It was not knowing how to connect, not watching the right TV shows, not liking the right music or reading the right books. It was made abundantly clear—I didn't like the right things, I didn't act the right way, I didn't deserve to fit in.

My undergraduate years in Dearborn came and went, and though I allowed myself new experiences, and new ways of reimagining identity, I kept myself shut off from identifying as Arab American. Completing research on queer Muslim communities made me feel as if I was exploiting my informants while also instilling a sense of longing—did I finally find my community? Was my exclusion from Arab communities based on something I didn't have words for? Did I exist at the margins of Arab identity because of my proximity to whiteness or my proximity to queerness?

One Facebook group led me to a few transformative friendships that I would have never made otherwise, but when we first met, we really only had each other. We had all been searching for some sort of community, to find other people who were queer and Muslim or queer and Arab—really just to find anyone who "got it" would have been enough. And regardless, I would still feel left out to a certain degree, never having been able to properly code-switch and ingratiate myself into an Arab or Muslim community.

One of the first times these new friends and I had all gotten together was to break fast at a restaurant in Dearborn during

Ramadan—something I had never done because I had always been the only Muslim in my friend group. Such a casual thing—so mundane—and yet I had never felt more like myself. There was no pressure to behave a certain way, order certain foods—it didn't matter.

Additionally, in the years since 2014, it seems as though queer Muslim and/or Arab visibility has absolutely skyrocketed, lending itself to the creation of various social spheres, art installations, and community resources. I was recently scrolling through Instagram and saw that a friend was working on (or had already hosted by this point) an art installation that centered queer Arab work—publicly, visibly, without apology. It brought me to tears for two reasons: they are active and highly visible in the metro Detroit area, something I never thought possible, and I felt I could never do something like that without feeling like some sort of fraud.

Sometimes I still feel like I'm co-opting my identity. I don't feel like it's my own. I don't intentionally engage in Arab American social circles, though it is trickier now, living somewhere where Arab Americans are not as prevalent. I still don't feel comfortable communicating in Arabic—at this point I've accepted that it will always go in one ear and out the other. I'm on the sidelines.

Tenth grade, maybe. Another banquet, deep in east Dearborn, this time to celebrate an organization my dad would end up leaving six months later due to some sort of personal drama.

We parked three blocks down from the venue, just my parents and me. My dad, dressed in a light brown suit if I remember correctly, black hair slicked down and to the left. Round glasses covering up the bags under his eyes, his smile looking as tired as ever—as if he could never just naturally smile—it always looked like it was hard for him. I don't remember if this era of my dad included a full beard, a mustache, or just a full face of heavy stubble, but no matter what, it was salt and peppered from stress, covering up wrinkles that always remind me of the lines inside trees.

My mom's hair at the time was shorter, blond as ever, pinned back at the sides with bangs resting on top of her glasses. Or did she wear contacts? It doesn't matter—we had both gotten my dad's approval to leave the house, so I can only assume we looked good enough. This banquet was an excuse to dress up, to braid my hair and do my makeup and probably not get yelled at as long as I could hold my own with my dad's friends' kids. Which I totally could do—with my eyes closed and heels on.

We walk into the sound of music buzzing, people chatting, serving trays clinking—a cacophony of celebratory noise—no one quite sure what it was exactly we were celebrating, but who needs an excuse to dress up and show off? My dad introduces my mom and me to all of his friends—they all mention that they knew me as a baby and I smile politely, show off the few words of Arabic that I know confidently, and then search the room for any familiar face.

Of course, no one else's kids are here. Just me, a trophy forced to be on display—the idea that I obviously wanted nothing more than to attend a banquet like this passive-aggressively being rubbed in all my dad's friends' faces.

My mom, white as a CW show in the early 2000s, drags me around to say hi to all the wives—they make eye contact long enough to let both of us know that each interaction they have with us is painful, and not welcome, and we should just head back to our table as soon as possible. This happens enough times that my mom and I do head back to our seats, whip out our phones, and talk only to each other. Through all six courses, every speech, countless hours of dancing, this is how my mom and I spend our night.

My dad stops by only twice—once to gently check in, the second to glare daggers at both of us for not engaging with anyone else. "It's embarrassing. People are going to talk. Why can't you two just sit with people." As though our presence doesn't halt every conversation in its tracks, as though we haven't been trying, as though it is also our own fault that no one has invited us to sit with them or come over to say hello. Nine thirty hits, it's a school night, and my mom insists we leave. I strut out with my head held high, knowing that if I'm going to be judged I might as well look good doing it, but no one is even looking.

Every banquet, barbeque or dinner my dad took us to was an exercise in isolation and resilience. I was teased mercilessly or just completely excluded from Arab spaces for not speaking the language, for being too awkward, for liking books, music, and TV shows that were considered white. Kids are mean, and it was never enough to just ignore me: sometimes it was laughing right in my face, grilling me about things I liked, asking questions in a tone that implied I was some sort of freak or just plain dumb. The implication always was that I acted too white, talked too white, didn't belong. Others made it clear to me that being part of that world was an unfortunate and punishable accident. These two identities—being white or Arab—became something I had to choose between, and I clearly could not keep up with being Arab.

I saw my experiences reflected in my mom's—when we attended community events, I'd cling to her. Her conversations were stilted, halted by the non-responsiveness of my dad's friends' wives or altogether ignored. My mom performed her obligatory social niceties for these women to openly reject, which they often did. As an adult, I try to have some compassion; there's nothing wrong with people not getting along or not wanting to defer to whiteness. And maybe the very act of including my mom and me would have been doing just that. As I grew up, we went to fewer and fewer family dinners or community events, something my dad always blamed us for. Why couldn't we just get along with everyone (never mind that we tried over and over and over again)?

Watching my mother navigate these spaces in the same way that I was—hesitant, uncomfortable, purposefully left on the outside, included only out of obligation or to be the butt of a joke—reaffirmed to me as a child that we would never fit in. At the end of the day, my

whiteness, or my alignment to whiteness, was viewed as an embarrass-
ment in the communities my dad participated in. And so, I leaned into
a white identity to build resilience. If I was going to be ostracized and
bullied in the spaces my dad forced me into, then I was going to have
to have some sort of armor.

I desperately wanted a group of friends in high school who could stay
out past 5 p.m., whose biggest worries were whether they'd make var-
sity soccer or get asked to whatever dance. I guess I did have that in
high school; I just had to sneak around and lie or flat out not participate. In this world, too, I was isolated, if only because the restrictions
placed on me were a burden, an inconvenience to anyone else who
didn't have to think twice. I didn't behave like how my dad thought
a good Muslim or Arab girl should behave—I wanted to stay out late
with my friends, wanted to wear shorts when it was hot out, wanted
to not feel quarantined or ashamed for participating in my own life.

Looking back, these gripes seem like incredibly small things, but
they were tied to my conceptions of who I was—was I really a bad
person for wanting to have a life like the kind you used to see on ABC
Family? Was it really being Arab American and Muslim that held me
back from having that type of life? It's interesting—I didn't see any one
of my dad's friends' kids experiencing life the way I was, and in hindsight I know it was less the social norms of Arab and Muslim culture
and more my father's expectations that tainted the experience. But at
the time, it felt like Arab identity was a prison—a series of rules meant
to confine, exclude, isolate, and punish any behavior considered incongruent with what it meant to be Arab American. I spent a lot of my
youth trying to fight back against this, against the increased amount of
shame I experienced for not being able to meet anyone's expectations.

Coming out and understanding my queer identity broke all the
rules. Coming out completely rebuilt how I saw myself, how I could
engage with my identities—it was one final act of freedom, one

deliberate choice that would have to force me to take "a side." But by the time I came out, I didn't want to take a side—I wanted to be all of me, all of the time. Realizing my queerness built the foundation for me to reengage and reimagine how I define myself as an Arab American.

I am half of a first-generation American, freckled with Lebanese, Syrian, Greek, Polish, and Hungarian roots. Thirteen years before I was born, my father landed in San Francisco, the result of a war his parents and grandparents had no stake in. My father immigrated to the United States in the late 1970s, fleeing the civil war that had broken out in Lebanon. He came from no place as well—in living memory his family had been expelled from Greece and grown up at the margins of Lebanon and Syria.

Baba recently reminisced, "It seems that I lived the life of an immigrant just like all my ancestors since 1897."

Baba's birth is shrouded in misremembered details. He may be fifty-six or just turning sixty—no one is quite sure. We all existed, and still exist, in governments that don't want us and account for us differently than they do for others. His great grandparents evacuated Greece due to colonial violence. Baba said he still dreams in Greek sometimes—a language he was forced to leave behind, in a country that was never his. Jasmine stopped growing on his front porch five years ago—around the time I came out.

My mother, born and raised in Utica, Michigan, one of seven in a Polish Catholic family, grew up equal parts cheerleader and band geek. She attended the University of Michigan-Ann Arbor before heading off to Kalamazoo for graduate school. She met my dad there; they were the only two students in the eighties who smoked cigarettes.

My mom can remember her grandmother speaking Polish, but her cultural connections are faded, surface level. We make pierogis from scratch every year, and she looks for any excuse to put on polka music.

Ours is the kind of identity that has been swept up into whiteness, which is inextricably tied to conceptions of American identity. We lean into the stereotypes associated with Polish identity, but effectively, my mom's identity is not tied to any type of -ish or -es. She has always had the ultimate privilege: freedom from cultural definition.

Due to my mother's roots, I pass under the category of "acceptable/vaguely ethnic," just enough to be called "exotic" in white circles, and just white enough to have felt left out of Arab circles. Being effectively white passing in most spaces means I have the privilege of invisibility—I can move through the world without ever being questioned for it.

Baba moved to Michigan in the summer of 1987, having been accepted to Western Michigan University for graduate school. This is his favorite story to tell. Baba had left behind his job as a restaurant manager in the small California town to which he had first immigrated to pursue a career in education. Leaving California with only ninety dollars in his pocket, my dad took his old Dodge sedan out on the road. Long days spent driving through the desert followed by nights sleeping in his car next to the highway, not knowing what he'd do should anything go wrong along the way. The story ends with him pulling up to my uncle's home in Kalamazoo and the car dying on the street that night. I always come back to this image when my dad talks about feeling trapped. School, marriage, and jobs lead my dad to Dearborn. He still lives in the house where I grew up. He once told me that every morning he dreams about moving back to Lebanon; not how it is now, with his brothers and sisters older and gray like him, but how it was when he was a child.

My mother had a childhood I can only think about in sitcoms: *That '70s Show*, *Freaks and Geeks*, *Happy Days*—where the neighbors are in and out of the garage and there's always a Big Game to cheer at or play in, a constant revolving door of community. Whenever she talks about high school or even her early years at the University of Michigan, you can't help but tune her out and instead hear John Mellencamp's "Jack and Diane." You can't help but see a montage of letterman jackets, milkshakes, long nights studying, and pep rallies—think *Saved by The Bell*, just in the Midwest.

She attended Western Michigan University for graduate school, gaining two master's degrees: one in pure math and the other in applied statistics. When we talk about Western and meeting my dad, she tells me that he was funny. He was smart, handsome, completely laid back—they had a blast, and he was unrecognizable from who he is as my father. He drank beer, they went to parties, they fell in love.

Things have since changed. My dad stopped drinking beer and will deny he ever did if you ask. My mom took a job at GM until she had me, and then my brother and sister followed shortly after. My dad got his PhD in systems engineering after almost eight years of working multiple jobs, switching advisers—I think even at one point he switched schools. My parents, I guess, had never talked about how they wanted to raise their children—and so what seemed like reasonable disagreements between them quickly became fundamental disputes about what kind of life one ought to live in order to be successful. "I am raising my children the exact way my parents did," was the unshakable foundation (and yet constantly moving goalposts) my dad laid down, and I think my mom did her best to follow suit.

My parents have been divorced for five, maybe six years now; it's hard to keep track. My father's foundation was built on a bedrock of what he thought a good Muslim should be, how a good Arab should act. His understanding of what it meant to be a good parent and raise a successful child didn't allow for the whiteness I inherited, and so it was an aberration, a problem he couldn't solve despite his best efforts.

I want to call out here that I vehemently do not and will not privilege one culture, race, religion, or any other identifier over the other. My father's behavior and how that impacted my understandings of Arab American and Muslim identity are what I am trying to get at by tracing his logic and its impact on my frame of mind growing up.

In any case, being raised this way was a breeding ground for resentment, shame, hurt, anger. I was told that I was not good enough, never going to be good enough, and that I would more or less be on lockdown until that somehow changed—something I was also supposed to be responsible for. I saw freedom as something distinctly separate from my cultural identity, as something incongruent with my father's conceptions of Arab identity, and something I would never be able to obtain so long as I lived in Dearborn.

Dearborn is a city that I cherish in hindsight, through my rearview mirror, only after I could come and go as I pleased. There is no other place in the world like it, but it took leaving for me to know that. Known by some as Little Lebanon, Dearborn has one of the highest concentrations of Arab Americans in the United States. I think this fact above all is why my father stayed, why he insisted my siblings and I grow up there. Arabic is offered as a language in middle school and high school. There are just as many mosques as there are any other house of worship, and a vibrant community of both Arab Americans and Muslim Americans. Living here may not have always been my father's dream, but his favorite theme to rely on is sacrifice—if he couldn't move us all back to Lebanon, he could at least surround us with it. If he couldn't raise us around his family, he could at least raise us around other Arab Americans, around other Muslims. He thought it would be the best place for the family to learn about our heritage and to be around our culture.

Growing up in west Dearborn, in a predominantly white part of town, my sense of self developed almost wholly in relation to what I saw on TV—how I assumed my friends lived. Watching *Lizzie McGuire* after sitting through an inexplicably long and terribly useless Arabic class (all the other kids were already fluent, I might as well have been invisible to the teacher, why couldn't I just *figure it out*) had me assuming that Lizzie's experiences, embarrassments, friend group, were all things I should have had but didn't. I was trying to understand a phenomenon not unique to me—not being able to fit in, not being sure of yourself or what it is you like—but complicated because of cultural dynamics.

I couldn't have had Lizzie's experiences because some of her experiences were not for "good Arab girls." That cloying phrase could be taken from literally any community or family member. It was something said to me any time I wanted to do something my parents didn't want me to do. My childhood brain connected the dots that what I wasn't allowed to do were things that were too white. That may not have always been the case, but it is still embedded in me. Even now, at twenty-six, buying shorts feels clandestine, a crime I might not get away with. A majority of my negative social experiences as a kid were tied to events focused on around identifying as an Arab American or as a Muslim. I was reminded constantly that though I did not belong, I had to participate and keep trying. I was the problem.

In hindsight, there were so many signs that I was not straight. Some as innocuous as the type of storylines in shows and books I gravitated to (a whole separate essay could be written on my love for LGBTQIA+ young adult novels), others as obvious as me telling my friends in high school that I was bisexual only to walk it back immediately every time it began to feel real.

Coming out was too risky, too big of a commitment for teenage me to make. It was hard enough to exist day-to-day, let alone try to figure out something that could end up being more dangerous for me in the long run. So, I never let myself think of identifying as anything other than straight as an option. Dating boys was so rebellious, so radical, so much effort. It pervaded my entire high school experience, emblematic of what was systematically denied to me as a result of my dad's interpretation of culture: freedom. And the thing is, no one else ever quite got it. I dated boys whose parents did not immediately associate talking with someone of the opposite gender as *haram*. I dated boys who would bail the second something seemed difficult or annoying—I don't blame any of them. It was exhausting to keep up the sneaking around and the self-preservation while still giving myself as many mundane experiences as possible.

See, the mundane was intoxicating—it didn't matter if I liked a boy or not (I did not like any of them very much at all, to be quite honest), but the experience of dating, of just being able to interact with other people without culturally enforced shame, felt like something that had been taken away from me. This was the crutch I latched onto as representing freedom, choice, and autonomy—all things that had been denied because it was not "what good Arab girls do." It felt like something I was wrong for wanting in the first place.

This desire for escape and conflating dating with freedom followed me all throughout college. I committed to a relationship for three years that was not at all healthy or positive for two reasons: that boy had a quintessential, stereotypically white life, one that I craved simply for its lack of adherence to anything; and that he stayed despite the cultural pressures my family put on me. Growing up isolated from both worlds, from most communities and social circles, I was desperate for anyone who would put up with me and all my cultural baggage. By staying despite my father's expectations, this boy seemed magical. I did not care about any sense of self I had, about any baggage, cultural or otherwise. I ignored warning signs that this was not a healthy relationship for him or for myself, and I stayed long past our even wanting to make things work. All that isolation growing up forced me to be hyper self-aware, but dating had always been a blind spot.

When we broke up, I lost it. All the rejection I faced as a kid returned. I took our breakup personally, as an affront to my Arab identity, policed by my dad and something I couldn't help or change. The breakup, though warranted and absolutely the best decision, felt like a rejection of everything outside of my control. If I couldn't make things work with the one white boy who was willing to deal with my father's cultural and religious boundaries, then it was clear to me that I would never be able to. I would continue to be trapped in the cracks of both worlds, with no ability to form any type of long-lasting connection that wasn't tinged with rejection of some part of me.

Almost immediately following this breakup, an opportunity to attend a leadership camp for LGBTQIA+ college students came up, and I took it without thinking twice. I had always identified as an ally (perhaps *too* eagerly sometimes) and thought it would be best to get away for a little while. So I went.

The eight-hour drive from Dearborn, Michigan, to Nashville, Tennessee, felt like entering a portal into a different world. Eight hours where we got lost on one of the freeways and ended up in Royal Oak for thirty minutes; where we stopped at a restaurant in Ohio to eat heated up frozen hash browns and take cute selfies; where we finally showed up on Vanderbilt's campus and scrambled to find the rest of the group.

Three other folks from the University of Michigan–Dearborn and I attended Camp Pride in the summer of 2014—the summer before my senior year of college. By this point in my life, I had resolved to be as identity-less as possible. There was no overarching group that I fit into, white or Arab or Muslim or straight or otherwise, and for the first time in my life, I was trying to just go with the flow.

We arrived at the end of den assignments and an info session that took place in the auditorium. At check-in, everyone else in my group had already been assigned a den, but as I was added to the trip last minute, there was no place for me just yet. We walked into the auditorium, and one of the program managers went up to the Pride Leaders in Den 6 and asked if there was room for me. By chance, but completely meant to be. They said yes, and I was immediately swooped up into a giant hug by one of the other campers who said that he, "never does this, [I] just love your aura."

Camp Pride was a week-long retreat for LGBTQIA+ and ally college students, hosted by the organization Campus Pride. When I attended in 2014, Camp was taking place at Vanderbilt University in Nashville, Tennessee. Similar to a conference format, campers attend various workshops, panels, and participate in exercises around identity, community, and advocacy for the LGBTQIA+ community within higher education. We had regular morning and evening check-ins with our den, composed of roughly eight other students and two Pride Leaders—the stewards of our individual dens.

That first night felt like nothing I had ever experienced before—a feeling of belonging. It was like a deep breath out, eating university cafeteria food and chatting with other students from all over the United States about their lives. So wonderfully mundane! No pressure to attempt to code-switch, no concern about getting punished for behaving in whatever ways my dad deemed unacceptable, no explaining myself as people looked on, already zoned out and tired. I tried to savor each moment, let it last as long as I needed it to. The first few days felt this way: I have almost no recollection of specific events, workshops, or conversations—just feelings. I remember feeling the sun on my skin, glowing; the sheer number of hugs to be had with almost total strangers; the way it felt to see the other people in my den smile or laugh; the immediate sense of safety, connection, and intimacy carefully curated by staff and attendees alike.

By the third day, at the morning check-in with our dens, I heard myself say out loud, "Well, I'm pretty sure I'm queer." That may not have been my exact wording, but it doesn't matter. We were sitting on the ground in a circle, all a little grumpy from lack of sleep. Everyone at the check-in shared how they were feeling—mostly thinking about when they could get up and get more coffee. When it was my turn to check in, my body spoke for me, and it was like a dam opened. One of the Pride Leaders, Ash, nodded and smiled, and it was like I was given permission to mean what I said, and that yes, those words really did come out of my mouth. I didn't know it was possible to feel so light, but there I was, coming out before I could overthink it or push it away. Outside of my body, giving myself to a life I had never once let myself think about. I said it, and everything in the entire world felt right. This was freedom.

Somewhere between the speaker sessions, icebreaker activities, and the scorching heat, I fell into a queer community. It didn't take more than a few days for me to say wholeheartedly that I'm queer, that this was the identity I had been missing, the piece I couldn't figure out all those years. I had never had a space before to simply *be*.

As much as it felt like I was in a new world, living a new life, things back home did not stop for anyone. During that week, my jidu (my paternal grandfather) passed away. I hadn't seen him since I was around thirteen, so in my early twenties it didn't even feel real. I remember the last time I saw him: We were in Syria, sitting on someone's porch. I was getting ready to leave with my uncle to fly to Cyprus—flying home that year included a lot of extra stops courtesy of the American embassy.

When I went to say goodbye, Jidu was visibly frustrated. He couldn't remember who I was, why I was trying to leave, and why was I interrupting his breakfast anyway?

The second to last night in Nashville, I got the news and ran out of the auditorium back into the dorm I was staying in to cry, for Jidu, for my dad, for myself. I felt so guilty for even grieving. I had thrown away homes we never even had so I could be at a college campus in the South, pining after girls with short hair. *Haram.*

Queerness had never been an option to me growing up. It wasn't necessarily condemned, just never mentioned. Just another thing that wasn't for me. My parents and I were always clashing about other behaviors that they considered culturally and religiously inappropriate: being around boys, participating in musical theater, studying literature instead of biology, wanting to wear some goddamn shorts! I never had the space to even think I could be anything other than straight. I always had thought, "No, not me. Dating boys was rebellious enough." Dating boys who were white and weren't Muslim was about as big of a risk as I was willing to take as a young adult. But during that week in Nashville, where it didn't and wouldn't matter if I did end up liking girls, everything smelled like jasmine. Colors were brighter, food tasted better, my whole world felt softer.

Haram means forbidden, something leading to sin, but to me, in the moment we were packing up to drive back home, it meant exile. It felt like Jidu's passing was the final cord cut, letting me go from everything that had never been ours in the first place. Maybe I should have been relieved, but all I felt was heavy. Jasmine choking my senses.

I came out to my mom immediately—pretty much the night after we got back from Tennessee. I called her on the phone, too chicken to do it in person, and through heavy sobs I managed to say that I'm pretty sure I'm bi, maybe, but who could say, but I'm definitely not straight and I've always known I just didn't actually know for real but now I do and I'm sure and that I'm sorry. A long, pointed, exasperated sigh was the response. "Well couldn't you just . . . choose a man, please, I know that's not how it works but . . . this is not good." My mom was support-ive but scared. We joke now about how some of her initial questions and thoughts were problematic, but she was just trying to find the best way to keep me safe. We didn't know how my dad would react—we assumed not well given his views on what was considered appropriate dating behavior. Being attracted to folks who did not identify as cis-gender men? Definitely haram in his eyes.

By this point in time, my parents were beginning the process of getting divorced—my mom moved into a new house, my dad back into my childhood home that we had been renting out in the meantime. At the beginning of my senior year, in between student government meetings, two jobs, and copious amounts of homework, I was moving boxes, sneaking cigarettes, and trying to keep everyone happy.

My dad and I had settled into a cadence where we'd argue about perceived cultural and religious differences for a week straight, and then go back to being fine. I had figured out at least how to code-switch when I was over there—a victory I would have once thought impossible to achieve. But coming out to my dad would have flipped the script entirely. It would have solidified to him that I was privileging white identity over his, since in his conception of Arab and Muslim identity, there was no room for queer people. And so, my plan was to keep up the charade and code-switch for as long as I needed to. My sexuality had nothing to do with our day-to-day conversations, and I could expertly avoid the impending marriage talk by just adding on more and more plans for graduate school. No need to rock the boat if there wasn't anything to rock the boat over, right?

And then, there was a reason.

I came out to my dad in 2016, just a few days before leaving for grad school. I had been with my partner for almost two years, and I was tired of hiding. I wasn't invited to community banquets anymore; my dad had stopped trying to force me into social circles where he knew as well as I did that I wasn't wanted; and by this point I had gotten to a place where I did not need outside validation to confirm all of my identities.

Coming out to him had been preparing for the worst—I assumed that he viewed queerness as the ultimate transgression from being an Arab and a Muslim, and he had said as much whenever my research on queer Muslims came up in conversation.

My mom came over to his house with me and from the moment we pulled into the driveway, I was shaking uncontrollably. Was he going to be violent? What was he going to say? We never had a real relationship, but something about this conversation felt so final—depending on his response, we never were going to have a relationship, and that would be that.

My uncle had been staying over and I asked him to step outside for a minute. He did, and my mom and I walked inside the home I grew up in. My dad looked so much older that night than he ever had—his beard more salt than pepper, his wrinkles weighing down his entire face—standing at the fan in the kitchen, smoking a cigarette like he knew what was about to happen.

We sat at the dining room table—I could only stare at the ripped and peeling wallpaper, the scratches on the wood floor, my old bedroom out of the corner of my eye. My dad had turned it into an office. My dad asks me to hurry it up—

"What's wrong, habibi Mariam?"

I stumble, my voice shaking and my eyes firmly planted on the placemat in front of me.

"Baba, Mom, I just have to say it out loud—I'm gay. I'm gay and I've always known, I've never known what to do about it but I'm gay and I can't change it and that's that. I just thought you should know."

And my mom begins waxing on about, "Oh, wow, I never saw this coming, oh wow, this is BRAND-NEW information to me."

My dad stands up, storms back to the kitchen, and lights up another cigarette. This is it. I see the light leave his eyes the second those words came out of my mouth.

"Baba?" I say, looking for a response so we can just keep the conversation moving. He could be so unpredictable, and I needed to know what was going to happen next.

"I should have known. I should have known! You were are always acting *weird*, even as a kid, and if you had respected my wishes growing up you wouldn't be like this," my dad says, talking more to himself than to us at this point. He starts smoking one cigarette after another, his hands shaking, his face red with anger.

I hold firm and keep saying what I promised myself I'd say—that this was who I am, that there is no changing it, that I am going to live my truth, and that I needed him to know that. I tune out the pleas, the anger; I offer to make sure the rest of his family never finds out, and that brings him back down—an olive branch in the middle of a raging storm. There was something different this time—he knew it and I did, too. In all of our previous fights, I would match his anger, scream, and yell until we were both red in the face. But this time, I didn't care anymore. I was calm—I just wanted to feel free no matter what his response was.

However, despite the anger and the blame, his final response surprised me.

"I am too old to change my mind, so please do not talk about this with me, but it's your life habibti. You are my daughter, and I will always love you. Just promise me this: do not let anyone in my family or friends know, that would end me."

To me, this moment was the best-case scenario. He wasn't happy, and indeed still isn't, but his words didn't have power over me anymore. I know he was thinking that if only he could have raised me as he wanted, as a good Arab and a good Muslim, without whiteness stubbornly interfering, I wouldn't have come out, or this wouldn't have happened.

It didn't really matter what he said, though. My culture was no longer a prison for me. Beholden to nothing after coming out to my dad, I was free to figure out that it wasn't my heritage or the religion I was raised with that monitored and determined my sense of worth. It was the ever-moving goalposts of expectation set forth by my dad, who was making these decisions based on his interpretation of Arab culture, coupled with how he was raised and his own interpretations of the Qur'an. I wasn't "kind-of Arab" or "sort-of Muslim" or "I'm half-white"—it could be everything all in one sentence: a queer Arab Polish American person who was raised Muslim and is just doing their best.

I now live in Minnesota, where the closest I can get to participating in Arab culture is going to the Lebanese deli down the street. For those from Dearborn, this deli is reminiscent of any and all banquet halls—a mockery of what could be found at any shawarma place in metro Detroit. The chicken is always dry, and the rice is always a little crunchy. I almost never go to eat there, but I make a point to walk by it every day. I actively try to cling to my identities—Arab, queer, sometimes Muslim—but they don't seem to mean anything the more I say them.

Claiming my Arab identity while still existing on its margins is not easy work. It is an act of deliberate vocalization—of allowing myself to take up space while recognizing all the ways in which vocalizing my experience could potentially do harm and mitigating that harm appropriately. To be Arab and queer is just as mundane as it is radical. To me, it is knowing that my family's displacement and trauma has led to a very specific search for what home means and that we all have had different ways of getting there. To be Arab and queer openly is to participate without guilt. To be Arab and queer is the smell of jasmine in the Midwest.

# NOT ARAB ENOUGH

*Jeff Karoub*

To live and work in the Detroit suburb of Dearborn in the early years of this century as the grandson of Lebanese immigrants is to sometimes, but not always, fit in with what the community has become. To feel a strong connection to the past yet some remove from the present. To almost, but not quite, be "Arab enough."

Dearborn, rightly dubbed "the capital of Arab America," is the only city in America where you can be called out for not being Arab enough. It's also true that in Dearborn, as in America, your pedigree isn't necessarily your destiny.

I am the youngest grandchild of Hussein Karoub, who came to the United States in 1912 from the Bekaa Valley, now part of Lebanon, but then it was Syria under Ottoman control. He was like so many other immigrants, going to work at Ford for the promised five dollars a day, but in short order he would distinguish himself as the first imam in the United States to lead a freestanding, purpose-built mosque in nearby Highland Park. He also ran a print shop and published newspapers, including *Al-Hayat* and *The American-Arab Message*.

He represented and served the community for decades, marrying, burying, and leading prayers wherever he was called to do so, but he also helped establish and presided over Dearborn's American Moslem Society, or Dix Mosque, not the first but easily the longest continuously operating Islamic house of worship in the state.

It would be a lot to live up to. One of his sons joined the family businesses, eventually running the print shop, publishing the newspaper, and serving as an imam. That was "Ummo Mike," or the Rev. Imam Muhammad Karoub. His youngest brother—my father—was invited to follow suit but had other dreams: Carl Karoub's calling was music, and he worked his way into the French horn section of the Detroit Symphony Orchestra and counted himself among the in-demand session musicians who played on so many indelibly classic Motown records by Marvin Gaye, the Supremes, and others. Before all that, his own father thought music "a good hobby," but ultimately came to accept it as a career path. Even while carving out his own path, my father would chauffeur his father, who never learned to drive, to various cities in and out of state to perform religious services.

My father married a Dearborn woman of varied ancestry—none of which was Arab. My mother, Deanna Lee Feldhak, descended from Germans, Norwegians, Scots, and others. Some family genealogical work suggests her ancestors in the United States reach back to the colonial era, perhaps even including prominent families. But in her more immediate line, she also was the daughter of migrants, at least of a sort: Her parents came down from rural northern Michigan in hopes her father, Sidney Feldhak, would find work at Ford. He succeeded, joining the ever-growing automaker a couple decades after Hussein Karoub.

I followed in the footsteps of my parents, who were among the first in their families to graduate from college. Like them, I also chose a path that was less publicly religious. My brother, sister, and I weren't raised attending a mosque, though we'd find ourselves occasionally in one for special services, family weddings, and funerals. I would watch my more observant cousins for cues on what to do during prayers. I found fellowship as a teen in a United Methodist youth group that didn't judge me or my background—and the pastor was a big Beatles fan. I'll neither confirm nor deny that this may have played a large role in my early fondness for Methodism.

As an adult, I married a preacher's kid and joined up with the Methodists, ultimately landing in a church just down the road from the one in which my maternal grandparents worshipped. I have since learned that I am not the only grandchild of one of the earliest imams in Detroit to have found my way to Christianity. Not by a long shot. For me, there is no abandonment or judgment in any direction—except against those who weaponize their religion. My grandfather and uncle preached unity, not only among Arabs but also the Abrahamic faiths. A couple years before he died, my uncle, the imam, offered blessings at my wedding, which was officiated by my Methodist minister father-in-law, the Rev. John Huhtala Sr. Their genuine respect and support for each other and my union certainly gave me hope and bolstered my notion of a big-tent faith.

I would also pursue elements of the paths chosen by my father and grandfather. Like my father, I became a musician. One of my original songs is called "Made by Motown," which pays tribute to my parents and grandparents and their contributions to the metropolitan area they have called home for a century. One line says that "sometimes I feel like the unlikely child of Henry Ford and Aretha Franklin." It often gets a laugh from the audience, but in humor there is truth. Like my grandfather, I became a journalist. My newspaper career sent me across Michigan, and I lived in the Port Huron, Flint, Lansing, and Ann Arbor areas before returning to metro Detroit. I was always drawn to tell the stories of Arab Americans in those places, from Port Huron's Helen David, the pioneering daughter of Lebanese immigrants who opened the Brass Rail Bar in 1937 and owned it until her death in 2006, to surviving elders of Flint's Hamady family, whose immigrant forefathers opened a grocery store in 1911 and grew the business into a chain that once comprised about three-dozen stores.

It was during my time at *The Flint Journal* that I encountered a man who might as well have been a lost uncle. Mike Rizik called my office phone out of the blue one day. "I saw your column in the paper," he said, a bit brusquely. "Now, Karoub—is that Lebanese?" When I told him it was, he seemed satisfied. "I'm taking you to lunch. When are you free?"

Mike was born in Flint in 1920 and lost his father in a train crash when he was fourteen. He served in the army during World War II as a second lieutenant and ranger, and ultimately opened an accounting firm and tax practice that he ran for nearly fifty years. He married Matilda (Til, as he called her) and they had seven children—doctors, nurses, and lawyers among them. He was a founder of Our Lady of Lebanon Maronite Catholic Church.

I heard about all of the above over that first lunch and many to follow. He would never let me pay—another sign he was a lost Arab uncle—and he made me speak Arabic words and phrases. He told me his father insisted they speak it at home—"You can speak the language of the dogs on the street," Mike recalled his father saying. His grown children sometimes came to our lunches and wondered what these meals with a reporter were all about. Fair enough. I justified them as work related because each time I came away with more knowledge of Flint's early Arab community. By that point, I had lost my grandparents, and his stories of family, faith, service, and entrepreneurialism—and balancing the Arab with the American—fit right in with theirs.

Those trailblazers I got to know and write about in Flint, Port Huron, and elsewhere have all since passed on. During those days, I would ponder what they had done in and for their respective communities, and it would remind me of my forebears. Yet it was during my work as a Detroit-area journalist—and especially living in Dearborn—that I began to think much more about my family's history and heritage: how it shaped us, what it offered us, and what the passage of time gives and takes away. Arab Americans often are frustrated that their long history in and contributions to the United States are forgotten in the wake of a heinous terrorist act or during wars with Arab countries, but Arabs themselves often forget or never knew about the accomplishments of the Arabs who came before them.

I found my familiarity with Detroit-area Arab and Muslim communities of some benefit to my work as a reporter: I often knew whom to call or where to go for experts or "real people." But I also made assumptions sometimes based on outdated or incomplete information and could overlook subtle but important differences, such as geographic or economic dividing lines between Arabs of different nationalities that those outside or on the periphery of the community couldn't see. I learned this early in 2007 when I walked into a Dearborn bakery, asking a worker if he would be willing to comment on the latest developments in the Iraq War. "Not Iraqi, Lebanese," the worker replied. He pointed across the street. "Iraqis are on that side of Greenfield." Being off by a block or two is close, but not nearly close enough.

My father and his siblings came of age during the Depression and World War II eras, a time when acculturation and assimilation were more common and even at times necessary. They adopted "American" names, some of which stuck, and sang patriotic songs and standards. We have recordings from the mid- to late 1940s, now housed in the University of Michigan archives, of my father playing French horn and the group singing songs of the day as well as an "Ara-glish" ditty called "Bint El Shufta on the Corner" (The Girl I Saw on the Corner), written by their uncle, Athman Karoub. This tongue-in-cheek lament was about American women taking all of his money. For me, the recordings my father shared were personal, cultural, and anthropological gold, providing a portal to the past through a language I understood: music.

It's historically common for Arabs to gather and share songs and stories, and the tradition continues and evolves. I recall being at family get-togethers when I was a kid where a darbuka drum would appear and all of a sudden we were singing Arabic songs. It didn't matter if you didn't know the words—you joined in and sang what you could. Sometimes the dabke would even break out.

My father still regularly assembles as many of his children and grandchildren as possible to join him in his basement music studio to grab an instrument and play. We often joke that my wife, Kirstin, was aces with him the second he learned she could play piano and accompany his command performances. While Arabic songs don't typically make the setlist today, the custom of communicating through music very much keeps with traditions passed down to him. And I carry it on, playing music for or with my wife and daughters.

I've since learned that you needn't be a century removed from your family's immigration or limited to speaking only a few words of Arabic to feel "not Arab enough." A local grocer told me he felt immediately less so after arriving from Lebanon in the 1970s. Like the new car losing a few thousand dollars off the sticker price the minute the new owner drives it out of the dealership lot. Growing or shrinking Arab identity is especially apt in Dearborn, which has been home to Arabs since the turn of the twentieth century but has become synonymous with its evolving Middle Eastern community as its population and influence has grown.

There is a shaping and a reshaping here. That's true anywhere, of course, but there is a key difference: People from Arab countries keep coming, maintaining an Arab vibe unlike other ethnically rich enclaves where the immigrants from one country or region are replaced by another. Since there are many Arab countries, there are subtle cultural differences that come along and add flavors that wouldn't otherwise emanate from one area. Though Lebanese remain dominant in Dearborn, the city and surrounding area over time has become a destination for people from Yemen, Iraq, Syria, and elsewhere. While differences and disputes bubble up, one community inspires another to open businesses, form organizations and run for office. Palestinian American Rashida Tlaib, now a Democratic US congresswoman from Detroit, was the second Muslim state legislator in Michigan; my uncle, James H. Karoub ("Ummo Jim"), was the first. While not all Arabs are Muslims and vice versa, they go hand in hand for many in and around Dearborn.

The constant replenishing and reimagining of Dearborn's Arab community sets it apart from virtually all others in the United States. What if it had been another "Little Syria," which once stretched for blocks across lower Manhattan? It was, as I wrote for The Associated Press (AP), "a slum and a promised land, way station and destination (that) served as an incubator for other Arab enclaves," such as the one in Dearborn. I toured the neighborhood, which wasn't hard to do: All that remains are three original buildings on Washington Street, as most of the rest was torn down in the 1940s to make way for the Brooklyn Battery Tunnel. Still, it's hard to completely erase history: When the cornerstone of a Syrian Maronite church was discovered in the rubble of New York City's twin towers in 2002, it offered proof that Arabs once lived, worked, and worshipped there.

If Dearborn had suffered a similar fate to that ethnic quarter, the "capital of Arab America" would be somewhere else, if one place could wear the title at all. To be sure, there are other pockets of Arabs, but in all likelihood no one locale is so large in area and so concentrated with people tracing their roots to the Middle East that you could feel free to express your Arabness to such a degree. Or ever stop to wonder if you were "Arab enough."

As expected over time, I hear about fewer personal interactions others had with my grandfather, who died in 1973 when I was four. Still, I've relished those interactions: A now-elderly woman told me with tears in her eyes that Imam Karoub "married" her and her husband. A prominent community activist who became known for his work in social and economic services fondly recalled being a Sunday school student of my grandfather's at the Dix Mosque.

I grew up in the 1970s and '80s in Detroit's Downriver area, next door to Dearborn. In many ways it might as well have been a million miles away because of the scarcity of Arabs in the region at that time. We'd make some Middle Eastern dishes at home, but only rarely would we dare to bring a sandwich to school in "Syrian bread," as pita was known then. Buying that bread and other Arab food staples would require trekking over a series of railroad tracks and past numerous factories to Dearborn's Southend and going to stores in the shadow of the mosque where my grandfather and uncle once led prayers. By that time, it was mostly a Yemeni neighborhood, as Lebanese were moving into other parts of town, but this was well before thoroughfares on the city's east side would become constellations of Arab-owned groceries, restaurants, cafés, and commerce of all kinds. It's worth noting that many Downriver communities have seen their Arab American populations grow in recent years, so my brown-bag school lunch menu would likely be a little more diverse if I were a kid now.

It's widely understood that when one loses a particular sense, such as sight, smell, or hearing, the remaining senses strengthen. So it is for me with the food of my forebears, as the language and other cultural and religious customs fell away. When I walk into a Middle Eastern grocery store, the pungent, pleasing smell of the big buckets of olives immediately transports me to those Southend markets, and, then as now, the language spoken by workers and customers is familiar even if I can't fathom most of what is being said beyond pleasantries. It all est

washes over me, and, for a fleeting moment, past becomes present. My parents and I (along with my wife and children) still regularly gather for meals, and not surprisingly those meals often are at Middle Eastern restaurants. There, we hear stories from my father about the old days in Highland Park and receive gastronomy lessons, such as the right way to pour olive oil over labneh. And, of course, this indispensable truth: Utensils often take a backseat to "Syrian bread."

As I embarked on a newspapering career, it became more common for people to hear my last name and ask if I was related to the state lawmaker-turned-lobbyist (Jim Karoub), the doctors (Muhammad Karoub's sons, Carl and Frederick), or the professional musicians (my father, Carl, and older brother, Mike). As our family branched out geographically and professionally, our ties to Dearborn loosened and the public connection to our patriarch lessened.

I have tried in fits and starts to keep alive elements of my heritage. In my early twenties, I took an evening Arabic class at Dearborn's Fordson High School with my father. He claimed to be rusty, but a session or two in, he could have been teaching us. It's obvious to me that he saw it as a way to refresh and reconnect with the "home" language of his childhood and bond with his youngest son. Regrettably, I didn't keep up with the flashcards or use what I learned enough to retain more than a few words and phrases. But I'll never regret the time with my father—that alone made the class more than worthwhile.

A few years ago, I wrote a song called "Sometimes the Sea," a simple, unadorned folk song that also possessed a stately, classical hymn feel. I "heard" a horn line in my head. I knew a guy. I jotted down my ideas in musical notation, showed it to my father, and asked if he'd come into the studio to record it. He took my ideas and made them better, and the resulting recording can still make the hair on the back of my neck stand up. Music has always had that mysterious power for me, and to have the person who inspired me to pursue music playing on a song I wrote is far more easily felt than expressed in words. To have him join me on local stages to play that song takes those indescribable, full-circle feelings even further.

When I finally returned to the Detroit area after a decade of newspapering stints across the state, the hometown of Henry Ford (as some
municipal manhole covers say) seemed like a welcome place to make
a home for my young family. My parents were pleased for us, and it
brought back a flood of memories for my mother, who grew up here.
It was where her parents remained until their deaths. For all of his
connections to Dearborn over the decades, my father actually only
lived in the city for less than a year in the 1930s: The lay leaders of
the Dix Mosque wanted my grandfather to live nearby, so he moved
his large, young family to an upper flat in the Southend. It wasn't to
my grandmother's liking, particularly the pollution, so after several
months they packed up and moved back to Highland Park. (Similarly,
his own mother followed her sons to the Detroit area about a decade
earlier but returned to their ancestral village after about a year.)

There's no denying that the overall experience for my own family
has been positive. I wouldn't want any of my reflections here to sug-
gest that I have felt marginalized or that there has been any form of
major discrimination at play in my life. I haven't faced the obstacles
that often confronted earlier generations. Instead, I benefited from the
strong foundations laid by my grandparents and parents. But it's only
natural, I would think, to feel some ambiguity in terms of my ethnicity
and sense of place—especially returning to the city that was a strong
part of that foundation.

It can certainly create cognitive dissonance from many sides: The
maitre d' at the Middle Eastern eatery who does a double-take when
I say my last name and he takes in my not-obviously-Arab counte-
nance. The non-Arab acquaintance who disparages Arabs but then
backtracks when learning of my ancestry: "Oh, but I didn't mean *you*,
Jeff." Or when my children get looks of astonishment or suspicion
from classmates when they say they are Arab. "Say wallah!" came the
reply to my middle daughter, Nora. My youngest, Charlotte, says she
would have to tell some disbelieving people, including friends, several times. My oldest, Anna, said if she added "I'm Arab on my dad's
side," they would quickly respond with "Oh, you're just half then."
She's a quarter Arab, technically, making the implication even more

clear: "not Arab enough" in Dearborn. No malice, perhaps, but still matter-of-fact.

Again, the end result hasn't all been negative: My kids have benefited from knowing and befriending people who share their ancestry—often at a greater level, sometimes the same or less. It's even been motivating. Nora, in particular, has been learning Arabic with the help of a first-generation friend and her family. She becomes "Noo-ra" (complete with the rolling R) when she is at their home and now proudly wears a cedar tree charm on a necklace, which they gave her.

What would Hussein Karoub make of it all? He lived long enough to see his children and even some grandchildren pursue fields and chart courses far different from his own—some that must have surprised him. He made the conscious choice to leave Majdal Anjar for whatever Amreeka could offer, so he would have known at least on some level that changes were inevitable from the moment he landed. It meant some of his descendants would find other paths, professionally and spiritually. But he was also among the people building the early Arab and Muslim institutions that would make it possible for a community to grow and thrive in the century that followed, whether or not they knew of him or could understand the accommodations he had to make as he forged a path.

I wonder if at least some amount of not feeling Arab enough comes from a lack of information about my grandfather's life leading up to and during his immigration. When I set out to share his story as part of a first-person narrative for the AP in the centennial year of his immigration, I was struck with some potentially fatal obstacles: First, no written record could be found of his 1912 passage, and a key story passed down through family lore—that his ship traversed the North Atlantic at the same time as the *Titanic* and in fact received its distress call after it struck an iceberg—was revealed to be a tall tale spread by relatives. Rather than recommend I abandon the effort, my editor, Ted Anthony, suggested it could be compelling to write what I didn't know and show how quickly these stories that become lost to time or myths can be used to fill in the blanks. It's especially common for Arabs whose ancestors came before Ellis Island and the creation of the National Archives to have holes in their migration stories.

The journalist in me wants to distinguish between myths and truths, even the painful ones within my own family. There's no glossing over the hard times: My father was born at the beginning of the Great Depression, and by the time he was nine he suffered the losses of his mother to kidney failure and his eldest brother and sister to tuberculosis and cancer, respectively. The nonagenarian great-grandfather still wonders what life would be like had they all lived and everyone else hadn't been forced to grow up a whole lot faster. Their presence might have helped shore up familial relationships and cultural traditions. In the aftermath, endurance and perseverance became the primary drivers and perhaps spurred his desire to maintain strong family bonds down through the generations, as well as a preference for living in the present and looking forward as opposed to excessively pondering the past.

What about the notion of feeling "not Arab enough"? While it *feels* real, perhaps it doesn't really hold up to greater scrutiny. There are many different Dearborns—over time and even at this moment. And, in the words of Sally Howell, a coeditor of and contributor to this collection: "There are as many ways to be Arab as there are Arabs." Even as the stories differ, most of us want to know who we are and where we came from—particularly if that place is fleeting and ephemeral.

Several years ago, I was talking with another grandson of Arab immigrants. He was a bit older and knew of my grandfather. He noted that we both had become more American than Arab, which likely explained why we were so interested in our heritage. Perhaps we were finally comfortable enough, felt like we belonged enough, to seek answers. For us, knowing our past and finding a place in the present were pieces of a growing puzzle. It became less about loss and more about gain.

The man thought Hussein Karoub might be a little "scared" when imagining his descendants' lives more than a century after he launched a new life and started the clock ticking toward becoming an American. Still, he reasoned, my jidu would be "even more proud" of what his multicultural, interfaith family had become—however much "Arab enough" we are.

# A CONVERSATION WITH RANIA MATAR

**Ghassan Zeineddine (GZ)**: What inspired you to come to the Detroit metropolitan area to take pictures?

**Rania Matar (RM)**: I had started this project titled "SHE," which is about young women in relationship to their surroundings. I always work with young women around the ages of my daughters. This is the work I received the Guggenheim Fellowship for in 2018, and I was a brand-new empty nester, so this was the first time in a long time that I could actually travel to make art. Most of my previous work took place in Lebanon or Massachusetts, which are my two homes, and now I was able to travel more widely within the Middle East and the United States I started picking locations where I knew people, as I needed to have a hook to work from. I knew you were in Dearborn and my web designer in Ann Arbor, so I made it work around both connections. But I also went to Oklahoma; I went to Ohio; I went to Utah; and more. I went to places I hadn't had a chance to visit before, and it was great because each location added another dimension to the work.

**GZ**: We'll come back to your new project a little later on. Tell me about your first impressions of the Detroit metro area.

**RM**: Dearborn felt very different from Detroit. I was agreeably surprised when I walked into stores and people just greeted me in Arabic; it was like being in Lebanon. Detroit has a very different feel. What I loved about Detroit was the texture of the place, and in the work *SHE*,

I'm very interested in texture and tactility, this sense of the surrounding and how it becomes part of the backdrop of the photograph. I loved Detroit for that, so most of the images in this book are actually from Detroit.

**GZ**: Among the urban spaces you visited to take pictures, was there a particular one that stood out to you?

**RM**: There were three places. The first one was a bit random, but often this is how I come across interesting places. I was driving with Rebecca [one of Rania's subjects], and once we saw this place with all the weeds, we stopped the car and jumped out.

The second place was an abandoned building next to Eastern Market, near Saad Wholesale Meats. The place had so much graffiti and texture it was really beautiful. It reminded me of some of the walls I like to photograph in Beirut.

The third place was Fort Wayne, Detroit, which felt like it was from a different time. The sky was very dark, the place was abandoned and overgrown with weeds, adding to this whole sense of mystery. One of the women in the photographs, Jodi, knew the place and helped me gain access.

**GZ**: Did working in the Arab community in the Detroit metro area pose any particular challenges for you?

**RM**: Not at all, actually. I work with young women who enjoy being part of the process. I first try to make the work feel very collaborative; I want them to feel empowered by the process, to have a say in it, to feel beautiful. If you pay the right amount of attention to people when you're photographing them, you really can get beautiful and intimate images, because people *are* beautiful—you just have to create the right level of comfort, trust, and collaboration.

**GZ**: A lot of your work focuses on women and female adolescents and the intimate spaces they occupy. In your previous books

*L'Enfant-Femme* and *A Girl and Her Room*, you showcase photographs of American and Arab young women, putting them in conversation with one another. You also capture the relationship between mothers and daughters. How do your photographs in this volume compare to your previous work?

**RM**: All my work follows young women close to the ages of my daughters. It's very much about my sense of identity and my daughters' identity as Arab Americans. So in all my work, I make photographs in the United States and the Middle East, and for me, it's not about comparison—on the contrary. It's about focusing on the shared humanity of growing up as a girl and as a woman, and about the universality of going through the transitions of life, even if the women's personal lives are different. Young women have their own uniqueness and individuality, but they are united by similar biological, physical, and emotional milestones of puberty and growing up at similar times in their lives, right?

My earlier work focused very much on the domestic and familial space, because my girls were living at home, and *A Girl in Her Room* is about a teenage girl and her intimate relationship to her bedroom. My newer work is more about young women who have left home. I started this work when my daughters were in their late teens and early twenties and had left for college. In Ohio, where you and I met and where I fell in love with the rural lush landscape, I realized how these young women [students at Kenyon College] who have left home and are making the exterior space, the larger environment and more global backdrop, their own space for a defined period of time. So I started focusing on the sense of texture, the physicality of the place. It eventually grew into a larger project and ties to the work I made in Detroit.

For instance, in the photograph "Zarghoona," I loved photographing Zarghoona because I loved the tattoos on her arms. All I could see were the flowers and the dress, and I think she was wearing jeans and she was putting the dress over it, but I loved the relationship she had with the texture in the background. She arrived late to the site, and I barely had time to photograph her (I was scheduled to speak to your class), but I love what we ended up creating together.

I told her: "I need to see your tattoos." I love that she has these unique tattoos all over her arms. A lot of times, in the West, we tend to judge women from the Middle East one-dimensionally, but for Afghan women, because of the news, the stereotypes rise to another level.

One of her tattoos translates to: "The enemies say it's the language of hell. I am going to Heaven with Pashto."

In another photograph, "Noor and Hajer," the picture is of two sisters. I love that they were sisters, and that one is veiled and the other isn't. When it comes to the hijab, some people tend to think that it's something that's forced upon women, and they don't get that there are so many layers to it, and a lot of times it is a choice.

We spent a long time here. I love the sense of tactility in this picture and how the hair is blowing in the same direction as the hijab. The whole sense of the different fabrics and the mystery that was created by the clouds, the wind, and the aura of the place added so much to the mood of the photograph. At the same time, the older sister is touching her younger sister; they were very close.

**GZ**: At the beginning of our conversation, you mentioned your new book *SHE*, which was recently published. Can you tell us more about this book and why you titled it *SHE*?

**RM**: I kept wondering if I'd keep that title until I realized I couldn't find any other title that expresses as much as this does. I found that being twenty today is very complicated, and I'm looking at it from the lenses of young women and girls. We tell them they can be anything they want to be, yet at the same time, they still have the same pressures traditionally placed on women: to be beautiful, by a media standard of beauty. I'm realizing how much pressure there is on them, especially with the bombardment of social media. In this work, I wanted to really focus on our sense of physicality rather than the digital world that so many of us are living in.

Zarghoona, Detroit, Michigan, 2019.

Zarghoona, Detroit, Michigan, 2019.

Rebecca, Detroit, Michigan, 2019.

Fatima, Detroit, Michigan, 2019.

Amal, Fort Wayne, Detroit, Michigan, 2019.
Images courtesy of the artist © Rania Matar.

# THINKING DETROIT

*Hayan Charara*

The past of my poems is usually called Detroit. But because I left the city for good in 1996 and return infrequently, the city exists for me predominantly as memory, and a lot has changed over the past two decades, so much so the Detroit I write about may not, in significant ways, correspond to the Detroit of the here and now. In *The Alchemist's Diary*, my first book, I describe the city as "a shithole" "where boys / are manufactured into men," where "Fords and Chevys, the carcasses / of car makers' assembly lines, / [are] torched and over- turned," where "rats cried for escape," and where "I was first called a sand nigger." Yet I also bestow upon Detroit the epithet of holy city, a nod to its stubborn refusal to die, its insistence on rebirth. And in a poem titled "Dandelions," a lone dandelion rising out of a crack in an asphalt parking lot symbolizes the city and its people. The dandelion is a weed, of course, a thing unwanted, that gets yanked out. But with its bright yellow petals, it's easy to mistake it for a flower. The dandelion insists on being:

> a show of survival, of getting through,
> of coming close to not making it,
> and then, all of a sudden,
> life where we never expect it.

Detroit is also where I witnessed, on a highway exit ramp, a man holding a sign that asked, "Why doesn't Jesus turn asphalt into bread?" It is where I heard the city's longtime mayor, Coleman Young, explain Detroit's decades-long decline by noting, "Neighborhoods collapsed

because half the goddamn population left!" Detroit embodies the inex-
tricability of the profane and sacred—a shithole, a holy city.

My take on Detroit—its complexity—arises out of facts, those which
any researcher, professional or amateur, can find supported not only in
other poems by other poets, in novels, films, essays, history books, and
government statistics, but also by simply speaking with someone who
has lived or still lives in Detroit. You could also visit the city and see
for yourself. However, I have to concede that despite the facts, the city
of Detroit, as I know it, as it appears in my poems, is probably more
imagined than real. Lately, I've been thinking about this a lot (probably
because I have surpassed the milestone of living more years in other
cities than in my hometown), and I have come to a few realizations,
one of which is that I can hardly tell the difference anymore between
thinking about the past and remembering the past. In fact, I am beginning to wonder, when it comes to thinking and remembering, if there
is any significant difference between the two.

Most people, myself included, view thinking as tied to the present
moment, as a here-and-now practice, whereas memory resides in the
past—remembering as a practice with the capacity for time travel. Our
everyday language reinforces the dichotomy. We tend to "think back
to" rather than "think on" or "think of" an earlier time. We remember
and recall events and people from the past, the re- prefix a reminder of
the returning, the going back. This division between past and present
is not quite right, though. A return to an event or idea via memory is
not a return to the original encounter. The re- prefix so often used
in the vocabulary of memory belongs as much to the new and now as
the old and then. When we return, recall, remember, remind, we must
also think of things that occur afresh and anew, and these necessarily
invoke the present moment, the right now.

In the strictest sense—literally speaking—every thought occurs in
the past. Whatever I think—or speak or write—at this very moment, the
moment, perceived as the present, occupies a space already a fraction
of a millisecond gone (the time it takes for the sensory experience of
an act or thought to travel to and register in the brain as the here and
now). Every moment experienced as *now* takes place *then*. However,

our brains simply cannot sense this infinitesimally small lapse of time. Maybe, then, we should regard memory (remembering, thinking about the past) as something that happens simultaneously in the past and present. This is what I do. You can do what you want.

Obviously, no single image or set of related images can possibly embody an entity as complicated as a city, a truism for cities both in the actual world and memory, cities of the past or present. Oddly enough, I found in the work of my forbears, Philip Levine and Lawrence Joseph, a Detroit all too familiar to mine, even though decades separate the Detroit of our poems and pasts. This speaks to endemic problems, often largely ignored or worsened by inept, inadequate, or misguided policies and politicians. It also brings attention to the way the past works—a city, or anything else for that matter, should be unchanged in the past. What happened then, happened once, is set in stone. Except—both in the real world and in the imagination—the past is anything but static. While the *actual* changes Detroit undergoes may be too slow or, for those who must bear the brunt of its ills, nonexistent, the Detroit of my memory-thinking is constantly changing—in some respects more often and more dramatically than in actuality. Which brings me to another problem I think a lot about—truth. I take truth to be an endpoint—at least an intention—of my poetry, and while no pursuit of truth is entirely innocent, mine follows the path of the poet, not a philosopher. In other words, or in Richard Hugo's, "The words should not serve the subject. The subject should serve the words. This may mean violating the facts." The poet, Hugo tells us in *The Triggering Town*, "owes reality nothing and the truth about . . . feelings everything."

While I never tell lies in my poems, I do violate the facts—innocuously, I believe. Worse than allegiance to the truth about my feelings over the facts, however, is my reliance on memory to arrive at truth. In its service, except to persuade, memory can be nearly worthless. Most lawyers will tell you—the one I'm married to tells me all the time—that eyewitness testimony (or "memory") may indeed be one of the most effective, persuasive kinds of evidence, but it is also possibly the most unreliable. In this way, the past mirrors a work of literature: open to multiple readings, interpretations, and, more importantly, open to misinterpretation. In the law, certain verifiable forms of evidence applied to eyewitness testimony (DNA in a criminal investigation, for example) show that even the most self-assured, without-a-doubt, under-oath memories turn out to be simply impossible. Like other poets who aim for truth, I don't place my hands on a Bible and swear to tell the truth, the whole truth, and nothing but. No poet—nor any witness in a court of law—ever swears to tell the facts, either. Other forms of speech—in particular, I'm thinking of legal and political speech—come with formal (public) rituals and oaths. Elected officials swear to do this and that; persons about to be married do the same. Poets have no such rituals. They do, however, engage in other rituals and commitments—the practices and pacts a poet makes with craft, with a reader, with his or her own censors—but these come about voluntarily, and they vary from poet to poet. If the facts can be disregarded or altered, and truths (definite or indefinite) depend on or emerge from feelings, then do I owe my subject any allegiance? What do I owe the city of Detroit, which, a quarter century after abandoning it, I still call my hometown?

The easy answer, which I had to learn, which every must poet must learn: nothing at all.

Louise Glück puts it this way: "The artist's task, then, involves the transformation of the actual to the true. And the ability to achieve such transformations, especially in art that presumes to be subjective, depends on conscious willingness to distinguish truth from honesty or sincerity." While poetry may depend on actual experiences, "honest speech" does not lead the poet, or the reader, to discovery. Honest speech is "the degree to which and the power with which the generating impulse has been transcribed. Transcribed, not transformed." The poet's work is not to transcribe but to *transform* experience into truth. The poet's experience serves as a lightning rod, but the truth isn't necessarily found in the lightning bolt. The poet must transform the experience so it may lead to a discovery. The poem that does this is one that "sounds like honest speech," but, Glück reminds us, sounding and being honest are not the same. The authentic voice is the one that rings true. "The true, in poetry, is felt as insight," Glück writes. It does not have to be lived, either. "It is, instead, all that can be envisioned." The advocacy here calls for an inventive mind and a bold mind. The poet can—Glück seems to be saying the poet *must*—transform lived experience. It has to be "changed—heightened, distilled, made memorable." She also advocates for "the true," which is the thing in a poem "felt as insight"—it is "*all* that can be envisioned." The emphasis is mine. *All* that can be envisioned requires, I think, a long-term, continual commitment to the truth—to return, again and again, to a previous realization or discovery, to a subject (to a city, for example—and if not a city, then to another subject, another *object* of attention until it becomes, in the ideal, an obsession). A poet may never get to "*all* that can be envisioned," but each return (to the poem, to its subject) is a step in that direction. This, Glück contends, is the "advantage of poetry over life." I would add politics and law to the list of things over which poetry has an advantage.

Poetic speech, it should be obvious, is not political or legal speech. Nor is poetic practice akin to its legal or political counterparts. Plain and simple, poetry is not politics, or law, or, for that matter, journalism, or history. Much as I write about Detroit and what has happened to it and to its people, my poems on the subject, concerned though they may be with truth, are not public records. They are private ruminations that come to be only barely, occasionally public. And, yes, I aim for them to speak a truth, and I believe many do, but no matter how apparent a truth in them may be, no matter how authoritative the poems or the truths in them, they are never authoritarian. You can undo them. But even if you don't, I have no doubt that eventually I will. I will try, at least.

Though I have spent more years living in other cities than in Detroit, I keep going back—that is I keep *thinking* about the city. Nostalgia—the pain, the yearning to return home—only partially and inadequately explains why I go back. I do so because I am, every few years, someone new—not a better human being, necessarily (though hopefully), but simply someone with another different perspective through which to make sense of the world—my world, in particular. Because I have changed, so has my past. A colleague of mine, lecturing on Aeschylus's *Agamemnon*, remarked that one of the frustrations of Greek tragedy is that no one has a second thought about a horrific crime or transgression until it is too late. Agamemnon may not be able to go back in time to the moment before he decides to murder his daughter; he seems incapable of this task, even in memory. But I am not Agamemnon, and having managed to avoid such darkness, most of us aren't. We can go back—we must go back—and when we do, we can rethink our pasts, and we return from the journey with either knowledge or pain, which is a kind of knowledge. Either would be fine. Both can be made into one of the many truths available to us over the course of a lifetime. I am convinced—more than I have ever been, probably because a little older I hope I am a little wiser—that this is necessary if only (but not only) because the truth possesses an extraordinary capacity for disappointment. Once made—you can say *discovered*, if you wish, or *realized*, or *arrived at*, but I'll say *made*—the truth wants to be exclusive; it does not wish to share space with other truths. But anything experienced in isolation ultimately gives way to an aching for something more, something else. With the truth, this is the beginning of its undoing. And to undo, we must first go back before going forward.

The poems of my first book try to make sense of the city, its meaningfulness, by way of presence, rootedness—the images concrete and definite: "Interstate 94, at milepost 210," "the city beside the strait," "Hart Plaza," "Eight houses from the birthplace of Henry Ford," and so on. In *The Sadness of Others*, written nearly a decade after I left, I go back to the city, but I think-remember Detroit differently. Having settled into a new life in New York, a city and a life so much unlike those I knew in Detroit, I ache for something new, something more. The city is transformed in these poems because I underwent transformation. No doubt—I can say this now—my mother's death loomed over this ache. She had been dead almost a decade—she died only months after I left home, left Detroit—and her death, the most literal, permanent embodiment of transformation, made it nearly impossible for me not to view almost everything in those days through this lens. And so the poems in *The Sadness of Others* turn to more reflective renderings and become more concerned with absence than presence—the images, the speech, the truths, less definite and more liminal, occupying the space of transformation, which inhabits both sides of the boundary separating past from present.

When past and present become enmeshed with one another or indistinguishable from each other, where do you stand, and what do you do?

You can forgive
the past. Or you can
forget it or curse it.
Either way,
it doesn't matter.
Soon enough, you'll sleep
in another city,
dream of bridges
with different names,
and somehow even the air
that rises above
the sewer grates
will smell like lilacs
in spring.

This is a kind of reconciliation with the past—*kind of*, because the terms of the agreement, the settlement, allow for acceptance or rejection, for reinvention, for wholly altering the past, or even as a last resort, for a mild embrace. Perhaps reconcilement is not quite right. A more accurate way to conceive this may be as a re-visioning of how to struggle with the past. Re-visioning allows us to do what could not be done when our actions, thoughts, and feelings first happened—to stop the forward march of time and consider them slowly, repeatedly, carefully, with all the benefits of hindsight and distance. This allows us to unmoor the past from time and place, to unfix the past.

This thinking appears in *Something Sinister*, my most recent work: "The past is a strange land. // Go because you can. / Go because you can / come back." Though I did not until recently come to this realization (that we can not only journey to the past but find it new each time we visit and bring back with us something new each time we take leave of it), I must have had some inkling of it early on. "Thinking American," a poem written on the occasion of leaving Detroit, ends:

> Listen,
> when I say Detroit, I mean
> any place. By thinking American, I mean made.

We live in places. Regardless of where on earth and when in time we live in them, and regardless of the extraordinary diversity of these places and of humanity across space and time, our joy and grief, our pain and happiness, remains much the same. How we encounter and reencounter those joys and pains also remains much the same. Whether in Houston or New York City, London or Madrid, on a trail in a forest or at a table in a coffee shop, when I think of Detroit in the years 1972 through 1994, which are all gone, or when I think of the house I grew up in on Carlin Street, which is gone, or my mother, gone, and everything else in the past which is always on the verge of coming to mind, when it comes, all of it, whether I want it to or not, it is always there, always here, and never the same.

# PERSONAL POLITICAL POEM

*Hayan Charara*


Around midnight I stalled
outside a police station
in Henry Ford's hometown.
The cops told me to keep
walking. A mile later

the Arab gas station attendant—
the name embroidered on his shirt
said Sam—he talked
and talked and talked.
He asked if I recognized him.

He said when we were young
we knew each other.
He'd been to the house
I grew up in. His father
loved my father, his mother

loved my mother.
He said he was sorry
for what happened.
He said we're all dying
but we should get to grow old

and *just like that* shouldn't be
how a life ends. He said
he was at the funeral.
Seeing me carry the casket
made him imagine

one day doing the same.
I said it was late, I needed
to get back, the cops
were going to tow my car.
He showed me a newspaper.

He said he was the guy
who pulled a drowning girl
from a crowded pool.
He pointed to the mayor
shaking his hand. He said

he went to high school with the mayor
who was the kind of guy
who would jab his finger
at your chest and say,
You don't look like a Sam.

There was something better
out there, he said. He knew
there was. For him. For me.
I told him it was true
he did not look like a Sam.

# THE DAY PHIL LEVINE DIED

*Hayan Charara*

My father never asked me
why I gave up
becoming a doctor
to be a poet.

I would've told him
because of a poem
by Levine
about a boy and girl

on Belle Isle
taking off their clothes
and walking
hand in hand

into the filthiest river
I knew, the Detroit River.
The poem
was beautiful

but I kept my mouth shut
about it and Levine,
sure he'd only ask
if the poet

was a Jew.
He only ever talked
to one Jew,
the owner of a furniture shop

by the Rouge,
and only to haggle
over the price
of a sofa or dining set

he wasn't planning
to buy.
He could've said a lot
that I might have

listened to:
poems won't pay bills,
and the companies hiring
don't give a shit

about all the poems
written in English,
or Arabic,
or any language.

He'd never read
a poem of mine,
and didn't bother
to ask if anyone

in the world thought
they were any good.
He might've
pointed out how poor

and destitute
so many poets died.
But he did none of this.
I told him

I was going to be a poet,
regardless of failure,
and he put a gun to my head
and said, "No."

# THAT SUMMER THAT YEAR DURING THE HEAT WAVE

*Hayan Charara*

What did we think sitting there
on the front porch, without fear, none at all,
no surprise or shock,
barefoot, slow breathing, the sun

unyielding even under elm and maple,
thirty-five years ago,
I wasn't yet twelve, my sister not ten, the city
months from the riots after the World Series?

Two men ran down the middle of the street,
the one in front yelling
(how far he made it—
the ice cream parlor, the diner, the liquor store, the bowling alley—

I can't say), and the other one,
chasing after him, aiming a shotgun, he looked at us
and smiled—
I saw all his teeth.

# 1979

*Hayan Charara*

We were stopped
at a red light, I was in the passenger seat,
and a guy crossing the street looked
at the Buick, then at us, flipped
us the middle finger and said,
"Go home, camel jockeys."
However hard I try, I can't remember
if, then and there, what the guy said
made any difference to me.
I was seven—what did I know
about crisis? As for the guy,
before the light turned green,
my father floored the pedal
and ran him over.

# APOKALUPTEIN

*Hayan Charara*

١

The Arab apocalypse began around the year
of my birth, give or take—
the human apocalypse,
a few thousand years earlier.

٢

I earn my living
teaching about the human condition, a composite
of violence, vengeance, and theft,
ingenuity, too, and forms of love unique
to men and women, the only species
that knows, consciously, what others of its kind
thought and did thousands of years before—
stories, myths, histories, philosophies,
all mirrors and constellations
showing humanity to itself,
none of which
will ensure our survival.

٣

A mile, a mile and a half from the border,
the Israeli border, Bint Jbeil,
the small city my father left
in 1967,
its orchards, hillsides, rivers,

roads, highways, bridges,
houses, schools, restaurants, coffee shops,
pharmacies, hospitals, cemeteries,
twice in his lifetime, obliterated.

ع

The Arab apocalypse began in the 1950s and '60s,
in Egypt, Tunisia, Libya, Syria, and Iraq—
the human apocalypse
in 1945, in a desert in New Mexico
where scientists exploded the first atomic bomb.

٥

In Beirut, snipers picked off children sneaking
to buy candy, yet the population grew.

٦

In 1972 my father paid $9,000
for a house in Detroit.
Forty years later, a foreclosure, it sold for $8,000,
its windows, doors, floors, walls,
the porch, the mailbox,
the tree in front, birch or poplar,
gone—now
weeds and bushes block the drive,
vines where the chimney once was
creep over the rooftop.

٧

"In free fall," an expert in urban decline
describes Detroit's population.
At the current rate, by the beginning of the next century,
stray dogs will outnumber people.

٨

Soon as I earned enough to get out, I got out.
Still a street comes to mind:
Forest, Grand, St. Aubin, Lafayette,
or the bridge over the river
to Belle Isle, or the tunnel lights
before Joe Louis Arena,
or, disappearing
in a rearview mirror, the horizon
with smokestacks, which once
upon a time I believed no other on earth
could match in perfection.

٩

The Arab apocalypse began on a piece of paper
in 1917—
the human apocalypse,
50,000 years ago,
when hunters wiped out
the giant kangaroo.

١٠

In politics, practically nothing is new.
Twenty-four hundred years ago
Plato worried about speech-acts,
what he called "craft,"
the crowd swayed so easily
by emotion and flattery, interest and advantage,
the logical failures to follow.

١١

Today, which poems will cause institutions to fail?
Who worries about that?

١٢

The city was here when lust lured us
away from the animals,
when kings and the children of gods hunted
side by side in the forests of lesser gods,
when Priam begged for his boy's broken body,
when Achilles, cruel and beautiful,
chose death for glory, when Abram became
Abraham, and Muhammad
heard God's voice in a lightning bolt—
it was here,
and the asphalt and concrete
won't reveal what it was, the rivers
won't either, or the trees or the soot turning
factory walls and lungs permanently black—
whatever it was,
swamp, forest, glacier,
it was there.

١٣

The apocalypse began
with a thousand hoofbeats
across a field, men
hollering, women wondering
where to hide
the children. "Here,"
a mother said.
"We will hide in the earth—
our ancestors are already there,
the rest will follow."

# URBAN NOMAD

*Teri Bazzi*

## FORTY-ONE

Starbucks. This is where I get most of my work done.

Iced coffee. Sugar-free vanilla, lots of cream. Trying to watch my sugar. I eye a donut. "Can I get a donut, please?"

Coffee and donut in hand, I mistakenly sit under a speaker. Lauryn Hill is serenading me a bit too loudly. I find solace in her lyrics as she is a badass. Badass. I have been called a badass. Am I a badass? How did I become a badass? I have been called a hero. I have been told that I am brave. I do not feel like a badass. I do not feel like a hero. I am not brave. I am tired of running and hiding from the atrocity that has been chasing me since I was a child. It so often eludes me, like a ghost passing through nightmares and terrors, moving through memory, space, and time.

A generation has passed. I am ready to tell this story. It needs to be told. I owe it to my daughter. To all of our daughters. Sons, too. I open the laptop, I sip the coffee, I bite the donut. Glucose straight to the abyss of malice that I have recently unearthed, its soil toxic and lethal. This soil is ready to be tilled.

## FORTY

"Happy birthday, Mommy!" Ah, I love them, I love them. I have been in this place a few times before, in complete and utter bliss. These are my people, my tribe, my home. They tell me they love me and I cry. Because this is forty. I have not yet arrived. I have not yet made my way. But I have these people that I madly love. I have raised the three of them well and we are secure. We are safe. We are home. We have love. "Daddy got you a cake!" my darling daughter says. My ten-year-old is carefree and full of sunshine goodness; she jumps up and down with excitement. I smile down at her innocent head. My heart swells because I am so blessed. I have escaped these clutches and here I am, surrounded by warmth and bliss. "Mommy! A picture! Let's take a picture!" She still calls me *Mommy*. I melt. My oldest boy takes the selfie. My first born, my Number One Son. He has the strongest arm. Sixteen and filled with sarcasm, angst, and wit. He has been with me the longest. He saved me. He saves me still. My middle child is a boy. He has dark golden curls and somber blue-green eyes. As his older brother stands tall, reaching over to enclose us all in this fleeting moment, my golden boy leans in for the shot. He knows this is important to me. And I am the center of his universe. To him I am paramount. I am vital. I am the rock. I do not know how I have earned this trust, this love, this loyalty. But they all are devoted to me. I do not understand the magnitude of this on my fortieth birthday. I realize it later on that year because I have found a freedom that is foreign to me. I have done well by these children who are gifts. The candles illuminate my face; I glow. The picture speaks a thousand words, and I am no longer broken, I am whole.

## FORTY AND SOME

"Mom, I don't like your dad." This proclamation from my golden boy catches me off guard. I try to contain my anxiety, but I laugh outright. He is my most careful child. He is sensitive, serious, and philosophical. He is thirteen and coming into his own. School bores him because he is too far above the nonsense that they are teaching him, as he already knows most of it. He embraces information, knowledge, facts. He needs life, not condescending social studies books. He knows things well before I do. Wise beyond his years. "Yeah, well. I don't like him either. As a matter-of-fact, I don't know many people that *do* like him. Why, babe? What's up?" I speak frankly with him. Very matter-of-fact. I always have. There are no shades of blue, green, gray, orange, or yellow with him. Nothing is gray. With this child, everything is black-and-white. The wildfire inside of me that I have struggled to suppress catches wind and ignites. I taste blood. I swallow hard. There is a despair that is forming in the pit of my stomach. Acid and fear. I have been in this place before. I do not welcome the familiarity. "He's a terrible person, Mom. Last winter, when I sat across from him at our cousin's wedding, after all of you left the table to go get dessert, he looked right at me and said, 'Jibraeel, did you know that your parents are pigs?' and he went about drinking his coffee. Mom, *why* did he do that?" I swallow the blood that is now in my mouth. It leaves a bitter taste on the tip of my tongue. It gets stuck in my throat. I will scream. But not in front of my child. Nothing with this child is unwarranted.

## STILL FORTY

I call my siblings. I call Mom. I let them know that I want blood. That I will get in my car and drive a half hour west in the middle of the night and I will murder him in his sleep. It is not enough that I have moved away from this terror, this dysfunction. It is not enough that I have shielded my children from him and that he barely knows them. It is not enough. I have done all that I can to protect my children from him, and yet he has managed to find a way. He has always managed to find a way. "He is senile, Teri. He doesn't know what he says," one of my siblings says. It is an absurdity to explain it all away. But my child is not yet made of marble or stone. I sang to him and I nursed him and I tickled his fat baby belly and I stroked his sweaty toddler head and I held him in my lap and I told him that he should always ride the waves and I read *The Giving Tree* to him and I told him stories and took him for ice cream and I introduced him to the beach and I let him love the water and I made the world conform to his temperaments and then I taught him to let the world in. I will protect this child because my mother failed to protect me. This reality has made me bitter, defunct, damaged. This child is pure. He is whole, and I will not let this transgression mold him as it once permeated my five-year-old soul. My child is thirteen and lovely and no harm will come to him. No harm will come to any of my children. I do not make excuses for my father, but I cannot tell my child the truth. I will not destroy him by giving him the truth. I tell my child that Jidu is a terrible man and that no one likes him, that he does not even like himself and that he is utterly miserable, and that misery loves company. My child does not understand idioms. Black-and-white. "Gabriel, there are 365 days in a year. Out of those 365 days, Jidu was horrible to his family for most of those days. If I had to count, I would say that he was the most horrible for three hundred of those days. So horrible that I often dreamed of running far, far away from him. But there were other days, too. And again, if I had to count, I would say that he spent thirty-five of them being just barely tolerable, and the rest of those days, the other thirty days of the year? Yeah, he was excellent. But thirty days as an excellent father is not enough. It is not acceptable." I tell him this and I swallow. Hard. The bile and copper taste in my mouth strong as steel. I tell a mistruth. But I am not exactly wrong. Those three hundred days of misery have always outweighed any good he ever did to any of us. I find myself questioning if evil is ever capable of good. The times that Baba taught me how to make Turkish coffee, took me on hikes through Belle Isle, brought me back jewelry from Lebanon, or taught me how to throw a punch does not alter any abuse he ever inflicted upon me. I will wait until Baba is on his deathbed. I will seek refuge in his death. There will be deliverance. My mother tells me that the doctor has discovered a black spot on Baba's lungs. But I know that what really ails him is the black mark on his soul.

## THIRTY-NINE

"Teri. The weight needs to come off."

Most days, I do not want to get out of bed, brush my hair, shower. But I do. I go through the motions. Call off work, clear my schedule, get the kids to school, and then crawl back into bed until it is time to go pick them up. I tell this to the doctor. I feel like a wounded animal, backed into a corner. I know that I am going to be caged. Do I tell the doctor about the emotional eating that has turned into binge eating? Do I tell her that the last family function triggered a violent and horrible memory that has sent me into a tailspin? Do I tell her that this downward spiral has no end in sight and that I have not yet reached rock bottom? Do I tell her that I send my kids in the house after we get home and that I sit in my driveway and scream and sob and yell myself into exhaustion? How much do I tell the doctor before she realizes that I am a threat to myself, and that if I were brave, I would have slit my wrists long ago? But I cannot, because my children, my children. What do I tell this doctor who is trying to understand why I am ruining myself? "You have put on more weight since the last time you were here. *What* is going on? You have a vitamin deficiency, you are dangerously close to having full-blown diabetes, you are malnourished, your liver is in trouble, you have high cholesterol, and, I suspect, sleep apnea. Tell me. Teri. What is going *on*?" So I tell her. I tell her and I tell her, breaking down in her office, and I tell her. Doc pulls up her chair to me. She offers me a box of Kleenex. I take the box, vigorously pulling out ten pieces of tissue. I dab my eyes and I keep talking. She listens. Her eyes never move from my face. She is taking this all in and I am filled with sorrow for what I am inflicting upon her. She is tall and blond and beautiful. She is a *good* doctor, an even better human being. She is goodness and wholesome. Heavily pregnant. From Canada. I wonder if I am hurting her baby. I cannot be censored any longer. I know that there are consequences for telling my story. I am thankful that I am in the privacy of this doctor's office, that I do not have an audience. But these things happen to little girls with neglectful mothers. I wonder if things like this happen in Canada. I don't know why I think this, but I do. This happens everywhere. She tells me to take a deep breath and start from the beginning and I do.

"Doc. I was five. . . ."

## THIRTIES

We have three kids. Rambunctious boys and a giggly, sunshine baby daughter. A girl changes my world. It's rowdy. I am forever busy. I

make myself busy as a distraction. This much I know. I am exhausted
most nights after PTO, soccer, mom life. I finally obtain my degree
from the University of Michigan–Dearborn (UM-D). I am always
mother, student, wife. I have no identity once I graduate. I struggle
with that. Student. I was content hiding behind the title of student.
UM-D honored me as a Difference Maker. A distinguished title, an
incredible accomplishment. Do I make a difference? Shit. If UM-D says
so, then I must be fucking spectacular. My days are filled with anger
and angst every waking hour. For the sake of my children, I suppress it.

## TWENTIES

Marriage, babies, community college. Extended family. Motherhood
is stifling, isolating, warm. It is a shuffle between sleep deprivation,
giggles, worry, and discovery. I try my best. I am not always my best.
I have nervous breakdowns. I sob. I have panic attacks. Nightmares.
Monsters want to steal my baby. Run away with my baby. But then I
have another one. I don't know why I keep having more. There are a
few good days. There are farms and pink skies and valleys. There are
tanks and wars and sunshine. There are beaches and waves and kites.
I try to play in the sand with my children, but I do not know how, so I
watch them instead. I want someone to tell me how to do this because
I don't know how. I was never taught how to be a mother.

## FIVE

"Teri. This is your father."

 I am five. On the street. Mom introduces me to him on the street.
He eyes me and it is not kind. There is no warm embrace, no affection, no pat on the head. He has dagger eyes. No pleasantries of long-
lost father-daughter attributes. I suddenly feel a whirl in the pit of my
stomach. I do not have the language yet to identify it. At five, it does
not have a name, merely a wicked and overpowering presence that is
an overbeating shadow, and it nearly knocks me down. I don't know
what this feeling is. I feel sick, there is a burn in my throat. It is acidic,

it tastes like danger and tainted brass. I do not like this man. Mom says he is my father. This is how I meet my father. In the street. There is no warning, no getting used to the idea, nothing to alert me. I wonder if this is some kind of adult game that Mom is playing, a game that I will never learn the rules to. I do not know this man. I have not ever seen him before. What is she doing? What is she trying to replace? Why are we here? Why have we moved, *again*? I don't like my new bedroom. I liked the other one way better. Am I supposed to hug him, go over to him? He is not approachable. He sly-eyes me while he takes a long drag of his cigarette. He nods. I take my leave. I can overhear Mom saying something to him that I cannot understand. The sounds coming from her are fragmented pleas. He shuts her up. I learn about terror and dread at five. There are bunk beds. I am five. I don't have the sophistication to ask Mom the questions that I need answers to. I stare into the dark, unfamiliar void. I want to crawl in another bed, someplace else, anywhere but here. Mom is in the living room. She is serving him. Tea, platters of fruit, and baklava. At that tender age, I know that she is trying to impress him, and I make a pact with myself to never ever impress a man, especially a monster of a man. I hear the clink of the tiny spoon hitting up against the tiny tea glass as the hot, bitter drink is stirred. I hear it again as the tiny spoon is rested against the saucer. This sound will unnerve me for the rest of my life. In my adult years, I do not care much for tea. I develop an aversion to tea packets and loose leaves. I do not drink tea when I am sick. When I have visitors, I do not serve tea, even though it is a custom. I refuse tea on social calls. Family members buy me ornate teapots from overseas. I have been given many tea pots as birthday gifts. I have managed to throw away any teapot that I have received. All Arab girls must have a supply of tea complete with a set of glass teacups, spoons, and a serving tray. This Arab girl does not. I have a set that collects dust. I have broken a few, many. I no longer care. The clink of a tea glass evokes silent fear. I am to call him Baba. I don't want to. For as long as I can remember, I don't call him anything. Over the years, especially in my teen years, this has earned me many beatings. Impressive beatings. Beatings with closed fists, backhanded slaps, kicks, flicks, metal spoons, shoes, rubber slippers, bricks, flipped tables, fence posts, hot forks, chairs. I even had a lighter ignite on my leg as it was thrown at me. But on this first night, in our new house with no escape, I am only five. And I am scared. The light turns on in our room and I think that it is Mom coming to tell me that this is all just a mistake and that we are going back to our real home. Or better yet, that she is staying here with Baba Monster and that my grandmother, Nin, is coming to get me. I wonder if Nin even knows about this. Nin would not stand for this. She would not allow this to happen. Nin takes good care of me when Mom sends me to her. She buys me pizza and chocolate milk and I have good pajamas at her tiny, comfy, little house. It takes forever to get to Nin's house. I know because when Mom drives to Nin's house, there are no stop lights for me to count. Mom doesn't like going to Nin's house all the time. She says something about gas money. But I know that Nin will give her money for the gas. Nin will sigh and give her a lot of dollars and then Mom will leave. But I don't ever mind. I will get to stay with Nin. I want Nin to know that Mom has moved us again. I want Nin to come get me. Nin does not come to get me that night. It is not Mom that has turned on the light and has come into my bedroom. It is not Mom safely tucking me in. Chasing away the boogieman. I learn that night that this bedroom is no refuge. It is not a happy place, and the boogieman is a real and heinous thing.

## TEN

Summer. Tank tops, ice cream, sprinklers, pool. Mom sends me out with Baba. I have on my favorite outfit: a red tank top and a pair of shorts. Totally eighties. Red paint splashes with red, orange, and purple X's and O's. I rocked this outfit. Nin bought it for me at Sears. Mom sends me with Baba. He is going to visit a relative and he wants to take the two-year-old boy with him. My sibling. And Mom sends me with him. The two-year-old is precious. I love this little boy despite the fact that Baba treats him like gold. It does not make me bitter. I love my younger sibling with a fierce protection that runs far and deep. Mom needs a break. There are new siblings now—this toddler and a new baby that never stops crying—and there is talk that Baba has a child back home. This child does not belong to Mom. When Mom and Baba were on a break, Baba went back home to Lebanon and remarried and had another child. But he abandoned his new, pregnant wife and came back to America to find Mom. And he discovered that Mom had a daughter. Perhaps this is what has caused all of the years of brutality. I am the defunct child, the outsider. Baba is within his right to question my paternity, and that is why I have been his target. My earliest memories include Baba calling Mom a whore, because when he got back to America from his extended trip back home, he found that she had given birth to a child while he was away. To my understanding, Mom and Baba had parted ways in the '70s before I was born, but she had already conceived me. Baba went back home to his country and broke off his relationship with her. He always questioned when I was conceived. I had heard it a thousand times. "Ya akrewti, hel bint badoo'aa. You whore. This girl is a bastard. She is not mine. You were sucking every dick in the Southend the minute I went back to Lebanon! You were fucking every bastard the second I turned my back on you! You are a whore. So is this girl. She is not mine. Whore, like you." Mom insisted that I belonged to him. I have been called a bastard since the day I met him. Mom is a whore. Whore. Whore. That is all he ever called her. I have known about whores, fucking, and dicks since I was five. He had beat her the morning of our outing. I was ten. I saw him grab her and hit her again and again and again, open fist, backhand, closed fist. She was black and blue and green by the time he was done with her. The toddler was screaming. I tried to pick him up. But Baba had grabbed me by the arm, picked him up, and went outside. I used to run to Mom after he beat her. But at one point I stopped. I didn't care that he beat her. It was her fault. She was a slab of meat, being pounded on again and again and the sound was deafening, blunt, solid. Her sounds were pathetic, void, shrill. The more she whined, the harder he pounced—again, again, again. And even though he beat her and left her black and blue and green, that afternoon, she sent me with him.

She sent me with him.

Baba and I left with the toddler after the beating. He told her to clean herself up and to shut up. He told her she was fat and ugly, a whore. She sent me with him anyway. I was ten. I did not know. We arrive at the relative's house where they dote on my sibling: chubby, agreeable, angelic. I am offered Kool-Aid and a nectarine. "Shukran," I say, staring at the ground. My sibling reaches for me and I take him in my arms, burying my shame in his light brown curls, taking in Johnson & Johnson shampoo, baby powder, lotion. Relief. The sight of Baba desecrating my mother still vivid in my mind. The other children are playing in the sprinkler. I join, taking my sibling with me. This child does not cry, only squeals with delight. I get to be a kid. Tank top, Kool-Aid, discarded nectarine; the sunshine drying up each water drop as it lands on my skin, hair, tank top. I find joy in the act of being a child in the summer with my darling sibling as he dances in each turn of the sprinkler, each trickle of water shining in the sunbeams, offering us all momentary relief from the scorching sun. I do not have to worry about vicious dangers lurking. I am a kid. Mom sent me with him. I am wearing my favorite tank top and shorts. I had been embraced in this warm summer day, the sun rays kissing the top of my head, and I feel safe in this false protection of innocent childhood play. I do not see Baba's wrath escalating from his placement among his relatives, and I have no warning as he approaches me. "My *mother* was married at your age," he sneers at me, grabbing me by the arm. He picks up my drenched sibling, who is startled but does not protest, and he bids his hosts a good afternoon. I try to climb in the backseat with my sibling, but Baba shouts at me to get in the front seat. I am grateful that the drive home is short. Grateful. It is short lived. "Just look at you. A slut just like your mother, you daughter of a whore. You are wet and I can see your tits. Do you like to be wet? Eh, is that what you like, ya bint sharmouta just like your mother?" He is driving away from the house. He keeps talking about shame and whores and tits. We reach the park. Our neighborhood park where I had played at the end of the school year on a class picnic. He pulls into a spot and he parks. I recoil and move as close to the car door as I can because I know something is coming but I am not sure what. My sibling is eerily quiet in the back seat. He is playing with a stuffed animal. Baba knows that I am afraid. I look straight ahead and as I try to turn away from him, he manages to reach over and pinch my pubescent tender breast, *hard*. With his other hand, he rubs the other breast angrily, over and over again. I am dirty. I am ashamed of my changing body. I am filthy because he has seen me, noticed my body changing. He violates me again and again, putting his hands on me, tugging at the strap of my tank top as I hold the collar tight. I try crossing my arms over my small, tampered body, and I am rewarded with a stiff slap. He violently caresses my breasts, again and again. He pinches the small buds, tells me that I have nipples and that I am old enough to be his wife. I try to move his hands from my body, I try to fight. He succeeds. After this assault, he rolls down the car window and spits. He calls me a daughter of a whore. All these years later I do not remember if I had tears in my eyes. But I do remember the sting of Baba's slap and his hands on me. I can feel his hands on me to this very day.

And it was my mother who sent me with him.

I am no stranger to this. It happens often. He likes to grab me, pin me down to the floor, in the kitchen, the living room, in full view. He lays atop me, breathing heavily on my neck. He bites my neck, he kisses my forehead. I squirm, I don't move, I wiggle, I play dead, I push. Mom tells me it's just a game. She caught me crying once and asked me, "You don't like his play, do you?" I violently shook my head, and at this she wistfully proclaimed, "Well, it's just *play*." No ally. No protection. No safe haven. I was fair game. Target. Prey. It is a strange phenomenon—what the body and mind will do trying to survive. The body and mind will create an alternative reality in order to survive trauma. But me, at the innocent age of five, six, seven, eight, nine, ten— I wanted to eat the pain whole. I wanted to regurgitate it and give it to my mother. She placed me there, time and time again. Each pat in the dark, each squeeze of the breast, each caress of the inner thigh, each time he pinned me to the ground and put his big body on top of my fragile, child-framed being, he broke me over and over again with his heavy breathing and sloppy kisses, his scent and saliva poison, acidic and torturous as he nibbled at my neck, my ear lobes, chuckled as he pinched my tiny breasts, always calling my mother a whore afterward. Whore she is, as she never intervened, never stepped in, never protected me or thought me worthy of saving. So he interpreted that as whore. She offered me up, over and over again, delivering me right to him. She either sent me on errands with him or sent me up to his room with a plate of fruit or a glass of Pepsi or a tray of tea, always setting me right before him. I relived what happened the time before and the time before that and the time before *that* each and every time he put his hands on me. He must've liked little girls, because once I was too big with developed teenaged breasts and hips, he stopped molesting me. Once I was older and he no longer fancied my small frame, he moved on to full-blown beatings, and I do not know which is worse.

Do I have to choose?

## FIVE

Baba often checks on me at night. On our first night there, he pokes his nose around my room, and I stiffen. I can hear the flap of his slippers lurking. He peers over the rail of my bed and I pretend to be asleep. A light flicks on. "Checking on them?" Mom asks, hopeful. How did she not know? "Eh," he mutters and walks out of the room. Mom turns off the light and closes the door. I wish it had a lock on it.

Safe for now.

Early the next morning, I get up. I am in search of Saturday morning cartoons and cereal. I am not sure where anything is in this house. I stumble out into the living room. There he is. Smoking, dagger eyes alight with malice. "Come," Baba says. "Do you have on underwear? Let me see," and he cracks a wicked grin. I have on my favorite Strawberry Shortcake pajamas. Strawberry Shortcake has red hair. I have strawberries on my sleeves. She looks up at me, her eyes no longer smiling. She whispers, "Teri, don't go, don't go to him. Go back to your room and close the door." I stand frozen in fear. I can see through the living room and down the hallway that my mother is asleep. Sheets are strewn about, blankets are crumpled about the mattress. I see her milky white skin, a soft pillow-like breast escaping the rumpled mess around her. His games with her were not enough. Now there are games with me. He wanted more. Did Mom stir his appetite? Or did I? I go back to my room. I shut the door. I stay there for what seems like hours. I am frozen; horror sets in. I taste brass in my mouth. The Strawberry Shortcake on my pajamas glances up at me, her eyes no longer smiling. She is sad for me. She knows that this will be a long and terrible ride. "Run!" she yells. "Get your backpack and throw some clothes in there. Grab Owl. Don't forget sneakers. You cannot run in flip-flops. Teri. RUN." All these years later, I wonder why I did not take Strawberry Shortcake's advice.

## FIVE, SIX, SEVEN, EIGHT, NINE

Baba checks on me. Every night. He takes my blanket away. I have on yellow striped pajamas. Strawberry Shortcake cannot bear any more. She closes her eyes now. Her eyes no longer smile. He tosses Owl on the floor. Covers come off. Yellow striped pajama top come down. Hands upon me, hands upon me. I sleep. I sleep. I squint my eyes and I pretend to sleep. Mom comes in. He stops. I cry into my pillow, and I want Owl. But he is on the floor winking at me. I hate Owl. I don't play with him anymore after that. Five, six, seven, eight.

## FORTY-ONE

My children are getting older. My oldest is approaching his final year of high school. Where does the time go? My middle boy will be approaching his last year of middle school, and my daughter will be approaching her final year of elementary school.

Many endings. So many beginnings. I have applied to grad school. I have been accepted. I am slowly beginning to heal. It is time that I talk. My siblings tell me that Baba is sick. There is a black mark on his lungs.

And I know that there is a black mark on his soul.

## FORTY-TWO

There is no reprieve.

There has not been since the day I shamed my family and took my story public. I shatter into a hundred million pieces every time an insult is hurled at me:

"You BITCH! Take it off the internet!"

"Wallahi, we will KILL you!"

"You are a whore, you DESERVE every bit of shit that comes your way."

"I have been to jail, I will come up to your house in front of your kids—I don't care—and by Allah, I will break every bone in your body."

"Make it stop. Dearborn is on fire because of you, just make it stop."

But of all these words, each syllable doled out like an unstoppable freight train, these hurt the most: "Don't talk to me, Teri. You are no longer my sister. Do not ever talk to me again."

## NINE

When I was nine, I looked him in the eye. He was giving an order. "Do you understand me? Kalbi! Understand! You do not tell them anything, fahmeni?" It was in his glare and contempt of me that I found my voice. It was a tiny little voice: It shook with fear and rage, and it was quiet and unsure. But it was a voice. And this voice was filled with courage. "So when they ask me what happened, you want me to lie?" And then we locked eyes. "Ya bint el sharmouta. Kilkhani, just like your mother."

## FORTY-TWO

I have been having nightmares, vivid dreams, night terrors. I am a home, my sister is a house. There we stand, side by side. My sister is the larger house, with more trees, fewer windows. There is a fence around her; it is a fortress. She provides me shade, the home standing next to her. I am filled with windows, flowers on my porch—there is a tire hanging from one of my trees, gently swaying in the wind. My yard is littered with bicycles, Rollerblades, a garden hose and Popsicle wrappers. Strewn about the pavement is sidewalk chalk drawings with hearts and rainbows, little messages of love addressed to Mommy. Children's laughter is abundant, it is sweet and quick. A barking dog is in the distance. My front door is open.

Yet the house next to me is looming; it hovers, casting a dark shadow. It begins to rain and thunder, but there my home stands, happy and proud, unaffected by the profound destruction that is happening on my neighbor's doorstep, my neighbor, my sister. I am protected and loved; the rain and thunder stays away. Children cheer for Mommy.

I am Mommy. My therapist tells me that this is the chaos in my brain. My troubled mind and my heavy heart are clearing out the cobwebs.

## NINE

"OK. Teri, is it? Where is your bedroom? We would like to take a look, talk to you privately, ask you a few questions. Is that OK, Mr. Bazzi?" He takes a long drag of his cigarette and then looks at me through slanted dagger eyes. He slowly nods, never moving his eyes from me. I hold his gaze. I do not waver. I do not fall. "Remember what I told you," he says in front of these nice ladies from the state. "Fahmeni?" I answer him back in English. "I understand."

## FORTY-TWO

He denounces me. Mom tells me that he has been getting harassing phone calls in the middle of the night, that people have spit on him in the street. I have committed the ultimate family betrayal and there is no compensation, no escape. I will not be excused or absolved of this. Yet I am elated. I have wings and freedom; I am being carried away from the calamity and strife that has imprisoned me all my life. I no longer carry the shame, and the family honor, tainted and fragile, has been compromised. My siblings have excommunicated me, and my mother is indignant with humiliation; even though she loves to chase a scandal at my expense, she has refused to shelter me from the blows that my siblings hurl upon me. My own mother, who once paraded me and my sister around town with bruises on our legs and faces, making a spectacle of our family dysfunction, begging any family friend or relative who would offer her an ear and a cup of tea for help, while my sister and I hid in the shadows, seeking protection, has told me, "Teri, this is not our way. We do not tell our problems to everyone on social media. We keep the family shame quiet and to ourselves."

After this devastation, I keep my mother locked away. She has been hidden and buried deep in the darkest place of my heart, far from my memories and my mind, away from my children who occasionally ask after Tata. Absent from milestones and events, purposely left off invites and gatherings, my mother cannot be a part of my life. This recent betrayal has left me exasperated, the fury too hot to address, the treason a treacherous display of disloyalty and destruction. My mother breaks me again and again. She could not protect me from Baba when I was a child, and now she refuses to offer me support and encouragement when I have finally broken free of his clutches. Mom has formed a new allegiance with my abuser. She has destroyed any hope of repairing the damage she has caused. I keep her distant. I get word that Baba is chain-smoking in his basement, seething over the mayhem I have caused, incensed over my rebellion.

I am the victor.

This is no consolation. Mom loved a good scandal. Even at the expense of her own children. I was twelve the first time I vocalized to Mom what Baba had been doing to me since I was six. "You think anyone will believe you? I will take you to Vista Maria where they send all the girls like you." And again, when I was fifteen and I had my first mental breakdown, Mom deserted me. Once I was a teenager, Baba could no longer hold me down and touch me. I was too mature for him to grope and grab, I was too big for him to pin down.

And that angered him. Instead, he resorted to a different kind of violation. He beat me. And he beat me on a regular basis. He beat me because I came home late from school. He beat me because I joined the basketball team. He beat me because I left my shoes out. He beat me because I read books. He beat me because I did homework. He beat me because I didn't turn the lights off. He beat me because I moved his cigarettes. He beat me because my mother didn't get dinner on the table quick enough. He beat me because I rebelled. He beat me because I defied him. He beat me because he couldn't get at me anymore. When I stood up against him, I had a mental breakdown, and my mother had no choice but to admit me to the hospital. Instead of holding a vigil at my bedside and swearing her allegiance to me, she left me alone in the hospital, bewildered and terrified. She left me with a social worker who refused to console me as I sobbed, on suicide watch. I begged the social worker to listen to me, to hear me out, to please believe me and let me out of my restraints. But instead, she abandoned me as I began to beg them to listen to me, to hear me out, to believe me. I pleaded with them, imploring them to let me out of my restraints. Instead, the social worker sat there, cold and inattentive, taking in a deep breath when I interrupted her concentration as she worked on her crossword puzzle.

My mother left me with an uncaring and unfeeling social worker so that she could run all over Dearborn to gather family friends and relatives to bring to my bedside, putting me on display. I was the main attraction at the circus; the back-alley sideshow that spectators gawked and fawned over, fretting and pawing over the display of grotesque horror, as some of these aunties smoothed my hair, muttering "Mashallah" and "Stakhfarallah," interested enough only to marvel in the realization that they were thankful that this train wreck was not their own. Yet now, decades later, Mom has managed to put me on display again. Mom is ashamed. Baba has been harassed, he has been spit on. She is the prize of these transgressions. The anxiety of these exchanges are ultimately dropped in her lap. She is sensitive to these mishaps, yet her constant betrayal leaves her in a juxtaposition of excitement and exasperation. She retells these rabid scenes to me with intensity and feigned piety.

This is what Baba's phone calls consist of: "How could you rape your daughter, Ramzi? How could you touch your daughter, Ramzi? God damn you to hell, you sick bastard!" The calls come at all hours of the day, some in Arabic, most in English. It is my mother who delivers this information to me. She is glad to have something to report. Baba doesn't understand at first, Mom tells me. He doesn't know what has

happened. Finally, it is one of my brothers who has to tell him. It is one
of my brothers who tells Baba that I have disclosed the family shame,
writing about this secret on social media for all the world and Dearborn to see. And then, the very thing that I have been wishing for all of
my life finally occurs. "You tell Teri that she is not my daughter," Baba
tells my mother. "You tell her that I disown her." Message received.

## NINE

"So, Teri. Tell us. Is this your bedroom?"

I stand there in my favorite one-piece jumper. It is white with rainbow stripes. The shoulders each have tie straps. I double knot both
strands just in case. I always double knot this jumper whenever I wear
it. I have learned to be careful. This is also the summer that I stop
showering. If I don't shower, I smell bad, and if I smell bad, he won't
come near me. I am pretty sure the nice ladies from the state will notice
that I do not shower. But maybe not since I spend every free moment
at the Hemlock pool. The chlorine takes care of that for me. But I am
messy, I am forever running, constantly playing in dirt, skinning my
knees, smudging mud on my face. My hair is short, but it is fried from
the sun and the pool, my skin ashy and taut. Despite my summer tan, I
have black circles under my eyes, I am underweight, small for my age,
exhausted for a child.

"Teri. Who do you share your room with?"

"My sister."

They look around the small room. In it sits one set of bunk beds, a
dresser. My copy of *Tales of a Fourth Grade Nothing* tossed on my bed.
I make a mental note to put it under my pillow as soon as I am done
with the nice ladies from the state. Baba does not like to see me read.
But Baba has been different since Mom put a gun to her head and told
my sister to inform the neighbors that she was going to kill herself.
That was the summer that Mom sent herself away, leaving us children
with Baba. Mom needed a break from him, so she grabbed his pistol
and calmly told my sister to take my brothers and me to the neighbor's
house and tell them that she was going to pull the trigger. My sister

was a compliant and dutiful child. She always did what she was told. And if this was some sort of game that Mom was playing to get Baba's love and attention, my sister did not question this: she simply did what she was told. She was the oldest child, and this was her responsibility. I followed my sister, astonished and baffled that Mom would do this to us. I stood outside with my baby brothers as my sister knocked on Ginny and Louie's side door. I could see that my sister had delivered some terrible news to our gracious neighbors. Ginny's face fell and Louie grabbed the phone. My sister stood in the middle of their kitchen looking at the floor with her shoulders slumped as arrangements were made. She was embarrassed, mortified that our family shame had come to the doorstep of these kind people. Ginny and Louie were gracious neighbors, old enough to be our grandparents. They kept an eye on us from their backyard, offered us tomatoes from their garden, fruit from their trees. As the sirens inundated the neighborhood and law enforcement taped off the area like it was a crime scene, Ginny shooed us away from the spectacle that my mother had subjected us to. But it was too late. The image of my mother being hauled away by the wailing ambulance, leaving us with the salacious predator who continued to torment us was forever imprinted on my broken heart.

Baba has not touched me or beat me since Mom went away. I can stay down the street at Susan Griffith's house all day if I want. And I do. Susan has a button nose that is peppered with freckles. Her golden hair, the color of straw, is always neatly braided. She smiles a lot and has a joyous laugh. There is nothing in Susan's life that keeps her from smiling. Her older brother is a pain, and he sometimes annoys us, but Susan and I ride our bikes and play with dolls and talk about Laura Ingalls. I wonder if she knows of the terror that I live just doors down from her. I know that there are things that nine-year-olds should not ever know, so I do not tell her. I study Susan's face. Her nose crinkles when she laughs, and I watch her as she interacts with her parents. She is well loved. Her parents are kind, and they invite me to stay for dinner. They never ask me to leave. And for that, I love them.

But I do not want to take any chances, even if Baba has left me alone. I pick up the book, leaf through its pages.

"Do you like to read?" one of the nice ladies from the state asks me.

"Yes," I say.

I sit on my bed, pretending to read. I do not waver. I do not fall.

"Teri, we would like to ask you some questions."

I look up at the ladies.

I hope they take us away from here, me and my siblings. I hope they put us all in a car and take us far away. Even to Susan Griffith's porch. They might not take in all of us, but Mr. and Mrs. Griffith will take me.

"Teri, does Baba touch you?"

I do not waver.

I do not fall.

"Yes."

The ladies from the state exchange a look. I know this look. I have seen it before.

"Teri, does Baba hit you?"

"Yes."

One of the ladies jots something down in her notebook.

"Teri. Can you tell me what happened to your legs? Did you fall off your bicycle?"

"No."

"Did someone hurt you?"

"Yes."

"Are you hurt someplace else?"

"Yes," and I motion to my back and shoulders with my thumb.

Last week Baba picked me up by the back of my neck and then he beat me with his plastic slipper all the way down my back. He did not stop at the backs of my legs even though it was summer and I wore shorts.

He didn't seem to care that I had his markings all over me.

My shoulders and back still hurt, and the plastic slipper left horrible marks. It still smarted.

The ladies were very interested in the marks going down my back.

So I told them.

## FORTY-THREE

Writing has now become more challenging, more intense. I have started thousands of paragraphs, written countless words. There are times when I get caught up in a trance. I am in my childhood home: I am four, I am ten, I am fifteen. I categorize each beating, each violation, each assault into the phases of my life. Groping and handling of my small, defiled body turns into slaps and kicks, shoves and pushes, jabs and smacks. Each blow is an insult and a curse. I think about these times and I cannot get enough paper and pen to make sense of them. I have a thrust and a hunger to get my story in print. It must be told, it must be documented, each transgression etched into parchment.

I write.

And I write.

And I write again.

I am cast from my community for telling my story. I am labeled and shunned and obstructed. But I rail against this force to silence me.

I am twenty, thirty, now in my forties. I have found my voice. I give it all to the blank pages as I write and try to heal.

# NOTES ON A DEARBORN

*Kamelya Omayma Youssef*

I sit down to write in a hookah lounge on Warren Avenue and Chase Road. I am three blocks from the house where I grew up at 7603 Orchard, a brown bricked duplex which has since been demolished and whose memory is preserved in some long-packed-away home videos in boxes in my mother's basement, and in a photo now at the Smithsonian archives, taken by Millard Berry, a photographer in the midnineties who was tasked with documenting the lives of Arab immigrants in east Dearborn. In the photo, family, neighbors, and friends sit on a cement porch in Dearborn, sipping tea and smoking argeila, legs crossed and hands gesturing in conversation, children leaning against their parents. It was a redbrick house. The photo is in black-and-white.

My memories in this house are sparse but rich in the way that memories of early and middle childhood tend to be, and I grasp for these memories in that almost state of mourning because I know the bulk of them may never find their way back up to the surface of my mind.

During my childhood summers at that house, royal blue convertible Mustangs would speed down Orchard with the speakers turned up all the way. They played songs by Amr Diab and Najwa Karam, and songs by DJ Kal, a local electronic music producer whose CDs we bought at Creative Image, the local Lebanese-owned beauty salon where Hisam reigned as king of all beard lineups and Fordson fades, and Faten waxed impeccable arches into the eyebrows of men and woman alike.

DJ Kal, DJ Refugee, DJ Syclone, and so many more who now have transitioned into careers as smoke shop owners and gas station owners and restaurant supply shop owners and pizza shop owners, all of them made freestyle music, a crossover genre between electronic music and autotune, with undeniable roots in Detroit techno and specifically ghetto tech. The boy DJs recruited their sisters and friends to record the high-pitched audio on their tracks, singing lyrics like "Chaldean Queen / you're always in my dreams / Chaldean Queen / please come to me / let me be your king," some odes to a "Lebanese princess," and the canonized: "Warren and Schafer all the way / we're rattin' Fordson every day / smokin' weed and we're getting high / Ford '99 baby is how we ride."

In my early twenties, I'd learn that freestyle music was known to have been popular in primarily three places in America: Miami, New Jersey, and my own Dearborn. I'd realize all three places are known to have populations of immigrant communities perpetually living on the border of whiteness: Italians, Cubans, and Arabs. In this are illuminations waiting to be excavated by some curious researcher out there, one whose ears are autotuned to nuanced liminality.

These, a little remains of my Dearborn of the 1990s. These, just a few years after the word Arab American officially entered the lives and consciousness of Arabs and other Americans alike. During his run for president in 1984, Rev. Jesse Jackson collaborated with Arab American community leaders and included them as people of color in the Rainbow Coalition. These are the years after the Iranian Revolution, when the Lebanese Civil War led to the massive wave of immigration of Arab Muslims into the United States, more specifically, Dearborn. My parents moved to the United States in the 1980s as a direct result of the Lebanese Civil War and the Israeli occupation, and my father attended Noam Chomsky's lectures at Wayne State University, not out of any interest in anarchism or in the concept of universal grammar, but because it was rumored that Noam Chomsky supported the Palestinians and therefore was a friend.

To identify just as American, though? I never crossed that border. My friends and I were Arab. If we were ever called American, it was by our parents when they scolded us because we had come home too late or wanted to wear shirts that showed slivers of our pubescent bellies, because we insisted on listening to rap music and going to the movies with our friends, without chaperones, without them.

The first time I knew someone in my family to own an American flag was five days after September 11, 2001, when my uncle put an American flag sticker on the driver's side window of his cobalt blue Astro van. His strategy, as he explained one evening at our house over tea, was that if he got pulled over by a cop, he would pull down his window just enough for the sticker to show, the first six stripes and forty-four stars peeking above his car door. He, he insisted, was American now, too.

Arab Americans from all around the United States would visit Dearborn for a literal taste of home. Places like Shatila Bakery and Saad Meats were long-standing culinary landmarks, the former edged with plastic palm trees like the ones standing right outside Beirut's airport welcoming and waving the arrivals home, the latter a walk-in freezer with lamb carcasses and beef shanks hanging on steel hooks, customers brushing past them quickly, unafraid to get blood on their jackets, unafraid of touch. For the Arab Americans visiting from Virginia and Ohio, from California and Utah, Dearborn was a pilgrimage, made once a year or once every few, a place that looked and sounded like home, a place that was a reminder, a reminder in place. For them, Dearborn might have been a place of the past—somewhere they could visit and a place for memories to visit them.

For us, Dearborn was not a museum of the past we could pass through. For us, Dearborn was home. We had no homes to go back to in Lebanon, nor did our parents have enough money to buy plane tickets for us to visit. We did not vacation. We bought clothes off the clearance rack at Kids "R" Us, Jacobson's, Mervyn's, and Hudson's. We hung out with our cousins and the kids of our parents' friends. We played on the lawn while our parents drank thick, bitter coffee in hand-painted fanajeen and occasionally smoked cigarettes. We saved our hand-me-downs to send back to our cousins in the village. We did not know the words colander or parsley because we only needed to know musfaye and ba'dounis.

If FBI agents existed in Dearborn before 9/11, we knew who they were. One lived at that house over there, with security cameras dotting his awning. We were careful not to let our bikes skid onto his manicured lawn. We were careful not to have crushes on his son. If anyone was watching us, it was our parents' friends peering out of their windows, as ready as an army to call my mother and let her know I had gone three blocks too far.

To say we lived a transnational life feels distant, trite. Things were how they were and there was no other way for them to be. The difference between here and there was a technicality. The difference between here and there was none. For many in Dearborn today, this still holds. The waves of immigrants have changed, sped up some years, slowed others. The number of FBI agents has grown. The Arabic festival where we would spend the early days of summer with our friends was canceled because of recurring bomb threats. At the last festival that was held, a group of conservatives showed up with a pig's head on a stake, goading our children. Right there, next to Hashem's Roastery. The warplanes fly ahead there, and now we are all here, finding home here, creating it.

*An outtake from the shoot for the Smithsonian photograph:*
*The cement porch. The metal railing. The brick in black-and-white.*
*The neighborhood in the background, children on sidewalks, a school,*
*other houses in a line. My mother sipping tea from a glass demitasse,*

The Youssef family visit with relatives on the front porch of Kamelya Youssef's childhood home in east Dearborn in 1995. Photo by Millard Berry.

*her hair pulled back. She's wearing an embroidered vest. Young Leila's face burrowed in her mother's shoulder. Her mother's gazelle eyes and stirrup leggings. The neighbor taking a drag of a cigarette, his daughter leaning against him, her wide eyes staring at the camera, her small fingers crossed. My long-legged grandfather with arms crossed stares into the distance beyond my father's lecturing gestures. My father's eyebrows raised. A tray on the table. Patches of white on cement ground. Trees. A car in motion. A small ceramic rabbit on a cement pillar. My grandmother in a dress, one hand resting across her belly, the other holding the argeila hose, smoking. Her pupil at the edge of her eye, barreling straight toward the camera.*

# AMERICAN ROAD TRIP

*Kamelya Omayma Youssef*

On historic Route 66 between freight lines and the I-15: The West at different speeds.

Doritos truck, Coachmen, Food/Gas, Use Bypass, Adopt-a-Highway, 1 mile, a cloud looks like a fist. My ears are popping or a more complex biomechanical phenomenon.

On this mountain highway, younger brother of Route 66, cousin of the freight lines. Seemingly infinite industrial capacity. Move. The 395. A bird flies. Hesperia.

359 miles. I wonder if I can get a vibrator in Utah, maybe attached to special Mormon underwear. Hands-free.

97 degrees. The city gives me anxiety.

Bear Valley Road. Roadside palm reader in Palmdale. Next Exit: Old Town Victorville. Dairy Queen. Shell. Subway. Motel 6.

My boyfriend says I make every conversation about Israel. Las Vegas—187 miles. Barstow is something closer. Maybe Israel butts into every conversation. Maybe it's not me. Maybe it's Israel. Rude.

I think I'm looking for America because of that part of me, that limb that creates that screeching dissonance when I try to tell myself that I am American. Just to see. Speed Limit 70. The voice on the radio just claimed that the University of Michigan was best known for its emphasis on the art of dissection. I graduated from Michigan with degrees in English and Middle East studies.

A Chevy truck painted in blue camo. Dirt Assault Unit, the decals above its back bumper proclaim.

From my perspective, the desert bushes are all standing in straight lines. I thought there were no straight lines in nature. Maybe the difference between man-made and natural is texture.

A bridge over the Mojave River dust and brown, loose rocks and gray bushes, most likely prickly pierced by the branches like a stake in a full fishing pond. The mountain ridges look pink from here. This road is adopted by the 12th Squadron. In large block letters: Peggy Sue's Diner.

Ft Irwin Road: Fort Irwin is known for its Box Tours where they have fake Iraqi and Afghani villages open for those tourists and supporters of our troops who have passed the background check (as FtIrwinITCBox@gmail.com told me). Watch us invade homes of fake Muslims. Practice.

There are real Muslims just a few miles thataway. They'll feed you for free—no practice invasion needed.

I'm listening to an audiobook about the 1890 Chicago World's Fair to which freight trains delivered entire villages from Egypt, including the villagers.

I wonder if my fellow travelers on the I-15 North with the back windows announcing their expected attendance of the Electronic Daisy Carnival know about the villages of Fort Irwin. Agrabas of the Mojave, Aswanis of the White City.

110 degrees Fahrenheit now. A car just threw out a Cheetos bag and liquid spilled out of it, orange vapor in the hot desert. The mountains look a dark purple. The mountains on the left a soft sage.

I only have fifty dollars in cash, a pack of cigarettes, a cup of coffee five-hours old (still warm), apricots, apples, cookies, salt and vinegar chips, a gallon of water, carrots, and a stack of CD audiobooks, including this one about the 1890 Chicago World's Fair, which, frankly, has rambled on for far too long about inane details.

You might as well start at the beginning. 111 degrees now. Is this America yet?

"For our nation, for us all / Marines: the few, the proud" billboard in grayscale, Marines staking an American flag, its colors electric, into what looks like a pile of limbs, also grayscale. I've seen this one before.

A wooden burger shack with a hand-painted sign that says Del Taco. Antique shop with GOOD STUFF on the building. Then: Ron Loves Mom. A little down the road, a farm: Kale for Sale.

111 degrees still. I am far away from my old apartment in Los Angeles, and I am closer to my mother's house in Detroit. In one direction, I am closer to my father's job in Saudi Arabia, and in another direction, I am farther from my grandfather's grave in Lebanon. Most of my belongings are in the trunk of my car. No place to stay not borrowed, no bed to call my own. An Arabic girl from Dearborn driving across a country she never knew she belonged to.

Another billboard two hundred feet into the desert to my right: HOT? HAUTE. A fading Denny's logo beneath the homonyms. The guys in the car next to me are smoking weed. I don't have any marijuana in my car because I'm afraid of Utah. The Mormonism here is as palpable as Islam in our Dearborn.

Rosinante, or my 2010 Jetta, Zzyzx Road, next exit. Audiobook Steinbeck says he doesn't write hot.

I am comforted by the Joshua trees to my left, my old friends from the first time I fell in love as an adult. The Joshua trees look older here, their chaos more infinite, their needles lighter, less green, faded in their Mojave domain, older siblings of those in Yucca Valley. These many dancers in the California desert, their soft green an accumulation of truths that come with witnessing.

The smoldering carcass of an F-150 straddling the ditch along the freeway median. Standing on its axles, tires melted away, hubcaps blackened. No cars stop at the ditch.

There's a boulder with a sign right in front, FOR SALE in red ink, a faded phone number, a forgotten Craigslist ad in the desert right before Exit 91: Moapa Indian Reservation.

I am in the shadows of mountains, the desert pastels fading into a darkness I have never passed through before, not alone. Orderville, Utah.

Stars and moon cascade into the Dixie National Forest, guiding light for a girl driving alone into the late night. Woman.

I am listening to Ziad Rahbani while driving across central Utah on I-70. I am thinking of permanence and those who believe in it.

Debt always had a seat at my family's table, a room in our house, a lease on our years. And now the crimson mountains of Utah.

No service for the next 110 miles, the billboard tells me, encouraging drivers to stop in Salina, which is also the name of a school in the south end of Dearborn, Michigan. Today, most of the students are Yemeni. Yesterday they were Lebanese and Palestinians. Before then, and beyond time, it is Anishinaabeg land. There's a big pipe going through the playground.

Soundtrack: Ziad Rahbani feat. Woody Guthrie. The Dust Tanjara. Sayed Darwish and Jimmie Rodgers. Sheikh Imam at Folsom in the seats, not on the stage.

I stop at Devil's Canyon, a cloth is laid out over the pavement to sell handmade jewelry. I buy a slingshot carved into a buck, his antlers the prongs.

I am too aware of being a settler in America to ask the Indigenous man selling it to me where he is from simply for the sake of a poem. He has a burn on his left arm. I thought it could have been a tattoo. I saw the texture of a scab and kept my question to myself.

His wife wraps the rubber band around the prongs and starts to hand me the slingshot. He gently takes the slingshot, leaning against the open trunk of his van, a blue Aerostar. He moves the rubber so the carved face of the buck faces the target, not the shooter.

"We're only here for the summer."

"Oh yeah, where are you going back to?"

"East of the Grand Canyon," he says.

Everywhere is east of the Grand Canyon.

I have a quarter tank of gas and there are only canyons in sight. Wind carved. Sepia. Reds. Spotted Wolf View Area, who named you?

My car breaks down on Colorado's I-70, the Rocky Mountains to my left and right.

A tow truck driver stops to help me. He's an Uzbekistani Muslim named John who has been in America for fifteen years. Started off working as a janitor in South Dakota. His ten-year-old nephew is in the truck with us on the way to Boulder. He's visiting from Uzbekistan and is disappointed that he hasn't yet seen any dead animals on the side of the road as was promised.

His name is Habiballah, which means loved by God.

# IT MIGHT HAVE BEEN OTHERWISE

## An Arab American Story

*Nabeel Abraham*

## ALEX

At 9 a.m. on October 11, 1985, Alex Odeh pushed open the door to his office triggering a thirty-pound pipe bomb. The blast blew off Alex's legs, burying him under a hail of debris. He would die on the operating table two hours later. Seven others were wounded by the blast, which halted traffic on the street. Terrified office workers poured out of the building, some running in panic down Seventeenth Street. The explosion that shook the town of Santa Ana, California, that morning might have had an analog in any one of thousands of action movies rolling off the production line in Hollywood, located only half an hour's drive north, but this blast was all too real and lethal. It left victims and onlookers thinking a sonic boom or earthquake had occurred. The FBI ranked it as the worst terrorist act on American soil in 1985.

More than two thousand miles away in Dearborn, Michigan, I sat in disbelief at my desk at a job I had started the previous month. I received a call from my associate Kathy Eadeh who was visiting the Washington office of the American-Arab Anti-Discrimination Committee (ADC). Kathy informed me of the horrible news. Alex was the forty-one-year-old director of the West Coast office of ADC, whereas I served the same function at the organization's Detroit office until I started teaching full-time at a local college. I knew Alex well from our work at ADC. A Palestinian Christian immigrant, Alex exuded dedication to the cause of Palestine and her much tormented people. He believed as I did that we were advancing the Palestinian cause in America by countering anti-Arab stereotypes and discrimination.

The explosion at the LA office cut close to home in other ways. Like Alex, I was outspoken in the local and national news media. The day before he was murdered, Alex had appeared on a local TV news program where he underscored Yasser Arafat's intercession in ending the siege of the cruise ship, the *Achille Lauro*, in the Mediterranean Sea. The incident, which ultimately centered on the murder of a Jewish American passenger, Leon Klinghoffer, drew widespread media attention in the United States. Because of the bombing, my ADC associates and I would henceforth need to take special precautions after doing media appearances, especially when going to the Detroit office. The FBI suspected the Jewish Defense League (JDL), a domestic extremist group, was behind the bombing that killed Alex. The FBI also considered the JDL to be a leading domestic terrorist group involved in the killing of seven individuals and the wounding of twenty-two others between the years 1968 and 1985. The mere mention of the organization's name made me sit up and take notice. Any one of us could have been targeted by them. My God, I thought, Arab Americans should not have to risk their lives just to speak their minds.

## "SOMETIMES YOU LOSE"

During my years as a political activist, I have interacted with many Jews, most of whom were supporters of Israel. But we weren't at war with one another. We weren't trying to kill one another. We debated and dialogued and talked like rational human beings who were trying to find a way out of the Arab-Israeli impasse. None of my interlocuters were affiliated with, let alone hardcore members of, the JDL. In fact, I had yet to see a JDL member in the flesh until I walked into a talk by the organization's founder, Rabbi Meir Kahane, on the Wayne State University campus in Detroit back in 1972.

Kahane was already speaking when I entered DeRoy Auditorium. I sat in the back. Scattered about the large auditorium were some fifty to seventy-five yarmulke-wearing men. Kahane was holding a mic in one hand and grabbing the lectern with the other, his black beard and yarmulke accenting his visage. He proved to be a commanding speaker despite his small stature. Kahane seemed to delight in driving his points home like a jackhammer. This was done using a tired refrain that can only be described as a "fatalistic sigh."

"The Arabs," he would say, "resisted our return to the Land of Israel. We Jews fought back. And guess what? *Sometimes you win, and sometimes you lose.* We Jews won; the Arabs lost."

It wasn't long before the audience took the bait like trained seals, reciting the refrain on cue, "And . . . Sometimes you win and sometimes you lose." I seemed to be the only one not in the chorus. I was surely the only Arab. Again and again, Kahane declared that Arabs had no place in the Land of Israel, no business dating Jewish women, no human or civil rights in Israel. His narrative turned every historic encounter between Jews and Arabs in Palestine into a life and death battle, and guess what? "Sometimes you win and sometimes you lose." Not surprisingly, the Arabs lost every time.

I slid down my seat with every reiteration of the refrain. Unable to slink any farther, I looked around the room and thought, *This is what it must have been like to have been a Jew in Weimar Germany as Hitler spoke to his admirers.* Not wanting to be there when the speech came to an end and the audience would be free to stand up and look around the auditorium, I slipped out as quietly as I had come in. Outside in the afternoon sun, I tried to shake off the gloom of having sat through a half hour of anti-Arab hatred and Jewish ethnic chauvinistic boasting.

I completed my undergraduate studies that semester and moved on, giving little thought to the experience. I hoped I'd seen the last of the Meir Kahane and the JDL.

## FACE-TO-FACE WITH THE JDL

Three years after the 1985 assassination of Alex Odeh, I arrived at the stage door of one of Detroit's majestic art deco movie theaters earlier than expected for the taping of a TV show I knew nothing about except that it would allow me to reach a national audience—the reason I was there. Waiting by the door were two other Arab Americans who I knew but was unaware that they, too, had been invited. They were equally surprised to see me.

After some small talk, one of them said: "They say JDL members will be representing the other side."

"The JDL?" I said. "I find that hard to believe. Do they have the temerity to show their faces after what they did to poor Alex?"

The thought occurred to me that an encounter with the local JDL on national TV might put us on their radar. "Fuck! Why the JDL?" I said. "There are dozens of Jewish spokesmen in the local community to choose from. Why the JDL? What's the point?"

We fell silent, like sheep at the abattoir gate, as the stage door opened. A stagehand checked our names against his clipboard and told us to follow him. He led us to a medium-size dressing room and told us to wait there. A pitcher of water and some plastic cups sat on a table in an otherwise spartan room. Raucous noise could be heard above: shouts, stomping, applause interspersed with heavy metal music. The three of us exchanged glances. The cacophony along with thoughts of having to face off with the JDL drove me into a funk. *What have we gotten ourselves into?* I thought. *I'm a college professor, for Christ's sake. What the hell am I doing here?*

I gave serious thought to calling the whole thing off. I took a hard look at the door and imagined myself walking back out into the sunlight. What stopped me was my sense of duty to my comrades. I couldn't just leave them to be slaughtered, lambs to the lions. Turning to them, I said, "We're going to do this. If the Jewish speakers turn out to be JDL, so be it. We're going to soldier through this. If the audience starts throwing tomatoes at us, we're going to stand our ground because our cause is just, and we know our stuff."

As we were shaking hands in solidarity, the door opened. A stagehand said it was time. We followed him up through a labyrinth to the stage. The din of the audience grew into a crescendo as we stepped out from behind the curtains onto the stage. The overhead lights were blinding. The sound was deafening. Stagehands wearing wraparound headphones and mics positioned us at various spots on a stage big enough to mount Verdi's *Aida*. My comrades were placed at a distance from me. I stood across from a bearded, burly guy holding a mic large enough to double as a club. I was handed a similarly sized mic.

The show's host, Morton Downey Jr., turned to the audience, calling them "loudmouths," and telling them to "zip it." The noise volume fell. Tall and lanky, Downey moved toward us mic-wielding Arabs and Jews. After puffing on his cigarette, he drew his mic to chin level and announced: "We're in Detroit this week, and this great city is being torn apart by violence. Many people here are accustomed to the daily sound of gunshots ringing out, firebombs being launched, cars being torched. Why? I'll tell you, pal. Because the largest community of Arabs outside of the Middle East lives right here in Detroit . . ."

Downey introduced the Arabs and Jews and their affiliations one by one. The rumor was true—the Jewish representatives were indeed JDL members. Downey threw out an old trope, that Arabs and Jews had been killing one another since "ancient times." I decided I was going to challenge his description of the Arab-Israeli conflict.

At the first opportunity, I cut in. "There's nothing ancient about the Arab-Israeli conflict. It is a very modern conflict . . ." I stopped. I could hear some in the audience shouting.

"Boring!"

"Let's see the A-rabs fight the Jews."

"Fuck you, camel jockey!"

Downey yelled back, "Shut the fuck up, Loudmouth! You there—zip it!"

A musical interlude followed as Downey announced, "We'll be right back after this message from our sponsors." Applause, shouting, stomping.

During the break, Downey addressed the Arabs and Jews on stage, telling us: "Get down to it! Tell us why these people"—head nodding to the audience—"should give a damn."

The music stopped. Downey turned to the audience and said: "We're back. Hey, you, zip it! Yeah, shut the fuck up!"

Downey looked at the heavyset JDL guy standing across from me and said, "The Arab spokesman over here said that the Arabs were driven from their land and they want to go back. What do you say to that?"

Burly JDL Guy: "We want to live in a Jewish state in Judea and Samaria in our ancient land that God gave us. The Arabs are invaders. They must leave; they must go! Every Arab is a threat to the existence of Israel. No Jew can sleep at night knowing Arab babies are born every minute in the Jewish state."

The mere mention of Arab babies being a mortal danger to Israel triggered a bomb in me. I lost it. Shouting into the mic to be heard over my opponent, over the din and even over the others on stage, I pointed to him while talking in the direction of the audience: "Did you hear what he just said? He said that no Jew can sleep at night because Arab babies are being born in Israel/Palestine. Babies! Babies! Anyone who talks about babies being a mortal danger is a Nazi. He's a racist, a Nazi!"

The JDL guy started shouting back that I was the Nazi. "He wants to kill all the Jews," he said pointing at me. The audience joined in stomping and hooting; the others on stage started shouting at their opponents. Trying to keep my focus on my opponent and not let what was happening on the stage or in the peanut gallery beyond distract me, I got lost in a back-and-forth shouting match with him. Him calling me a Nazi and a terrorist; me calling for a binational state where Jews and Arabs could live as equals.

Downey ignored us, refocusing on the other guests located closer to the audience. *This is crazy,* I thought. *I might have a heart attack right on this stage. Now, wouldn't that be one hell of a message to send to a national audience?*

After cooling down, I looked at my burly opponent and said to him off camera, "Hey, why don't we try to be constructive and use this opportunity to get our messages across to a national audience in an orderly manner rather than have everyone think we are a bunch of barbarians?"

He stared back with a puzzled look before turning and walking away. Feeling alone and exposed on stage, the futility of whatever we were doing hit me. I lost hope of getting a coherent message across. I quit trying. I shut down. Frankly, I can't recall after all these years if I spoke on stage again or not.

Later that evening, I realized that we—Jews and Arabs—had been played. There was nothing noble or even educational in what we did. We weren't gladiators in a coliseum attempting to out club one another in a test of strength and endurance. Rather, we were scorpions in a bottle, a bottle in the hand of Morton Downey Jr. With occasional and calculated shakes of the hand, the show's host could get the Arab and Jewish scorpions fighting and stinging each other for the amusement of the audience and the show's ratings. So embarrassed by my performance and ashamed of my hubris, I buried that episode of my life in the darkest recesses of my mind until now.

## THE BEST OF TIMES, THE WORST OF TIMES

The zeitgeist of the seventies and eighties for Arab Americans amounted to openly racist, demeaning stereotypes and political cartoons about Arabs that were so crude and extreme as to be utterly incomprehensible to today's readers. Cartoons of the Palestinian leader Yasser Arafat, for example, often depicted him as a jumping ape wearing his traditional checkered Palestinian headdress. Other cartoons depicted the Palestine Liberation Organization leader with a hooked nose, exaggerated lips, and a stubble beard—much like discarded antisemitic caricature traits used against European Jews in the past. Arabs in general were depicted as irredeemably violent and brutal terrorists; greedy and cruel oil sheiks; or ugly and lecherous sheiks surrounded by veiled, submissive women. Images of this sort appeared freely in the print media, in op-eds in major newspapers and in made-for-TV and Hollywood movies. I found it impossible not to be offended and demeaned by them. The way ADC and other Arab American organizations attempted to counter such damaging stereotypes back then was to ask editors if they would have run the same cartoons and editorials if the word "Arab" was replaced by the word "Jew." That is, would they allow such overtly racist and demeaning tropes be used to refer to Jews or Black people? The answer was, "Of course not." Then why allow such tropes to be used on Arabs? Over time we got results.

Sad to say, however, that demeaning media stereotypes of Arabs, Middle Easterners and Muslims continued to infect ordinary Americans long after they disappeared from the news media. Here's an example of what I mean.

One warm Saturday in the fall of 1980, my friend Kamal, a grad student in nuclear engineering at MIT, and I decided to spend the afternoon visiting the New England Aquarium in Boston. It was a planned escape from our work—Kamal's doctoral research and my daily responsibilities as director of the Association of Arab American University Graduates (AAUG). We got in the ticket line. Here we were, two olive-skinned men, looking out of place among families and their excited children. Kamal, a Palestinian Christian from the West Bank town of Bethlehem, was conversing in a mix of Arabic and English, as was his habit.

From behind came a voice, "Excuse me, what language are you guys speaking?" The questioner was a white, middle-aged woman.

"Arabic," I said.

Before I could divert her query into safe waters so that we might continue enjoying our outing, Kamal interjected, "We're Palestinian."

"Oh, Palestinians! Where are your machine guns?" she said, laughing and motioning as if she were firing a machine gun, pretending to spray fire back and forth sideways.

I took umbrage at the automatic connection of Palestinian and terrorist and told her as much. Perhaps I shouldn't have. I can see in hindsight that she was being playful, failing to consider that her willingness to interact with us was perhaps a positive sign. As it happened, we went our separate ways.

Another incident occurred in late November 1979, as I happened to be riding in the back of a taxi in the nation's capital along with two visiting Arabs from abroad. On a break from the annual convention of the AAUG, we were headed up Massachusetts Avenue to have lunch at a Lebanese restaurant, when traffic came to a crawl.

Our Nigerian driver said, "I think something is going on at the Iranian embassy."

The embassy stood as an imposing landmark in the capital. Across the street milling about were at least two dozen demonstrators wearing Halloween masks depicting hook-nosed, thick-lipped Middle Easterners in turbans waving gas cans and carrying signs to bomb Iran. It was an ugly display of American anger at another gasoline shortage due to events taking place in the Middle East. At the sight of the demonstration, my friends commented softly in Arabic about checkpoints during the Lebanese Civil War before falling silent as one and then a second demonstrator approached our car. We held our breath, the tie around my neck feeling tight as I imagined the demonstrators in their ugly masks opening the back door and pouncing on us "Iranians!" Even our Nigerian driver froze and kept his gaze straight ahead as if he were a statue. One big-lipped, big-nosed turbaned mask wearer stopped by the rear side window and peered in as if looking for something. No one moved. The Nigerian cabbie inched the car through the congestion until the street opened before us. He stepped on the accelerator the first chance he got. Everyone exhaled, and the Arabic conversation picked up again as if nothing had happened. The earlier remark about checkpoints was a reference to how civilians were often pulled out of vehicles during the Lebanese Civil War and interrogated, tortured, and even shot if they were from the other side. I thought back to that moment in front of the Iranian embassy several years later when I watched the horrifying scene in *Gandhi* wherein a trainload of Indian Muslims, on their way to the newly created country of Pakistan, are pulled off the train and set upon by angry mobs of knife wielding Hindus. I have occasionally reflected on that moment in front of the Iranian embassy and sighed, "It might have been otherwise."

## THE EYE OF MORDOR

Nothing focuses my mind like government threats to round up people on a national security pretext. With its awesome power and resources, the federal government is the closest thing in our world to the Eye of Mordor. I didn't always feel this way. Back in the late sixties/early seventies, a seemingly inconsequential congressman from the other side of the state, Gerald Ford, publicly warned that Maoist-trained Arab guerrillas were hiding among Arab students at American universities. I brushed off Ford's comment, feeling that I had little to fear from the police or federal authorities even though it was known that they were actively surveilling Arabs in America. Looking back on my brashness as a youthful rebel, I marvel that I made it to old age without ever getting arrested or clubbed by the cops. Although I was not doing anything wrong or subversive, that alone was no guarantee of immunity from the Eye of Mordor and its informers.

## "WHERE ARE THE GUNS?"

One night, two of my brothers and I finished running off a newsletter in the Arab Club located on the edge of Wayne State University campus where we were undergrads. We loaded three boxes of newsletters into the trunk of our car, which was parked across the street on Cass Ave. Just as we closed the trunk lid, a car pulled up behind us. Four police officers jumped out of the unmarked car and ordered us to place our hands on the car.

Policeman: "Where are the guns?"

"Guns? What guns? We don't have any guns," I said.

"We know you have guns. Where are they? Are they in the trunk of the car?"

Meanwhile, the other policemen patted us down.

"Look, we don't have any guns, just newsletters," I said.

"Open the trunk. We saw you put boxes in the trunk."

"I know my rights. You need a search warrant to search the car."

"We can arrest you on suspicion and then get a warrant, if you want."

One of my brothers said, "Let 'em look in the trunk."

"Okay," I said.

I popped open the lid, saying, "Like I said, newsletters . . . ink on paper, that's all."

The cop ordered me to step away from the car. Fearing he might plant a gun, I strained to watch as one of the cops blocked me. The lead cop looked up from the trunk as if he had just come across a dead rat.

Turning to another cop, he mumbled, "There's nothing here."

"We heard you were moving guns out of the clubhouse; where are they?"

"I told you we don't have any guns, but here you are wasting your time and our time looking for them. Maybe you guys shouldn't believe everything you hear."

"What about the clubhouse. You're hiding guns in there, aren't you?"

"No, we don't have any guns in there. But you'll have to get a search warrant 'cause I can't give you permission to search the place."

The cops finally gave up and let us go.

I later related the incident to attorney Abdeen Jabara in a boastful way, assuming he would praise my tough stance with the cops. Instead, a pained look came over his face. He gave me some advice. "Next time, cooperate with the cops. Don't give them any lip. They could have beaten you up and even jailed you on some pretext. In court, it would be your word against theirs. Judges side with the cops. You were lucky it ended the way it did."

## LA EIGHT

My naivete as a young radical could have turned out badly as Jabara had suggested. His advice sobered me up. Over time, I started to develop a robust wariness of law enforcement, especially the feds. With the 1985 murder of Alex Odeh still unresolved, agents from the FBI and INS arrested seven Arab students and a student's Kenyan wife in Los Angeles on what turned out to be trumped up terrorism charges. They were shackled and detained for three weeks Gitmo style. One detainee, Khader Musa Hamide, thirty-two at the time, described his three-week detention:

> They put two of us in a six-by-ten cell for 23 hours a day. For the first two days, the lights were on 24 hours a day and a camera was pointed at my head. We were allowed no phone calls, not even to our attorneys. I did not know day from night. I did not know where my wife was. I did not know where my friends were . . . some of the guards called us many racist names and made sure we could hear the racist jokes they were telling.

The detentions occurred in 1987, fourteen years *before* 9/11. It wasn't an isolated case, either. A young Palestinian American female college student in LA was similarly arrested and detained on the heels of the LA Eight arrests. After an uproar ensued among civil libertarians and influential newspaper columnists, charges were dismissed against six of the eight. Legal battles dragged on for years before the government, having lost its case, relented. These and similar arrests cast a pall of fear over me and other Arab Americans, which I believe was the government's intention all along—intimidation. Like the young LA students, I wasn't doing anything wrong or illegal, but I, nevertheless, learned to fear the awesome power of federal and state authorities. Having watched what activists like Angela Davis and others went through, I knew that the authorities could make a person's life a living hell if they chose to. I never stopped speaking out, writing, or making media appearances, however. As an Arab American activist, I was wary but not deterred, believing that the best way to lose your rights was to not use them.

The most alarming revelation to emerge from the LA detentions was a leaked document detailing a secret plan to detain and deport large numbers of Arab and Iranian students, permanent residents, and even US citizens during a presidentially declared national state of emergency. Oakdale, Louisiana, was designated as the site of one of the planned detention centers. The mere mention of the words "detention camps" and US citizens in the same sentence sparked images of gray, austere housing on a desolate plain surrounded by barbed wire fencing interspersed by guard towers. It was too easy to imagine Arab and Iranian Americans replacing the 100,000 Japanese Americans forced into the internment camps during World War II.

So, when I received a call from David Cole, one of the lawyers representing the remaining two LA defendants in the early nineties, I was vexed. Cole asked if I would testify as an expert witness. He thought testimony from someone like me, a scholar of Arab Americans, about the political culture of Palestinian Americans might help his clients whose "crime" seemed to have been selling Arabic-language magazines produced by the Popular Front for the Liberation of Palestine (PFLP). If I agreed and the court consented to allow my testimony, I would be given a ticket to fly to LA to testify. As an admirer of Cole's work and someone committed to civil liberties, I readily agreed, even though I realized that testifying for the defense might put me in the government's crosshairs. I could recall the time anti-Vietnam War intellectuals, like Eqbal Ahmed, and activist priests, like the Berrigan brothers, and nuns were arrested and charged with plotting to kidnap Henry Kissinger, Richard Nixon's national security adviser, in the early seventies, based on the word of a paid FBI informer. The much-celebrated case made national headlines. Nevertheless, I resolved to suck up my anxiety and await further details. They never came. For unknown reasons, I wasn't called to testify. Incidentally, the LA Eight case had a terrifying two-decade run, reaching the Supreme Court of the United States along the way in 1998, until it was closed in 2007.

Not long after 9/11, I had another brush with the feds. The assistant US prosecutor in Detroit who was in the news for prosecuting local terrorism cases called me for a favor. He asked in a friendly but hurried manner if I would come downtown to speak informally to him and his staff about the Detroit Arab community. Not wanting to disappoint, I agreed. But then regretted my decision mainly because I was critical of the cases his office was prosecuting, which seemed to me and civil libertarians to be based on flimsy grounds, designed to intimidate the community while advancing the careers of prosecutors rather than ferreting out actual threats to society. In fact, most of the terrorism cases were either dismissed or resulted in plea bargains over incidental violations of the law. I also feared that by speaking at a gathering in the prosecutor's office, I might also be inadvertently putting myself in the crosshairs of ambitious prosecutors hungry for more targets of opportunity. Vexed over the matter for days, I called the prosecutor and told him that I would have to decline his invitation. Might my decision have been a missed opportunity to educate the prosecutor's office? Possibly. Yet, I wonder, is it possible to get bloodhounds off the trail of their quarry?

## POST 9/11 VIGNETTES

### The Men's Room

It was the morning after . . . September 12, 2001. I stepped into the men's room down the hall from my office. I greeted Greg, a colleague whom I liked and worked closely with. Greg (not his real name) was washing his hands while looking up at my reflection in the mirror in front of him.

He asked, "What do you think of what happened yesterday?"

"What do *I* think? My hunch is," I ventured, "that the attacks are most likely the work of a little-known Islamic fundamentalist group headed by an obscure figure named Osama bin Laden. I don't know much about him other than that he had mobilized support among Muslims in Saudi Arabia and elsewhere to aid the mujahideen resistance against the Soviet Army in Afghanistan back in the eighties. The US backed him and other Islamic fundamentalist groups. Ronald Reagan's CIA head, Bill Casey, openly declared that he intended to create a 'Vietnam' for the Soviet Army in Afghanistan.

"My guess is," I continued, "bin Laden's aim is to draw the US into multiple wars in the Middle East so as to wear it down, the way the mujahideen wore down the Soviets in Afghanistan. He believes that the Soviet defeat in Afghanistan brought down the Soviet Union."

A pained look came over Greg's face: "I asked you what you thought, and you gave me an analysis as if you were the BBC." I looked straight at Greg and he at me before he turned and walked out of the room.

Now I was looking at my own refection in the mirror wondering what the fuck had just happened. If I were the volatile type, I might have punched the mirror. Instead, I had to coax my shoulders, which were reaching for my ears, back down. I tasted humiliation mixed with disbelief.

Back in the office, I tried to make sense of the insult Greg had thrown my way. Maybe I should have just expressed my outrage at the brazenness of the attacks. Maybe I should have expressed my shock and revulsion at the turning of planes loaded with passengers into missiles, and what an abomination it was to hurl those missiles crammed with innocents into buildings filled with other innocents. Why had I kept my outrage bottled up? Hubris, I suppose. Hubris that I had detective-like figured out what the planners of the attacks were probably thinking. To be sure, the terrorists were mad, but they were mad in rational, calculating ways. I wanted to put my knowledge and sleuthing abilities on display. But what quickly emerged was the realization that nothing I could have said would have sufficed. Greg was angry and wanted to take it out on an "Arab," and I made for a convenient target.

Had Greg simply wanted reassurance from me, the only "Arab" he was acquainted with, that not all Arabs were cold, calculating killers who hated America, I would have gladly obliged. My BBC-like dispassionate response to him was my way of distancing myself from the emotional fires consuming America that morning and the billowing hatred toward Arabs and Muslims as whole categories of people and nations. As a Palestinian American, I knew that the trail of violence did not begin on that fateful day in September 2001. The Gulf War ten years earlier and the ensuing economic sanctions on Iraq had resulted in immense death and suffering of Iraqi civilians, mostly children. I was, of course, also familiar with the untold suffering and violence endured by the Palestinians. Most Americans weren't aware of these things or the fact that successive American governments were complicit in that violence and suffering. None of this, of course, justified the 9/11 attacks by any stretch of the imagination. My disgust with and opposition to violence against civilians was total and absolute. And although I couldn't justify the September attacks on moral or even tactical grounds, I could comprehend their insanity and translate it to others dispassionately as an observer of contemporary Middle Eastern affairs. In the final analysis, however, I was trying to retain my own sanity in what was an utterly insane moment in history. But in the men's room that morning my ethnic identity, not my expertise as a Middle East scholar, was sought as a punching bag.

The horrors of 9/11 ignited a latent fear in me of the federal government clamping down on Arab Americans and American Muslims. Memories of the LA Eight and similar cases came alive in my mind. It was all too easy to imagine myself in Oakdale, Louisiana, along with thousands of fellow ethnics. The "good" news is that history had contrived an experiment with which to test my fears. The terrorist attacks of 2001 could have activated the government's secret plans to detain thousands of Arabs and Muslims in special camps. Fortunately for everyone concerned, as well as for the country as a whole, America failed to repeat its shameful treatment of Japanese Americans. For that, I am eternally grateful. My worst nightmare never came to pass. By the same token, federal authorities did clamp down on an untold number of Arab, Muslim, and Iranian immigrants, in many cases violating their civil rights, arresting, detaining and even summarily deporting hundreds if not thousands. The government also seized greater surveillance powers, a move that continues to alarm civil libertarians.

The expected backlash at the popular level—everything from jingoistic taunts to violent outbursts up to and including the killing of several individuals in the weeks following the 9/11 attacks—did materialize around the country. For a brief moment, President George W. Bush added fuel to the fire by referring to the war in Afghanistan and the war on terror as a "crusade," reviving centuries-old battle cries between the Christian West and the Muslim East. Fortunately, rational heads prevailed, and Bush quickly disavowed his unfortunate use of that loaded term. Washington, after all, couldn't afford to start a war with the entire Muslim world. In fact, it had far more Arab and Muslim allies than enemies.

## Maoist in Mecca

In the weeks following the 9/11 terrorist attacks, I received a curious message in my inbox at work. It was an email from a fellow named Moe (not his real name) inquiring if I was the same person he knew when he used to hang around the Arab Club at Wayne State University in the late sixties, early seventies. From the descriptions he provided, I was certain he was indeed the guy he claimed he was.

*Why after thirty years is Moe contacting me?* I wondered. *And why now, so soon after 9/11?* The prompt flashed impatiently on the screen next to his message.

Moe and I were never close. At most, we were sparring buddies over Palestinian politics. He was an admirer of the PFLP, which had engaged in airplane hijackings and espoused Marxist leanings. Even as a nineteen-year-old who read Marx, I opposed those hijackings on moral and tactical grounds and felt they were highly counterproductive. Moe, who from all signs did extraordinarily little reading, openly declared himself a Marxist because the leader of the organization he supported called himself a Marxist. The ultimate irony was that Moe, who grew up in a Palestinian refugee camp around the Jordanian capital, started out politically as a member of the conservative Muslim Brotherhood, the antithesis of Marxism.

The question kept nagging me: *Why is Moe trying to contact me in the aftermath of the 9/11 attacks?* I wondered. *Does he have some connection to the attacks? Or is he trying to get a reading of the reactions of Arab Americans?* I can't deny that I was curious about him, but I also suspected that the government must be monitoring communications between the United States and the Middle East. Was it worth it taking a risk to satisfy a curiosity?

I recalled that Moe was prone to saying off-the-wall things, like the ridiculous comment he made one night maybe fifty years ago, which has stayed with me like an old bite mark. One evening Moe and I found ourselves alone in the Arab Club staring at a large map of the Arab world Scotch-taped to the wall. News out of China at the time centered on the Cultural Revolution, which was gripping Mao Tse-tung's China. Moe seemed entranced by the Cultural Revolution's power to sweep away ancient Chinese cultural thinking and institutions, replacing them with a new order.

"Do you think," I asked, "China's Cultural Revolution would have any applicability in the Arab world?"

Moe pointed to the map and replied, "Of course! Especially this bastion of reaction, Saudi Arabia," he said, sweeping his hand over the map for emphasis.

"And, what about the holy city of Mecca?" I asked sardonically. "How would hundreds of millions of Muslims react to a cultural revolution engulfing Mecca?"

Moe paused momentarily before blurting out, "The Israelis can bomb it for all I care!" Amused by his own suggestion, he repeated his statement with an impish smile, "Yeah, let Israel bomb the Kaaba." He laughed gleefully.

Stunned by his suggestion, I said, "I doubt very much that Israel is stupid enough to inflame the passions of over a billion Muslims around the world." I should point out in this regard that not many years later, news leaked from Jerusalem that a Jewish organization there is dedicated to rebuilding the Jewish Second Temple on the very location of the Islamic Haram el-Sharif. Doing so would by necessity require the destruction of the Muslim shrine, said to be the second holiest in Islam. Thus far successive Israeli governments have thwarted attempts by Jewish fanatics to blow up the shrine.

Moe's quip about bombing the Kaaba was so outlandish when first broached five decades ago that I have been unable to rid my memory of it. The very thought of Islam's holiest of holies being bombed is so phantasmagorical as to be beyond the ability of the mind to contemplate it, at least for Muslims. Once rung, the bell cannot be unrung. My conversation with Moe is illustrative of a salient fact running across my youth—Arabs have said wild things to me in private that they would not otherwise say publicly to fellow Arabs.

I lost touch with Moe after I graduated. Many years later, a mutual friend informed me rather indignantly that Moe, his erstwhile comrade, had slid back into his Muslim political roots after accepting a job in, of all places, Saudi Arabia.

Sitting at my desk looking at Moe's email, I felt Uncle Sam's breath on the nape of my neck. I took a deep breath and moused the cursor over Moe's email and clicked "delete" while exhaling.

## Kufrproof

Kim S. was a young mother and student of mine. She elected to do her second-year honors research project on how metro Detroit Muslims fared in the aftermath of the worst attack on the United States since Pearl Harbor. Emotions were still raw. Kim did not grow up with Arab Americans around. But she could sympathize with them, arguing they had nothing to do with the actual 9/11 attacks. I agreed to supervise her project and suggested that we do an interview with a Sunni Muslim clergyman named Sheik Ismail. I didn't know Sheik Ismail. I knew of him only through some of my Muslim students who performed the Friday communal prayer at the adjacent campus to ours. My students had informed me that I was on his radar as a secular Arab American. I asked Kim if she would like to do a trial interview with Sheik Ismail since he was nearby and I could accompany her. She nodded.

Through intermediaries, Sheik Ismail agreed to meet with us after the Friday prayer in the room the university had set aside for Muslim students. It was a warm, fall afternoon when we arrived. Leaving our shoes near the entrance, Kim and I walked toward a youthful-looking sheik seated in the corner of a spacious, carpeted room. He didn't rise to greet us, motioning instead with the wave of a hand for us to sit on the floor across from him. My suspicions were already aroused by the sheik's youthful age as well as his sudden appearance on the Detroit scene.

We exchanged some pleasantries in Arabic before I asked him about his background in English for Kim's benefit. We learned that he and his father, Palestinians both, had come to Dearborn to help give the "neglected" Sunnis an alternative in majority Shia Dearborn. Sheik Ismail didn't try to hide his sectarian biases, especially his anti-Shia bias. Turning to Kim, he said, "Your professor here is at fault for allowing the Shia students in his classes to define Islam *the wrong way*."

"Sheik Ismail," I interjected, "we didn't come here to get embroiled in Sunni-Shia sectarian divisions. Ms. Kim is doing research on the post-9/11 backlash faced by Muslims."

Kim asked about complaints of harassment and discrimination encountered by his congregants as well as himself. He told her that anti-Muslim harassment is a problem *only* if Muslims do *not* heed the message and return to their countries of origin! "Muslims, good Muslims, should be in their home countries fighting foreign invaders and internal enemies," he said.

"Excuse me," I interrupted, "but what are you doing here then?"

Sheik Ismail retorted that his role is to warn the good Muslims about the various enemies facing Islam. Turning to me, he added, "That includes people like you, Mr. Nabeel, who attempt to undermine Islam in the classroom. We know about you and are keeping a record of your anti-Muslim activities; your kufr opinions."

Facing poor Kim, I told her that the sheik had just called me an infidel, and that was our signal to leave. Truth be told, I began worrying that we might be in danger, especially because a half dozen young men were milling about in a corner of the room. We got up and left quickly.

On the walk back to our campus, Kim asked what had happened; why had the sheik said those things? I told her that I, as a secular Arab Muslim, was the wrong person to accompany her to the interview. But on second thought, given Sheik Ismail's mindset that real Muslims shouldn't even be residing in the land of the infidels, the interview probably would have gone south no matter who might have accompanied her. I suggested she check out an anonymous website, Kufrproof.com, which I suspected reflected Sheik Ismail and his isolationist school of thought.

Kim went on to interview about a dozen Detroit-area Muslim clergy, all of whom were gracious and generous with their time. They uniformly saw the upsurge of interest in Islam provoked by 9/11 as an opportunity to showcase their religion as an antithesis to the 9/11 attackers. And Sheik Ismail? Word reached me shortly after our encounter that the FBI had arrested him and his father on charges of running an auto theft ring. I heard he was eventually deported, a win-win for both our country and his philosophy.

## George the Greek

To non-Arab Americans, I am an Arab American or simply an Arab. And as such I am often the closest person they know with whom to share their feelings about Arabs, as demonstrated by my encounter with Greg back in the men's room. A situation like that happened to me in November 2001, when George (not his real name), a Greek American writer, turned to me at a social event, leaned in, and said point blank: "You know that I live in New York City, right? Well, 9/11 was a living hell for us."

"Yeah," I nodded.

Leaning closer, George looked me in the eye and said: "I'm warning you, if it happens again, it's all over for you guys. Got that? It's all over. It better not happen again, got that?"

I stared back. "Um-hum."

Whew! I didn't know what to say. Since I didn't want to fight with George, I resisted pushing back. Still, till this day I can't get his words out of my head. George's admonishment caught me off guard not only because he was such a close friend of two of my Arab American friends but also because he was a progressive thinker. There had to be more behind his anger. We had just left an academic panel discussion where he was the commentator on the presentations. Perhaps the discussions about the fallout of 9/11 on Arab and Muslim Americans triggered him somehow. If they did, he didn't appear perturbed. Of course, there was the trauma of being in New York when the attacks occurred. I had friends and former students who were also in the city when the planes struck the World Trade Center, but none of them directed any anger at me or at Arabs in general.

I wondered if there wasn't more to George's admonition. Perhaps he was associating me with our mutual Arab American friend, Ernest, who in his typical prankster fashion had sent George a postcard several weeks after the 9/11 attacks poking fun at New York Mayor Rudy Giuliani. Ernest and George were childhood friends. Even so, George took exception to the prank, sending Ernest a scorching letter warning that their lifelong friendship was on the line. Still, I felt there must be something else behind George's ire. I had heard that his mother, a Greek immigrant, had grown up in the Anatolian town of Smyrna, a prosperous port city that had a large Greek and Armenian Christian population and a smaller but significant Turkish Muslim population. After the breakup of the Ottoman Empire at the end of World War I, Greek and Turkish forces battled for control of the town and surrounding area. Both sides engaged in widespread massacres, each attempting to ethnically cleanse the region of the other's ethnic population. George's mother escaped on the last boat after the defeat of Greek forces in 1922. Her hometown and Anatolia were incorporated in the new Turkish republic.

George doubtless had grown up hearing about his mother's connection to Smyrna and her traumatic departure from the city, just as I had grown up hearing about my mother's connection to Jerusalem and her departure as her half of the city fell to the new state of Israel following the ethnic cleansing of the city and major regions of Palestine. Perhaps, just perhaps, George's childhood transference of his mother's trauma had been awakened by the Muslim fanatical attacks of 9/11 on New York. But regardless of his motivation, I was again being put in the role of an ethnic punching bag for a non-Arab/Muslim needing to vent his fear and anger at the closest "stand-in" for the people who had made him feel so vulnerable.

Speaking my mind as an Arab American elicited pushback from the unlikeliest quarters: friends and colleagues. In the weeks following the 9/11 attacks, for example, I was quoted in a national newspaper as saying, among other things, that "I loved my country." I'm fairly certain that I had never said those words up to that point in my life, for the simple reason that I had always conflated "my country" with the government in Washington, whose policies, especially its foreign policies,

I invariably found objectionable. So, when I uttered those four words to a reporter, images of a vast continent blessed with majestic beauty flashed before me along with the freedoms accorded me in the Bill of Rights. Had I conjured the typical image of the Bush administration waging war against Iraq, those words would have been stillborn. Yet in no time, my words about loving my country were shot down in print by a Palestinian American acquaintance, who wrote that he couldn't imagine loving "something so abstract and imponderable as a country." Yet, it is a fact that people the world over, first and foremost the Palestinians, are prepared to die for their country presumably because they *love* their country.

On a different occasion, as George H. W. Bush was putting together the Coalition of the Willing to oust the Iraqi Army from Kuwait without even trying to negotiate a withdrawal, I was quoted in a national paper as an Arab American who felt so alienated by the upsurge in jingoism around me that I wondered if I should move to another country. The next day, Joe, a colleague at the college where I taught, appeared at my office door to tell me that he was in disbelief that I would say I was "ashamed" of my country. He was incredulous that any American could feel that way.

Joe was apparently threatened that I, as an outspoken Arab American on campus, would question the decisions of my government during wartime, especially in a prominent newspaper. I suspect that I was a stand-in for the Dearborn Arab American community in his mind. I knew Joe had German heritage in his background and that his wife was of Lebanese descent. So, I suppose it was only natural that Joe and his wife had learned consciously or unconsciously to display patriotism in times of war, by which it was understood to avoid speaking critically about the actions of government. I asked Joe if he had read the news story in question. He admitted he hadn't. I suggested that he read it and perhaps then we could talk about it. He never returned.

One day, long after 9/11 and the Iraq War, another colleague with whom I had worked closely with for many years approached me in a tizzy.

She got right down to it, asking, "Nabeel, do you deny that the Holocaust happened?"

Before I could open my mouth, she added, "I just had an Arab student tell me that he didn't believe that the Holocaust happened. Do you feel that way?"

I had to fight the urge to chew her head off. I wanted to say to her, "How long have you known me? How many Jewish speakers have I brought to campus?" Instead, I pulled hard on the reins and calmly said, "No, I don't. You might ask your student about the traumas he and his family have suffered and find out where he is coming from. It might be something as simple as his attempt to deny victimhood to the people who are oppressing him and his people. It can be cleared up."

Over the years, I have learned to never assume that the people around you perceive your ethnicity. In 2005, I moved back to Dearborn, Michigan, population 100,000, of whom half or so are Arab American. My non-Arab wife Lisa, her two children, and I moved into a predominately white neighborhood of vintage homes on the city's west side. We invited some neighbors over for drinks one night. Two of our guests were admiring a lithograph over the fireplace mantel. The contemporary artwork consisted of block Arabic script that isn't readily apparent to the uninitiated eye. Suddenly, one neighbor turned to me and said, "I didn't know that you were . . . you know . . ."

"Arab?" I volunteered. He genuinely seemed surprised, even shocked.

How he missed the cues, my name and olive skin, was beyond me. I assumed that non-Arabs would know to pick up the telltale features, especially in Dearborn, but my neighbor appeared clueless.

Not many weeks later, another white neighbor whom I didn't know at all, greeted me one evening, with "Happy Eid!"

Go figure.

## ME IN THE WORLD

In the eighth month of the COVID-19 pandemic, I stood in the checkout lane at Target in a small town in mid-Missouri in the region where my wife and I had relocated three years ago. Fearful of catching the virus at my age and with my preexisting condition, I was protected to the hilt with a plastic face shield over my mask, a long-sleeved shirt, and full-length pants, all topped with a baseball cap. I had carefully scanned the various checkout lanes searching for one having masked as opposed to unmasked shoppers in line. Missouri being a solid red state, mask ordinances are only found in a handful of cities and university towns. And even when merchants, typically big box stores, require masks and social distancing, they are reluctant to enforce their own policies lest their hapless employees get into fights with irate non-maskers and quit.

Not long after I squeezed into the lane between displays of bubble gum and candy on either side of me, I sensed a shopping cart perilously close to my backside. I turned and saw a middle-aged white woman wearing a mask below her nose, loosely covering her mouth.

"Excuse me," I said, "would you mind backing up a little so as to maintain the six-foot rule?"

Shopper X: "You called me a bitch, so no, I'm not backing up!"

"Excuse me?"

Shopper X: "You called me a bitch; I'm not backing up. So there!"

"Look, I apologize if you misheard me, but I didn't call you bitch; it's not my style. I'm a college professor. I'm also a cancer patient and can't afford to catch the virus. I really would appreciate it if you would back up a few feet."

Shopper X: "You called me a bitch. So, no!"

Feeling trapped in the aisle with Shopper X behind me, I pulled my cart back with an abrupt jerk at which point a surprised Shopper X backed up a little.

Turning toward her, I declared: "OK, you can have the lane, I'm getting out."

I swung my cart around in a semicircle toward her cart whereby the tip of my cart caught the edge of her cart, hitting it, prompting Shopper X to declare: "That's assault! You assaulted me! I'm calling the police." Shopper X reached for her cell phone and started dialing.

Having completely swung my cart around and moved away, I said, "I didn't call you a bitch before, but I'm calling you one now!"

I maneuvered down a different checkout lane and stood across from a cashier who asked how my day was going. I responded that I've had better days. Shopper X stood behind the cashier talking on her cell phone providing a description of me at the checkout. She called out to me with a question. I didn't look up. Shopper X moved to my side of the checkout lane, standing about five feet behind me, cell phone in hand, demanding that I answer her. I pretended not to hear her. She described the type of boots that I was wearing and the color of my shirt and trousers, presumably to the police.

I paid the cashier, collected my bags, and left the store like a raccoon chased by hound dogs. In the parking lot, I ran, pushing my shopping cart ahead of me. A gust of wind blew my baseball cap off my head. I stopped, turned around to retrieve it. Looking up, there was Shopper X coming toward me, still talking on the phone.

As I reached for my cap, Shopper X shouted: "Assault! That's assault!"

"That's not assault!" I yelled back, before running in the direction opposite my car. I tried ducking behind a van, hoping to elude my stalker, but realized it was futile. I decided to return to the store to seek help from the manager. On the way back, I noticed a police car pulling up to the store's other entrance.

The store manager and her assistant were sympathetic, volunteering that they found Shopper X's actions bizarre.

"You can stay here, we will protect you," the manager said.

I waited for the police to approach. Officer Shear, who appeared to be in his mid-thirties, asked my side of the story. He also asked to see my driver's license. He made an effort to pronounce my name, surprising me. I helped him by offering the nickname that I adopted in Missouri. I mentioned my concern about keeping distance due to my cancer. He asked about the type of cancer I have.

"Prostate cancer."

Officer Shear informed me that Shopper X was accusing me of assault.

"I don't understand, I never touched her."

He explained that there are four levels of assault in Missouri. I was facing a charge of the lowest level of assault because my shopping cart hit Shopper X's cart. Officer Shear would review the store camera tape and make a determination sometime tomorrow. Before I left, Shear returned to my cancer. He was curious about the various treatments I had had. We talked a bit as his partner listened.

On the forty-minute drive home, I beat myself up over why I had engaged Shopper X in the first place. I had come to Missouri, after all, to live in a small town so I could live in peace and tranquility as an average Joe. Now, here I was embroiled in a tiff with someone who clearly had a chip on her shoulder. Did my request that she allow safe distancing provoke a Trumpian impulse in her? Or was it my over-wrought face mask and shield that provoked her? Or did she feel insulted as a feminist because the request was coming from a man? If she thought she heard me say "bitch," why did she reject my repeated denials? Because my ethnic features were concealed under my mask and face shield, Shopper X had no other social cues about me. I was baffled.

The next day Officer Shear called with his verdict after reviewing the store tape. He failed to see any evidence that I had assaulted Shopper X, even though he could tell that I was angry when I turned my cart around. Had I rammed my cart straight into her cart forcing it into her, that would have been evidence of assault. Shear volunteered that Shopper X remained adamant that I be charged with something. He told her that he could charge me with disturbing the peace, but he would also have to charge her as well. She rejected that option. I was, of course, relieved that no charges would be filed against me, and thanked him for his scrupulous review of the incident. We talked some more about my cancer, and he appeared sympathetic. I thanked him for his concern and expressed my appreciation for his fair review of the incident.

## WHO AM I?

I can't get over the many ways the incident at Target might have turned out badly. I could have lost my head and deliberately slammed into Shopper X's cart and faced a fourth-degree assault charge, which might have entailed a thousand-dollar fine and a fifteen-day jail sentence. Or

Officer Shear might not have been fair in his investigation and charged me with assault, forcing me into court to prove my innocence. Even worse outcomes are imaginable. This being Missouri, where many residents carry guns on their person and in their cars, Shopper X might have pulled out a gun and shot me, claiming self-defense because I had "assaulted" her. Fortunately, I drew an even-handed policeman who did what was expected of him: He weighed the evidence against the accusation. The irony of the moment did not escape me, either. I had gratitude for a white policeman because of his attention to detail during a time of racially charged nationwide protests against police brutality.

The simple fact is that so much of my life—not just the incident with Shopper X—might have turned out differently. I might have been targeted by the JDL, beaten up by their goons like others have been. The bomb that killed Alex Odeh might have found me instead. I might have been beaten up by the police, even jailed, because I refused to let them inspect my car without a search warrant. I might have been innocently caught up in an FBI sting operation and found myself on trial for allegedly providing "material assistance" to a foreign terrorist organization based on the testimony of a paid government informer. I could have been found guilty of a crime I hadn't committed and wound up in prison, pleading with the Innocence Project to rescue me. I could have been attacked by Sheik Ismail or some of his congregants for heresy or some such. Or, worse, I might have been interned in Oakdale, Louisiana, along with Sheik Ismail, in a truly Kafkaesque twist of fate.

There was a time in life when I used to ask the question, "Why is such-and-such happening to me?" I now realize that that is the wrong question because the answer invariably leads to self-pity and to a sense of victimization. Neither of which is helpful. Of late I have learned to ask a wholly different question: "Who did I think I was when I reacted the way I did when I told the cops they couldn't search the trunk of my car or when I went on the Morton Downey Jr. Show without looking into the show's format?"

Who did I think I was when I asked Shopper X to observe social distancing? My best guess is that I was the young Nabeel growing up in a family of five brothers forced to share two small bedrooms. As the eldest, I grew up with a sense of loss, of having (for a very brief time) the world to myself only to find the world around me increasingly crowded with the addition of another sibling, four in all. The choice back then was stark: Either share and cooperate or fight for your share of storage space, toys, dessert, choice of bunk bed, etc. Adulthood only muted my idiosyncratic ways; it did not eliminate them. My knee-jerk response to infringements on my personal space is to attempt to control the environment around me—temperature, lighting, seating, view, and the like. I fidget until I get the environment to adapt to my comfort zone. Viewed this way, I can see that my interaction with Shopper X on that fateful day was prompted by a lifelong desire to protect myself, avoid illness, and to control (fidget with) the environment around me. That is probably one reason why I loved teaching so much—so long as I could control the classroom—and why my political philosophy is predicated on the proposition that things don't have to be the way they are.

So, who am I? The short answer is I am my past rolled up in an enchilada of the present, oozing with multiple experiences: being a male, an Arab American, the eldest of five brothers, etc. By the same token, I am whoever others see me as. Shopper X apparently wanted me to be a male who "insults" and "assaults" women like her. A woman in Boston heard that my friend and I were Palestinians and linked us to "terrorism." Others see me as an Arab Western Union, the person through whom to deliver messages to "the Arabs," and when all else fails, as someone to use as an ethnic punching bag. To some Arabs, I am the person to whom you can spill your darkest thoughts you might never share with "real" Arabs. To the JDL, I'm the Arab enemy threat who should be eliminated. To many Jewish community activists, I'm a Palestinian nationalist despite my insistence that I'm a universalist. To my students, I'm a teacher, professor, and program director who happens to be Arab or Arab American—or just a bald, olive-skinned guy with a strange name. In graduate school a fellow Arab American student from Toledo, Ohio, once called me the "resident revolutionary." Not wanting to be typecast, I reacted negatively. He never repeated it. The great irony is that I know I am more than what I might appear to be. All I ask is the freedom to define myself.

# MY DEARBORN

*Sally Howell*

The bridge on Miller Road is under construction again. While this is great news for Dearborn and for Ford Motor, it means that the Southend of Dearborn is truly cut off from the rest of the city right now. The Southend has always been cut off, of course. The Rouge Factory, which is over a mile long and includes more than a hundred miles of rail lines, has its own special entrances to both I-94 and I-75, but it stands like a mountain range between the Southend and the rest of Dearborn. Now, residents have to trek their way around the southern end of the plant, cross the Rouge River at that out-of-place-seeming drawbridge, and circle around through Melvindale, or they can go north on Wyoming to Michigan Avenue, where Dearborn and Detroit share their most prominent border, in order to engage with the rest of town.

It is May 22, 2020, the last day of Ramadan. I am taking the Melvindale route. I have always liked seeing the industrial wasteland that exists just across the Rouge River in Melvindale. The oil refineries, junkyards, giant mounds of slag, cement manufacturers, endless trucking garages, and for a little variety, a gentlemen's club called, of all things, Charmed. As I drive past this place and notice the name again, I look around to see if any of the other drivers nearby are also amused. This is when I notice a bright white Land Rover following close behind, looking very out of place. Hajj Hass Chami is behind the wheel—a young guy I have taken to calling "Mr. Dearborn" because he seems so tuned in to his generation's values, experiences, and expectations. He is a pharmacist and pharmacy owner who is busy raising a young family while helping his larger family manage a local restaurant. He has on his COVID-19 mask, so I can't really see his face, but I can see him giving me a WTF look nonetheless. Can it be that he has never been here before? Never seen the underbelly of the Rouge?

Michigan has been under stay-at-home orders for the past few weeks, so Dearborn has had to Ramadan-in-place. All the excitement of last year's Suhoorfest, and the other, smaller street festivals that were set up in and around Dearborn for the holiday are gone this year. It has been a quiet and subdued season—one of reflection and time spent with family. I've been working on an exhibit about Muslim visibility in the Detroit area with a small team of collaborators, and since our exhibit was shuttered prematurely, we've kept busy interviewing Muslim leaders about how they are surviving the COVID-19 pandemic. Somehow these conversations led us to partner with Hass (the creator of Suhoorfest) and the Michigan Muslim Community Council to host a Ramadan Lights Contest in greater Dearborn. Hass and I are on the way to the home of the Alzookery family, district champions for the Southend, to present them with their award, our last of the day.

We take Dix Ave. to Vernor, turn right at the mosque, follow Riverside as it curves alongside Baby Creek and the cemetery, and then head north again at the southernmost tip of Salina. This is where the Alzookerys live in a small bungalow. The sun is still out, so the bling of their light display is not yet impressive, but I have seen the videos and love what the family did, both inside and outside their home. The Alzookerys are expecting us, but only one person stands outside. I get out of my car and grab the lawn sign and sweets I have brought with me to present to them. Hass gets out of his car and begins to wrangle a large cluster of balloons out of the back. We'll need to tie them to the lawn sign.

We had begun this strange, rolling, socially distanced award ceremony a couple of hours earlier in Dearborn Heights at the home of the first district champions, a couple Hass had gone to high school with. As we moved from neighborhood to neighborhood and house to house, we figured out a protocol of sorts. We would tie a dozen balloons to a sign, place it prominently in the winner's yard, safely hand over the tray of baklawa Shatila Bakery donated to the project, and pose for a photograph with the family. All of this was livestreamed on Facebook and Instagram, of course. We also developed a running joke of sorts, as we've moved through town, perhaps more of a friendly competition, a pissing contest, over who knows Dearborn better, Hass or Sally.

Hass had been surprised to always arrive well behind me at each of the houses we visited. I hadn't bothered with GPS and just drove from place to place, whereas he tended to let his device guide him. At the Saab family home, near Fordson High School, Hass wanted to know how I was already out of my car, speaking to the family, and arranging things with the photographer when he pulled up. How did I know my way around town like this?

"I lived here back in the '90s," I told him. "My daughter was born one street over, on Middlesex."

"Well, my uncle lived right on that corner," he replied. "I spent every weekend here as a kid on sleepovers with my cousins."

Point Hass.

But now that we are getting out of our cars together in the Southend, I can see that Hass is out of his element. He is nodding his head in disbelief as he approaches me.

"How did you know your way here?" Hass asks. "I think I've only been here once in my whole life."

"You've got to be kidding. This is the Southend, where it all started for the Arabs of Dearborn. This is the place."

"I know I've seen that mosque before, but it is kind of crazy to be here."

"That's the oldest mosque in Michigan. Not the first, but the oldest. Established in 1938."

Hass stares in confusion. He wasn't expecting a dissertation. "There used to be another mosque on Dix—Hashmie Hall," I continue. "It was the first. It was Shi'i, and the Dix Mosque is Sunni. Hashmie Hall was the point of origin for the Islamic Center of America [the city's largest and best-known Shi`i mosque]. But Dix, the one we drove by, it is the oldest mosque in Michigan—the American Moslem Society."

"How the hell do you know so much about the Arabs of Dearborn?" Hass asks. "Do you realize you are obsessed?"

I laugh and remind Hass what I do for a living. I am a historian, and I run the Center for Arab American Studies at UM-Dearborn. I'd better know a thing or two about the Arabs of Dearborn.

"I like to bring my classes to the Dix Mosque," I tell him. "The Lebanese students, most of whom have never been to the Southend before, are always surprised to see how active and vital the place is. How big. How many people show up for the different prayers. I am always surprised by how little they know about the Southend." The neighborhood had once been home to the Lebanese community, to the families that came to Detroit in the 1910s and 1920s and first followed Henry Ford to Dearborn when he began construction on the Rouge, but now it is a majority Yemeni neighborhood.

As we stand in the street, me wrestling with too many things in my hands, a lawn sign, a certificate, and a large tray of baklawa, and Hass with his overflowing array of balloons, we get into it.

"My parents grew up here," he said, referring to the Southend.

"Well so did I, in a way. I worked here back in the 1980s and 1990s when I first came to Michigan. I worked at the old ACCESS—the one on Saulino Court—the original ACCESS. I was schooled on local history by Don Unis, Aliya Hassen, Ish Ahmed, Helen Atwell, Joe Borrajo, and so many others."

Most of these names have no meaning to Hass.

"My parents were in middle school then. They went to Lowrey."

"I used to teach the teachers at Lowrey about the Arab community, back before they had Arab teachers."

Hass stares at me in disbelief. Finally, he comes out with, "You are a freak!"

"Yes," I agree, having finally and decidedly won the competition. "I am a freak!"

As the two of us burst into laughter, the cars with our other team members arrive. Now that our videographer and photographer are here to record the moment, we plant the yard sign, gingerly hand over the baklawa and the award certificate to Mr. Alzookery, and, now that some of the children have come out to join us, we line up for a photo.

Sally Howell and Hassan Chami present the Al-Zookery family with a District Champion Award for the 2020 Ramadan Lights Contest in Dearborn's Southend. Photo by Razi Jafri, Halal Metropolis Project.

Hass in his mask on one side and me in my mask on the other, standing at an odd distance (six feet) from the family themselves.

Once the photo op is over, we return to our individual vehicles and to the realities of social distancing. Everyone but me is fasting, so they are eager to head home for their last iftar of the season and to get ready for the festivities of tomorrow—strange and muted as they will be with all of the city's mosques closed.

Ordinarily, we would have eaten together as a group. Instead, I hunt around for a place that is still open, hoping to take something back to Ann Arbor with me for dinner. I get onto the eerily empty highway and reflect on my exchange with Hass.

I am a freak, I realize. But the Southend of Dearborn is one of those special places that has exerted a genuine pull on many people, not just me.

In 2018 I attended the hundredth anniversary of the Salina School, the neighborhood's most vital and enduring institution. It was packed to the gills with people—standing room only for every single part of the festivities. It was amazing to see the history of the neighbor-hood represented in the flesh—as it were. The older, very gray-haired crowd, a mix of Poles, Romanians, Italians, Maltese, Lebanese, and the occasional southerner, were seated together—often with walk-ers and wheelchairs at the ready. Slightly younger people, in their fifties and sixties, were more likely to be Arab, mostly Lebanese, but with plenty of Palestinian and Yemeni couples as well. Those in their forties and younger were increasingly Yemeni, as were all of the chil-dren on hand. Today the neighborhood is overwhelmingly Yemeni, with a spattering of Sudanese, Somali, and other Black Muslims. And despite this obvious transition from one social group to another over time—from a highly diverse group of working-class immigrant Whites to still-arriving Yemeni Americans—the crowd was loving and affectionate. People expressed over and again how their experiences of growing up in this marginal space—this isolated, low-income, and environmentally hazardous place—had been a delight. Whichever generation they were a part of, they had in common immigrant par-ents, the isolated, tough, but tightly knit community of the Southend, along with that lack of pretension and openness that gives the place its personality. And they had stories to share. So many stories!

I did not attend Salina School or grow up in the Southend. Nor am I the daughter of immigrants.

I visited Dearborn for the first time in 1986. I was one year out of col-lege and looking for work. I had heard about this place called ACCESS in Dearborn. ACCESS was the Arab Community Center for Economic and Social Services, and they were said to be doing great work in the Arab American community. This is really all I knew about where I was heading. I had just moved to Ann Arbor with my new husband who was studying anthropology at Michigan. We had spent our honeymoon traveling around the Middle East, especially Yemen, where Andrew had planned to do his dissertation research. And I had also worked the pre-vious year for a couple of different Arab American groups in Washing-ton, DC. While I might have seemed out of place in Dearborn, I was hoping to get a job for the next year or two in an environment where I could improve my Arabic, especially the Yemeni dialect.

I remember that I drove right through the Southend without noticing it on my first try. I was worried about being late and was driving too fast, but as I retraced my steps—this time approaching from the east on Vernor Highway—I took the time to notice things. The Ford Rouge Factory made quite a backdrop to the neighborhood with its iconic blue oval and three giant smokestacks. And there on my left was a large mosque with a bright-green dome, a row of restaurants, grocery stores, coffeehouses, and travel agencies with names like Arabian Village, Uncle Sam's, and Red Sea. This time I observed Yemeni men in footahs and kufiyyahs walking along the sidewalk. This was Dix, the heart of the neighborhood. I found my way to the Humood Center where ACCESS was located, and pressed past the crowd of Arab women, several of them wearing Palestinian thobs, who were lined up in the hallway. This was pretty cool, I thought. This must be Dearborn.

I spoke with Ismael Ahmed, director of ACCESS, about the work I had done in DC, my education, and the experiences that had led me to be interested in the Middle East in the first place. He introduced me briefly to the work and needs of the still-small ACCESS. I had good recommendations with me from Washington, and a bit of experience writing grants. Ish had been looking for someone to go after arts grants for the organization, perhaps to build a small museum, perhaps to replicate some of the progress that had been made along these lines by another neighborhood group (the Southeast Dearborn Community Council) that was now defunct. After the assistant director, Hassan Jaber, gave me a brief quiz in Arabic, Ish was kind enough to take a chance on me and to offer me a job. He hedged his bets—offering me a half-time job at a very low wage for six months. If, at the end of this time, I had raised enough money to support myself and the program, then I had a real job. What a deal!

Ish then took me out to lunch—why not get started right away? He wanted to fill me in a bit on the history of ACCESS and the neighborhood in which it was located. I have no idea where we went to eat, but I do know that I was mesmerized right from the start by his stories.

He took me past the Rouge Factory and told me about the Detroit Hunger March of 1932. There was the pedestrian overpass where a famous labor battle had taken place in 1937. I learned about Harry Bennett's goon squad (Ford's union-busting enforcers who had included plenty of Arab muscle from the neighborhood). And I learned about the earl UAW organizers who had included another Arab American, George Addes, in their posse. I observed the vast empty parking lots across from Ford's while Ish told me that the factory had once been the largest industrial complex in the world, employing over 100,000 workers. Raw materials were shipped in from the river, and completed Model Ts rolled off the assembly line at the other end.

As we passed the intersection of Michigan and Wyoming, Ish switched gears and told me about Dearborn's long serving, segregationist mayor, Orville Hubbard, who had stood defiantly on this spot in 1967 with a shotgun in his hands and ordered the National Guard to "shoot any looters on site." The uprisings in Detroit had been the deadliest (forty-three killed) and most destructive (over 2,000 destroyed buildings) in the country that long hot summer remembered now for its contagious civil unrest. Now, twenty years later, the city had a Black majority and was synonymous with the drug wars, unemployment, and crisis, while the metro region was commonly referred to as the most segregated metropolitan region in the country.

This was a lot for me to take in. I had been raised in Louisiana and North Carolina. I didn't know anything about labor history, the Arsenal of Democracy, the urban uprisings of 1967 and 1968, the Great Migration, or racial segregation in the North. If anything, I shared the underlying anti-union bias of my native region and thought of Ford through the acronym my brothers had taught me—Fix Or Repair Daily.

I had come to ACCESS looking for Arabs, and what I got instead was this heavy dose of Americana. Of American history. Of drama on a grand, national scale.

This place mattered.

And, there was more. Starting in the 1950s, the city of Dearborn teamed up with Ford and the Levy Asphalt Company (that effectively made up the eastern boundary of the Southend) to rezone the neighborhood for heavy industry and tear down all of its housing. Under

Hubbard's leadership, they succeeded in destroying over 300 homes, but the community had fought back. They took to the streets, stood down the city's bulldozers, and won their day in court. What's more, the people who had organized this campaign to save the neighborhood were, by the end of the struggle at least, Arab Americans. Arabs had fought the longest and hardest to save the Southend because their mosques were there. Their only mosques. And, by the 1970s, when they finally won the court battle, a new generation of Arab immigrants were beginning to make their homes there, too: Yemeni sailors and auto workers, displaced Palestinians, and families seeking to escape the ever-escalating Lebanese Civil War. These new immigrants were poor, like their predecessors. They lacked English. They lacked the kind of job skills that would have enabled them to thrive in Dearborn. But they kept the Salina School full, the mosques and coffeehouses along Dix very busy, and made the neighborhood vibrant and essential again.

And the people who had fought city hall and won were still, for the most part, right there in the neighborhood. Some still resided there, but others were connected to ACCESS in one way or another. Most were very eager to share their stories: Aliya Hassen, Don Unis, Joe Borrajo, Helen Atwell, George Khoury, Hassan Newash, Abdeen Jabara, Barbara Aswad, Ron and Alan Amen. In my early days at ACCESS, I would sit with Don in the restaurants on Dix and watch him chain-smoke and sip coffee while regaling me with stories about his uncle and Pancho Villa or about his father and "the old man"—Henry Ford. From Don I learned that the *Titanic*'s sinking was "an Arab American tragedy." (There were over one hundred Syrians on board, several of whom survived and one, Fatima Muselmanie, who settled in the Southend.) From Don I learned that Arab Americans were on both sides of the struggle to unionize Ford, and were, perhaps, responsible for the disappearance of Jimmy Hoffa. From Aliya Hassen I learned that she and other Arabs had played a significant role in bringing Malcolm X to Islam and encouraging him to make the hajj. From Joe Borrajo I learned about the decades-long campaign to clean up the air, water, and soil of the neighborhood from the devastating realities of living downwind from Ford's smokestacks. From all of these storytellers I learned about the 1967 uprising in Detroit and how it had scarred the city—how it had hardened Black-White divides and reinforced the stark and devastating segregationism of the region. And everyone had stories to share about Orville Hubbard who presided over Dearborn for thirty-six long years, all the while doing his best to "keep Dearborn clean," a well-known euphemism for keeping it White.

I worked at ACCESS from 1987–1995, with a couple of years spent in Jordan and Yemen sandwiched in the middle. These were important years for Dearborn as the Arab community was growing rapidly then, swelling beyond the Southend and becoming the dominant group in east Dearborn as a whole. As they revitalized one business district and housing market after another across the city, the powers that be began to take notice. And because I was the cultural arts director at ACCESS, it became my job to know and share these stories, among many others, in grants, documentary videos, museum displays, and books like this one. I left Michigan in 1995 when Andrew got a teaching job at SUNY Buffalo and returned in 2000 when I began graduate school myself at the University of Michigan. I focused my dissertation research on the history of the Muslim communities of Detroit, which enabled me to elaborate on, add to, and update the core set of stories I learned at ACCESS—work I have been doing ever since. And now, in my role as a history professor at UM-Dearborn, I get to share these stories with a new generation of students. More than that, I consider it my job to empower a new generation of Arab Americans to learn and tell these stories for themselves. And to tell the equally compelling stories of their own generations. Now that Dearborn's Arab communities make up over half the population of the city and have spilled into the surrounding communities of southwest Detroit, Warrendale, Melvindale, Dearborn Heights, and Garden City, it is many times easier for others to see Dearborn as I always have—as a very special, very American place, whose story has been shaped and shared by Arab Americans.

So, yes, Hass Chami was correct about me. I am something of a freak, but a very lucky one to have found this special place worth devoting so much of my career to. And I was correct about him as well in calling him Mr. Dearborn. Not only did his grandparents first settle in the Southend and raise their children there, but Hass is raising his children in Dearborn and has dedicated his own efforts to improve the quality of life there. By creating Suhoorfest and events like the Ramadan Lights Contest, Hass is shaping the future of the city and region as well, bringing new energy and new traditions to local celebrations of the holidays and everyday life.

As Hass and I reminded one another during Ramadan, this place matters still.

# Acknowledgments

We thank our families for their love and support. We are also grateful for the Mcubed grant the project received from the University of Michigan Office of Research. Our deep gratitude goes to the wonderful team at Wayne State University Press for believing in our work and treating it with care. Special thanks to Marie Sweetman for her unwavering positivity and encouragement, and to Annie Martin and Emily Nowak. Thanks also to Dr. Siwar Masannat and Lena Hakim for their help at different stages of the project.

Dunya Mikhail's poem "Baghdad in Detroit" previously appeared in her collection *In Her Feminine Sign* (New Directions, 2019). Hayan Charara's work first appeared in the following publications: "Thinking Detroit" in *The Poem's Country: Place & Poetic Practice* (Pleides Press, 2018); "Personal Political Poem" in *West Branch* (Winter 2018); "The Day Phil Levine Died" in *Miracle Monocle* (2018); "That Summer That Year During the Heat Wave" in *The Recluse* (Issue 15); "1979" in *The Normal School* (2014); and "Apokaluptein" in *The Adroit Journal* (Issue Twenty-Five, May 2018).

# Contributors

**Nabeel Abraham** has devoted his life's work to the study of Arab Detroit and Arab Americans generally. His writing on various aspects of the community span four decades. He coedited, with Andrew Shryock and Sally Howell, two volumes of the *Arab Detroit* series (Wayne State University Press), as well as other collections. He contributed numerous essays in various journals, books, and encyclopedias. Abraham taught anthropology at Henry Ford College in Dearborn, Michigan, for three decades, where he also directed the Honors Program until his retirement in 2013. Abraham served as executive director of the Association of Arab American University Graduates, Inc., from 1979 to 1980. He also established the Detroit Office of the ADC, serving as its local spokesman and adviser from 1980 to 1985. Abraham's experiences growing up in Detroit starting in the 1950s provides much of the material on which he draws for his current work.

**Yousef Alqamoussi** was born in Kuwait in 1987 and immigrated to the United States when he was three. He is the author of several books, including *poems (2019), chapter one: Costa Rica,* and *The Massacre of Heartbreak Morrow.* He teaches English and History in Dearborn, Michigan.

**Teri Bazzi** was born and raised in the Detroit area. She is a graduate student in the School of Social Work at Wayne State University. Her writing has appeared in *Read the Spirit* and *The Big Read Dearborn*, and she has contributed to online platforms such as Muslimgirl.com and StoryCorps. Teri has also spoken at community events that raise awareness about domestic abuse and sexual assault. Teri has three children who are the focus and light of her life. After graduation, she plans to advocate for survivors and help them find their voice as she believes that an untold story never heals.

**Hayan Charara's** poetry books are *These Trees, Those Leaves, This Flower, That Fruit* (Milkweed Editions, 2022), *Something Sinister* (Carnegie Mellon, 2016), *The Sadness of Others* (Carnegie Mellon, 2006), and *The Alchemist's Diary* (Hanging Loose, 2001). He is also the editor of *Inclined to Speak*, an anthology of contemporary Arab American poetry, and series editor and co-founder, with Fady Joudah, of the Etel Adnan Poetry Prize, which publishes first and second poetry books by poets of Arab heritage writing in English. His honors include a National Endowment for the Arts fellowship, an Arab American Book Award, and the New Voices Award Honor for his children's book, *The Three Lucys* (Lee and Low, 2016), about a child's experience during the July War in Lebanon. Born in Detroit in 1972, he has earned degrees from Wayne State University, New York University, and the University of Houston, where he is currently a professor in the Honors College.

**Sally Howell** is associate professor of history and director of the Center for Arab American Studies at the University of Michigan–Dearborn. She received her PhD from the American Culture Program at University of Michigan in 2009. Her books include *Arab Detroit 9/11: Life in the Terror Decade* (2011, Wayne State University Press), and *Old Islam in Detroit: Rediscovering the Muslim American Past* (2014, Oxford University Press). *Old Islam in Detroit* was named a Michigan Notable Book by the Library of Michigan and given the Evelyn Shakir Award by the Arab American National Museum. Howell is also a curator of the Halal Metropolis exhibition series exploring the political and cultural impact of Muslim visibility in greater Detroit.

**Mai Jakubowski** is a genderless queer Muslim dyke living, working, and writing in Minneapolis. Though their day-to-day work involves community engagement in the service industry, their creative endeavors are ultimately focused on interrogating how we define home, the frameworks we use to navigate our world, as well as what bonds people decide to forge with each other. They are currently working on a memoir project that centers on sexuality, loss, and connection. This is their first published work.

**Jeff Karoub** is a writer and musician of Arab ancestry who lives in Dearborn with his wife and three daughters. He worked across Michigan for nearly thirty years as a journalist, including more than a dozen years as a Detroit-based reporter and editor for the *AP*. Karoub was a founding member of AP's national race and ethnicity team focusing on Arab and Muslim communities. He was a finalist in the Religion News Association's Annual Contest for Religion Reporting Excellence in 2012. In early 2020, he joined University of Michigan as a senior public relations representative. He writes about faculty research and other developments related to business, public policy, economics, and innovation. Karoub also is a singer-songwriter and multi-instrumentalist who has released four solo albums and performed or received airplay on WJBK-TV, WDET, WUOM, CKLW, and other radio stations across the Great Lakes region. One of his compositions, "Breathe for Those Denied," was selected as a featured work in University of Michigan's 2020 Diversity, Equity, and Inclusion Summit.

**Rania Matar** was born and raised in Lebanon and moved to the United States in 1984. As a Lebanese-born American woman and mother, her cross-cultural experience and personal narrative inform her photography. Her work has been widely exhibited in museums worldwide, including the Museum of Fine Arts, Boston, Carnegie Museum of Art, National Museum of Women in the Arts, Minneapolis Institute of Art, and more, and is part of the permanent collections of several museums, institutions, and private collections. A midcareer retrospective of her work was recently on view at the Cleveland Museum of Art, the Amon Carter Museum of American Art, and at the AUB Museum. Matar received a 2018 Guggenheim Fellowship, 2017 Mellon Foundation artist-in-residency grant, 2011 Legacy Award at the Griffin Museum of Photography, and 2011 and 2007 Massachusetts Cultural Council artist fellowships. In 2008, she was a finalist for the

Foster Award at the Institute of Contemporary Art in Boston, with an accompanying solo exhibition. She has published four books: *SHE*, 2021; *L'Enfant-Femme*, 2016; *A Girl and Her Room*, 2012; and *Ordinary Lives*, 2009.

**Dunya Mikhail** was born in Baghdad, where she worked as a journalist and translator for the *Baghdad Observer*. Facing censorship and interrogation, she left Iraq: first to Jordan, and then, in 1996, to America. New Directions published her nonfiction book *The Beekeeper: Rescuing the Stolen Women of Iraq*, as well as four poetry volumes: *In Her Feminine Sign*, *The Iraqi Nights*, *Diary of a Wave Outside the Sea*, and *The War Works Hard*, chosen as a New York Public Library Book to Remember. She is also the editor of *15 Iraqi Poets* and has received a United States Artist Fellowship, a Guggenheim Fellowship, a Knights Foundation grant, a Kresge Fellowship, and the United Nations Human Rights Award for Freedom of Writing.

**Yasmin Mohamed** was born in Yemen and raised in the Southend of Dearborn, Michigan. A graduate of the University of Michigan–Dearborn, she currently teaches social studies at the same school she attended as a child.

**Hanan Ali Nasser** completed her bachelor's degrees in philosophy and biochemistry at the University of Michigan–Dearborn. She is currently a graduate student in the School of Medicine at Wayne State University. In 1997, Hanan and her family fled their hometown of Baghdad, Iraq and have lived in the Detroit metropolitan area since their arrival to America in 1999. She currently resides with her family in Dearborn Heights, Michigan.

**Yasmine Rukia** is a first-generation Lebanese-American-Shia-queer experimental poet, mother, and short-story smith from Dearborn, Michigan. Her work appears in *Mizna*, *PAPER Magazine*, *Cliterature*, *Red Fez*, *The Gordon Square Review*, *The Porter Gulch Review*, and elsewhere. Google the name and see the memes. She loves mangos, and her parents are still disappointed she isn't a doctor.

**Kamelya Omayma Youssef** is a poet, educator, and literary worker. She is the author of *A book with a hole in it* (2022, Wendy's Subway), and the co-writer of the play *Kilo Batra: In Death More Radiant* (2021, A Host of People). Her poems and lyric essays have been published by *Mizna*, the Academy of American Poets, *Michigan Quarterly Review*, *Poet Lore*, and elsewhere. She is currently an MFA candidate at New York University. In her spare time, she develops creative workshops with her friends.

**Ghassan Zeineddine** is an assistant professor of English at the University of Michigan–Dearborn. His fiction has appeared in *The Georgia Review*, *Michigan Quarterly Review*, *Witness*, *TriQuarterly*, *Pleiades*, *Fiction International*, *The Common*, *Epiphany*, and the *Iron Horse Literary Review*, among other places. He is currently working on a collection of linked short stories about the Arab American community in Dearborn, Michigan, where he lives with his wife and two daughters.